NAGUIB MAHFOUZ

THE PURSUIT OF MEANING

Naguib Mahfouz is the most important Arabic fiction writer of this century. Born in 1911, his long and prolific writing career represents the evolution of the novel genre in Arabic literature. His books are a rich record of the tragic tensions attendant on a nation's quest for freedom and modernity. In 1988 he won the Nobel Prize for Literature.

This is the only comprehensive study of Mahfouz's achievement. Rasheed El-Enany presents a systematic evaluation of the author's life and environment; local and foreign influences on him; elements of his thought and technique and the evolution of his craft. While each work is discussed individually, emphasis is laid throughout on elements of continuity in his work, whether thematic or aesthetic. In particular, Dr El-Enany challenges the traditional classification of Mahfouz's work into four chronological phases – historical, realist, modernist and indigenous or traditional. It is demonstrated that elements of these forms recur throughout Mahfouz's varied and experimental writings.

This book is the story of Mahfouz's rejection of Western moulds of fiction to express his own vision of man and society through forms inspired by the traditional arts of storytelling in Arabic.

Rasheed El-Enany is Lecturer in Arabic and Islamic Studies at the University of Exeter. He is the translator of Mahfouz's *Respected Sir* (1986) and also *The Caravan or ᶜAlī Janāḥ al-Tabrīzī and his Servant Quffa* by Alfred Farag (1989).

ARABIC THOUGHT AND CULTURE

This new series is designed to provide straightforward introductions for the western reader to some of the major figures and movements of Arabic thought. Philosophers, historians and geographers are all seminal figures in the history of thought, and some names, such as Averroes and Avicenna, are already part of the western tradition. Mathematicians, linguistic theorists and astronomers have as significant a part to play as groups of thinkers such as the Illuminationists. With the growing importance of the Arab world on the international scene, these succinct and authoritative works will be welcomed not only by journalists, travellers, teachers of English as a second language, and business people – in fact any who have to come to an understanding of this non-western culture in the course of their daily work.

Also available in this series:

AL-FĀRĀBI *Ian Richard Netton*
AVICENNA *Lenn E. Goodman*
IBN KHALDUN *Aziz Al-Azmeh*
IBN RUSHD (*Averroes*) *Dominique Urvoy*
MOSES MAIMONIDES *Oliver Leaman*
THE ARABIC LINGUISTIC TRADITION
Georges Bohas, Jean-Patrick Guillaume, Djamel Eddine Kouloughli
THE CLASSICAL HERITAGE IN ISLAM *Franz Rosenthal*

Forthcoming:
IBN ARABI *Ronald Nettler*

NAGUIB MAHFOUZ

The pursuit of meaning

Rasheed El-Enany

London and New York

First published 1993
by Routledge
11 New Fetter Lane, London EC4P 4EE

Simultaneously published in the USA and Canada
by Routledge Inc.
29 West 35th Street, New York, NY 10001

Typeset in 10/12pt Bembo by
Ponting–Green Publishing Services, Chesham, Bucks
Printed and bound in Great Britain by
TJ Press (Padstow) Ltd, Padstow, Cornwall

British Library Cataloguing in Publication Data
El-Enany, Rasheed
Naguib Mahfouz: Pursuit of Meaning. –
(Arabic Thought & Culture Series)
I. Title II. Series
892.735

Library of Congress Cataloging in Publication Data
El-Enany, Rasheed
Naguib Mahfouz : the pursuit of meaning : a critical study / Rasheed El-Enany
p. cm. – (Arabic thought and culture)
Includes bibliographical references and index.
1. Maḥfūẓ, Najīb, 1911–
–Criticism and interpretation.
I. Title II. Series
PJ7846.A46Z597 1993
92-28677

ISBN 0–415–02286–X
ISBN 0–415–07395–2 (pbk)

For my son, Sami

He was overwhelmed by a feeling of having been the victim of a heinous aggression – a conspiracy against him by fate, the law of heredity and the class system. . . . He appeared to himself a wretched soul standing alone against these forces combined. His wound was bleeding and no one was there to tend it.

Palace of Desire (p. 347)

CONTENTS

PREFACE AND ACKNOWLEDGEMENTS

A new book on Naguib Mahfouz has long been overdue. All existing studies, whether in Arabic or English, were written at a time when the novelist was still at the height of his energy and inventiveness. Thus the last twenty-odd years of his creative life (specifically since the late 1960s) which saw his imagination take new turnings and some of his most important works written have remained largely unresearched and the link unestablished between the two halves of his *œuvre*. The last two decades have also seen a steady increase in the realization of the originality and human significance of Mahfouz's work in the West – a realization which culminated in the award of the Nobel Prize for literature to the author in 1988. Today, with virtually half his novels in English translation alone, several more currently under contract, and with translations being published on a wide commercial scale as opposed to the narrow semi-academic circulation of a few years ago, the need for a fresh and thorough evaluation of the novelist's achievement (and one which addresses itself as much to the general reader as to the specialist Arabist) is all too apparent. This book, it is hoped, will be seen as an endeavour in that direction.

Critics have tended to classify Mahfouz's work into three chronological phases (historical/romantic, realistic/naturalistic and modernist/experimental), and more recently they have added a fourth, usually labelled 'the phase of indigenous or traditional form' (*marḥalat al-shakl al-aṣīl aw al-turāthī*) – the products of which I will choose to refer to subsequently in this book as 'the episodic novels'. This approach may have served a purpose while the author's development was still an ongoing process, namely to draw a demarcation line each time he broke new aesthetic or formal ground. However, now that his achievement is near complete, such an approach based on chronology alone would seem somewhat artificial, and it has not been adopted here. The very variety and unpredictability of the aesthetics of his work has in fact always defied neat classification. Thus critics and academics who happily talked for long about a romantic/historical phase of his work tucked away tidily at the beginning of his career must have been taken by surprise to find him writing historical novels again forty years later and this time without a trace of romanticism. Again the so-called modernist phase of his work is unanimously demarcated at *The Thief and the Dogs*, while *The Cairo Trilogy* is seen as the peak of his realistic phase. In fact, an intricate symbolic pattern (as will be shown), extensive use of the internal monologue, an intense heightened prose (especially in Part II), and a complex agonized sensibility (Kamāl's) all go to endow *The Trilogy* with the right to claim a place under 'the modernist phase' as much as it has always enjoyed one under the 'naturalistic/realistic' label for other considerations. To give yet another example, Mahfouz's indulgence in episodic writing does not begin until the 1970s, but is the much earlier *Children of Gebelawi* not an episodic novel? Indeed, is not *Midaq Alley*, too, episodic in its own way? Nor should we forget that throughout 'the episodic phase' proper, Mahfouz continued to write non-episodic novels as well.

These and other reflections have encouraged me to disregard the principle of absolute chronology in my examination of the author's work in favour of groupings of units within it which, in my opinion, have emphasized our sense of the elements of coherence and continuity in his thought. Chronology, however, has been preserved whenever it was found not to be in conflict with this scheme of things. Any classification is bound, nevertheless, to have an element of arbitrariness in it. Single works may qualify under more than one class, but in the end a choice has to be made. One problem I faced was where to place *Before the Throne*. Few works can be more 'episodic' and fewer still can be more 'historical'. My preference was to examine it in the context of the rest of the historical novels, rather than that of the episodic ones. In the end, however, any such disparities of organization will be consumed in a sense of the ultimate oneness, across single works and whole phases, of the novelist's vision – something I have tried always to remember in the course of this study. With regard to the short stories and the plays, I have chosen not to mix these with the novels, devoting to them an independent chapter at the end. I have, however, attempted to underline the strong thematic and aesthetic link between the two groups both in that chapter and via cross-references in the notes throughout. In my survey of the short story collections I have abided by the chronology of their publication.

As every writer will know, an important factor in a book of a prescribed length is allocation of space to individual subjects of discussion. In the present instance, individual novels often tended to claim their own worth of space within the prescribed limits. Hence the relative length of my discussions of works like *The Trilogy* and *Harafish*. On the whole I have felt that the novels of the 1970s and 1980s which have received scant consideration so far ought to be treated generously. Similarly, a feeling that some of the old novels of the 1940s (e.g. *Midaq Alley*) were ripe for reappraisal dictated again a relative liberality in allocation of space. If this has resulted in some stinginess towards the novels of the 1960s, my only consolation is that other scholars and critics have treated them lavishly, no less in English than in Arabic – a fact that a glance at the bibliography at the end of this monograph should not fail to confirm.

I have given preference here to the popular French-based spelling of the novelist's name (as it appears on the covers of his translated works) over the transliterated version usually favoured by Arabists. To avoid confusion I have stuck to the popular spelling even in my transliteration of titles of Arabic sources citing the author's name. I have, however, felt obliged to maintain the transliterated version of the name where I quote titles of English sources using it. Another choice of convenience and in deference to readers not conversant with Arabic is my adoption both in the text and its notes of the titles of all published translations of Mahfouz's novels and my rendering in English of the titles of those works as yet untranslated. Arabists, however, will be able to establish what the original titles are through the briefest glance at the bilingual list of works at the end. Finally, I must point out that all quotations from Mahfouz's work are my own direct translations from the Arabic originals (even where published translations exist) and that all the page references given in the text are to the particular editions cited in the bibliography.

Now for a few expressions of gratitude. It was my friend and colleague Professor Aziz al-Azmeh who first suggested that I should write this book. To him, for this and much else, my first thanks go. I also wish to record my grateful appreciation to all my colleagues in the Department of Arabic and Islamic Studies at the University of Exeter for allowing me a generous study leave without which the writing of this book would have taken much longer. I would like to acknowledge with gratitude the help (always forthcoming) that I have received over the years from Mr Paul Auchterlonie, the Arabic specialist librarian at the University of Exeter Library, who has also compiled the index for this volume, Miss Heather Eva, director of the inter-library loans section at the same library for running an excellent service, Mrs Aleya Serour at the American University in Cairo Press for providing me with useful bibliographic information on Mr Mahfouz's works in English translation, and Mrs Sheila Westcott for typing the text of this book and rendering valued assistance over the years in many other ways. The greater part of this book was written in Riyadh where I spent the period of my study leave. To Professor Fatma Moussa-Mahmoud at King Saud University (formerly Professor of English at Cairo University), for her treasured friendship and generous hospitality towards me and my family, for granting me free access to her private library and bringing to my attention several sources on the subject that otherwise might have escaped my notice, I would like to express the deepest affection and gratitude on my own behalf and that of my family. To Mr Abd al-Aziz Muhammadayn (also at King Saud University) and his family, for their spontaneous friendship and countless kindnesses and help throughout our stay in Riyadh, my family and I will always be their debtors. Finally, to my wife Wafaa and my children for their love and support, and for virtually relinquishing every claim on my time during the many months it took to produce this volume, I owe more than I can say.

I am also grateful to the British Society for Middle Eastern Studies for permission to use sections of my article 'Religion in the Novels of Naguib Mahfouz' (*BRISMES Bulletin*, vol. 15,

1988, pp. 21–7), E. J. Brill for permission to use sections of my article 'The Novelist as Political Eye-Witness' (*Journal of Arabic Literature*, vol. 21, 1990, pp. 72–86), and Curzon Press for permission to reprint with some alterations my chapter on *Riḥlat Ibn Faṭṭūma* in I. R. Netton, ed., *Golden Roads*, London, 1993.

Rasheed El-Enany
Exeter, June 1992

1

THE WRITER AND HIS WORLD

CHILDHOOD, FAMILY AND LOCALITY

On 11 December 1911, in al-Jamāliyya quarter in the heart of the old city of Cairo Naguib Mahfouz was born. Though he only lived there up to the age of 12 (in 1924 his family moved to the then new Cairo suburb, al-ᶜAbbāsiyya), there is a sense in which we can say that he has never left Jamāliyya, or in other words that it has always lived in his mind and consequently in the creations of that mind. Most of the novels of his early realistic period are set in Jamāliyya, notably *Midaq Alley* and *The Cairo Trilogy*, while in later works such as *Children of Gebelawi*, *Fountain and Tomb*, *The Epic of the Harafish*[1] and many others, though not mentioned by name and not recreated with the same meticulous detail as before, Jamāliyya continues to haunt his work in various mantles of disguise and lends to it many of its typical characters and physical assets. The *ḥāra* (plebeian street/quarter) with its warring *futuwwas* (thugs) and their gangs, its mystery-enveloped *takiyya* (dervish-house), its *qabw* (dark vault or arch which once housed a city gate), its ancient *sabīl* (drinking-fountain), its shops, its café and the adjacent *qarāfa* (cemetery) – all these components which make up the distinctive features of much of Mahfouz's work in the past twenty years originate in the old quarter of Jamāliyya whose images were indelibly impressed on the novelist's consciousness during his childhood years.

Jamāl al-Ghīṭānī, a well-known novelist in his own right and a confidant of Mahfouz, who also grew up in Jamāliyya and remained emotionally bound to it ever after, has retraced the steps of Mahfouz's characters in the quarter and attests that

'*Khan al-Khalili, Midaq Alley* and *The Trilogy* are accurate documentations of the features of the area during the period of their events'.[2] Mahfouz himself stresses the importance of Jamāliyya, or 'the *ḥāra* world' as he refers to it sometimes, as a source of inspiration for his work throughout his creative life: 'It seems to me that [a man-of-letters] must have a tie with a certain place or a certain object to form a point of departure for his emotions.'[3] He admits that Jamāliyya was reflected in his work and goes on to add that even when he started to treat issues of an intellectual or symbolic nature, he still went back to Jamāliyya for his background. 'What really moves me is the *ḥāra* world,' he proclaims. 'It is my favourite world.'[4] Mahfouz's dependence on the *ḥāra* world as a background for his fiction and a medium for rendering his vision of man and society has noticeably increased in his old age, particularly from the mid-1970s onwards. He explains this aptly:

> With the advancement of age one realises that his origin is his true refuge. . . . In the tumult of this strange world, one takes refuge in his childhood, in the security of his past life. This explains my nostalgia for the *ḥāra* and [my use of it] as a source for the *Epic of the Harafish* ...[5]

During Mahfouz's childhood the *ḥāra* was very different from what it is today. Today a *ḥāra* or back street in Jamāliyya or elsewhere in Cairo is exclusively inhabited by the lower classes of society. During the author's childhood however, the *ḥāra* was in a sense a model of the Egyptian society. He tells us that in those days all the classes of the Egyptian people were represented in it from the very rich to the very poor and that blocks of flats where whole families lived in single rooms with common facilities stood in close proximity to majestic mansions surrounded by gardens.[6] This strange composition of the Egyptian *ḥāra* (which according to Mahfouz survived until the 1930s)[7] can certainly explain his frequent use of the *ḥāra* as a comprehensive model of society and indeed of humanity at large in *Children of Gebelawi* and many later works.

One of the main features of the *ḥāra* as Mahfouz knew it in his boyhood was the *futuwwa*, a character type that was later to play a major symbolic role in his fiction, notably *Children of Gebelawi* and *Harafish*. In his memoirs, recorded by Ghīṭānī, he tells us that in those days every quarter or *ḥāra* had a *futuwwa* and goes on to describe some of the great battles of the warring gangs to which he was an eye-witness.[8] Elsewhere he defines the part played by the *futuwwa* at the time as not to 'oppress' the *ḥāra*, but to 'protect it'. Significantly, he goes on to add that 'as with some rulers, the protector sometimes turned into a usurper'.[9] Mahfouz often speaks with unconcealed admiration about *futuwwas*. He describes one of them whom he was able to watch at close quarters in his capacity as café-owner and manager after retirement from thuggery in the following terms: 'He had an awesome appearance; he resembled a party leader or a big general. He was quite a character! Very gallant and possessing an attractive personality! A [true] knight!'[10] The novelist also emphasizes the nationalist role played by the *futuwwas* during the popular uprising against the British occupation in 1919 as well as their part in supporting the Wafd, the nationalist anti-British, pro-democratic party, in general elections.[11] Mahfouz is indeed happy to admit the symbolic part played by the *futuwwas* in his fiction. He argues that in *Children of Gebelawi* 'they stood for brutal force', while in *Harafish* they were more 'like rulers, sometimes just, sometimes oppressive'.[12]

Another feature of the *ḥāra* which was to figure centrally in his work, especially *Fountain and Tomb* and *Harafish* was the *takiyya*.[13] He refers to it briefly in his memoirs: 'there was also a *takiyya* inhabited by Persians or [perhaps] Turks whom we used to see from a distance.'[14] Those mysterious strangers with their enigmatic songs made an impression on the budding consciousness of the author which apparently continued to haunt him until it found artistic expression much later in his life in the works mentioned above.

Mahfouz's childhood observations and experiences in Jamāliyya were not, however, confined to the local scene, for in 1919 when the author was only 7 years old,[15] the quarter, together with the rest of the country, was engulfed in a popular uprising against the British. It was in those days that the author probably first came to experience the meaning of nationalist feeling. About the events of that period he says:

> From a small room on the roof [of our house] I used to see the demonstrations of the 1919 revolution. I saw women take part in the demonstrations on donkey-drawn

> carts. . . . I often saw English soldiers firing at the demonstrators. . . . My mother used to pull me back from the window, but I wanted to see everything.[16]

From his elementary school opposite al-Ḥusayn Mosque, he was able, he tells us, to see the bodies of the dead and the wounded laid on the ground. 'You could say', he proclaims, 'that the one thing which most shook the security of my childhood was the 1919 revolution.'[17]

There is no exaggerating the lasting effect that those public events had on the awareness of the young boy, Mahfouz. For the rest of his life, as his works attest, he was to remain a child of that golden era of the national struggle and a spiritual follower of the liberal, democratic principles of the Wafd Party which inherited the revolution. The events of 1919 are widely recreated and affectionately celebrated in a great many of Mahfouz's novels, and especially in *The Trilogy*, as will be shown later in this book.

Fountain and Tomb, as an autobiographical *Bildungsroman*, is another major work where Mahfouz remembers the 1919 revolution at some considerable length. Tales 12–16, 18–19 and 23 are entirely devoted to the revolution out of a total of seventy-eight episodes in which the more salient memories and impressions of the novelist's early childhood are recollected. All the main events of the revolution from its eruption to the death of its leader, Saᶜd Zaghlūl, in 1927 are covered by the tales. What is particularly interesting about the account in *Fountain and Tomb* is that it is given through the highly excited and only half-comprehending consciousness of a child. Reading the book's account of the revolution we cannot help but see it as the reduction to its raw emotional elements of the elaborately recreated scenes in *Palace Walk*, the first part of *The Trilogy*.

Mirrors is another semi-autobiographical work where ostensibly personal memories of the 1919 events are recalled, though less extensively than in *Fountain and Tomb*. Of particular interest here is the episode of 'Anwar al-Ḥalawānī' where we can recognize without much difficulty what must have been the real-life origin of the character of Fahmī ᶜAbd al-Jawwād in *The Trilogy* I. The viewpoint here, like that later used in *Fountain and Tomb*, is that of a child. Here is how he describes the murder of Anwar, the son of a neighbouring family and, like

Fahmī, a student at the Law School at the time of the revolution:

> That morning I learnt that our neighbour Anwar al-Ḥalawānī had been killed in a demonstration with a bullet fired by an English soldier. Thus I came to know for the first time the meaning of the act of 'murder' in a real-life experience rather than through fairy tales. I also heard for the first time about the 'bullet' as one of the achievements of civilization.[18] And again there was a new word, 'demonstration' which required a great deal of explanation. It was perhaps also then that I first heard about the representative of a new human race in my little life: the Englishman.[19]

I have quoted Mahfouz earlier as saying that the events of 1919 could be said to have been what most shook the security of his childhood.[20] A review of the information available on the novelist's childhood (whose source is largely himself) appears to confirm that he grew up in a secure and stable family environment, nor did his immediate family seem to be directly affected by the public dramas of 1919 in any calamitous way. The main sources about the author's childhood are to be found in *The Trilogy* (especially the character of Kamāl ᶜAbd al-Jawwād) and *Fountain and Tomb*, a fact which the author has repeatedly admitted.[21] *Mirrors* is another significant source, though to a lesser extent than the other two. Finally there is his own direct, personal account given in interviews.

The author describes his childhood in the following terms:

> I grew up in a stable family. The atmosphere around me was one which inspired the love of parents and family. . . . The family was a basic, almost sacred, value of my childhood; I was not one of those who rebelled against their parents or rejected their authority.[22]

The sentiment expressed in his last statement is one which was to stay with Mahfouz translated into the wider context of respect for authority, moderation and a preference for gradual political and social reform, rather than outright revolution – all of which are values which clearly emerge from the totality of the political themes in his work, as I hope this study will later show.

The author tells us that although he was the seventh and last child in a family which already had four boys and two girls, he was virtually deprived of natural fraternal relationships. This was, he informs us, because the youngest of his brothers was ten years older than himself:

> I did not have the kind of brother or sister that I could play with, go out with, or confide my secrets in. There was between me and them the kind of barrier which existed between a child and his parents. . . . Because of this, friendship played a very important role in my life from a very early age. It provided the necessary substitute for the missing fraternity.[23]

One must observe here that his last statement is amply substantiated in his two most autobiographical works, *Mirrors* and *Fountain and Tomb*, where sketches of scores of friends, albeit touched up for artistic purposes, are to be found. Mahfouz himself has a comment to make on the influence of the absence of this relationship from his childhood on his fiction. 'For this reason,' he tells Ghīṭānī, 'you can notice that I often portray in my work the relationship between brothers; it is because of my deprivation of it. This is obvious in *The Trilogy, The Beginning and the End* and *Khan al-Khalili*.'[24]

The author describes to Ghīṭānī the family house in which he grew up in Jamāliyya. The description seems largely to tally with that of the house of the Aḥmad ᶜAbd al-Jawwād family in *The Trilogy*. He also tells us that the house is associated in his memory with play, particularly on the roof where house provisions were stored, poultry raised and various potted and creeping plants grown.[25] In this connection, readers of novels like *The Trilogy, Khan al-Khalili* and *The Beginning and the End* will recall how the roof figures as an occasional scene for family gatherings and the secret assignations of lovers. Mahfouz also says that, in addition to the roof, he used to play in the street with the children of neighbouring families.[26] Memories of those young friends and their common street adventures are affectionately recreated in both *Fountain and Tomb* and *Mirrors*.

About his parents Mahfouz does not say much and about his brothers and sisters he says next to nothing. He is at pains, however, to dissociate his parents from the most famous couple of his creation, Aḥmad ᶜAbd al-Jawwād and Amīna of *The*

Trilogy. He stresses that the fearful character of ᶜAbd al-Jawwād is not modelled on his father, but the head of a neighbouring family in Jamāliyya whom he used to visit as a child with his mother. He describes his father as having been 'old-fashioned', but in possession of a gentle temperament. Unlike ᶜAbd al-Jawwād, he spent most of his evenings with his family. He used to be some sort of book-keeper or accountant (we are not told exactly) in the civil service until he took early retirement to manage the business of a merchant friend of his.[27] Mahfouz's account of his father appears, however, to contradict that of Adham Rajab, a lifetime friend of his who knew him well during his adolescent years. Mr Rajab states that the author's father was so strict with his family that the young Mahfouz's friends were never able to visit him at his home. He says that the writer's eldest brother was also strict and surmises that the character of the fierce patriarch Aḥmad ᶜAbd al-Jawwād in *The Trilogy* must have been based on those two models. When faced with these revelations in 1970, Mahfouz accepted them as true.[28] Surprisingly, however, he was a few years later to contradict himself in the manner explained above.

The novelist emphasizes that patriotism was one basic value which he picked up from his father in his childhood:

> My father always spoke enthusiastically about our national heroes. . . . I grew up in a home where the names of Muṣṭafā Kāmil,[29] Muḥammad Farīd[30] and Saᶜd Zaghlūl[31] were truly sacred. . . . The strong emotion with which my father spoke about political figures would make you feel as if they were his personal enemies or friends. My father however was no exception here; this was the public spirit which dominated the country during my childhood.[32]

Much of this public spirit and of the infiltration of national politics into the life of the average Egyptian home the reader will immediately recognize in *The Trilogy*.

Religion was another important value in Mahfouz's family, whereas culture was absent: 'You would not have thought', he tells an interviewer, 'that an artist would emerge from that family.'[33] Mahfouz painfully fails to elaborate on what he calls 'the purely religious climate at home'[34] during his childhood. On what it was like and what his response to it was he leaves us totally in the dark. To answer these questions we have to go to

Kamāl in *The Trilogy* whose gradual disenchantment with religion is described at great length. It is interesting to note here that, while the value of nationalism (in which were also embedded the values of liberalism and democracy) was one that he nurtured and upheld all his life, that of organized, prescribed religion was one which he was to question and finally reject as he reached intellectual maturity.

Of his mother Mahfouz tells us that she was of a 'somewhat nervous temperament' and that there was little that she shared with the character of Amīna in *The Trilogy.* Unlike Amīna, and the women of her generation generally, she appears to have enjoyed a considerable amount of freedom. Interestingly, he tells us of her passion for ancient monuments. He remembers that when he was as young as four she would take him to look at the Pyramids and the Sphinx or the Museum of Antiquities, and especially to the Mummies Room.[35] This piece of information is illuminating when we consider that the author was later to develop a strong interest in Ancient Egyptian history and that his first three novels were to be devoted to the subject.

Around the year 1924, when Mahfouz was 12 years old, the family moved to ᶜAbbāsiyya, 'but I remained attracted to Jamāliyya, always hankering back for it',[36] says the novelist. He also tells us that the suburban quarter they moved to in the twenties was very different from today's over-crowded ᶜAbbāsiyya:

> The ᶜAbbāsiyya of old times was lush with greenery and had few buildings. Houses were small, consisting only of one storey and each surrounded by a garden, while open fields stretched as far as the horizon. . . and the silence was deep.[37]

Next to Jamāliyya, ᶜAbbāsiyya appears to be the only other place to have made a permanent claim on both Mahfouz's consciousness and his art. All other Cairene districts that serve occasionally as background for action in his novels are there only in their capacity as realistic detail. The same is also true of his descriptions of the Alexandrian scene as in *Autumn Quail, The Search, The Beggar* and *Miramar.* It is only when he evokes Jamāliyya and ᶜAbbāsiyya that he seems most at home and that we feel that we are in communion with some part of his innermost soul. Again, it is only evocations of Jamāliyya and ᶜAbbāsiyya that are employed symbolically in his work to stand for more than their immediate realistic reference. While to Jamāliyya he owes his many recreations of the *ḥāra* with its traditional features, he has the old ᶜAbbāsiyya lying on the edge of the desert to thank for his evocative descriptions of the *khalā'* (open space, emptiness, wasteland). In works like *Children of Gebelawi* and *Harafish*, to name but two, he annexes the *khalā'* of ᶜAbbāsiyya to the *ḥāra* of Jamāliyya to form his unique Mahfouzland which stands for all the world and all history.[38] In this personalized world-picture, *khalā'* is the scene for murders and clandestine burials and bloody warfare among rival gangs – it is the scene where some of the wildest human passions are set and where the inner loneliness is enhanced by the emptiness outside. But paradoxically, *khalā'* is also a place of refuge from the brutality of the world, of soul-searching, of communion with the vast and mysterious universe above, and of visions of goodness and reform. To ᶜAbbāsiyya and the many friends he made there during his adolescence he is also indebted for a great number of the fifty-five character vignettes that constitute *Mirrors*. In his old age, the novelist's nostalgia for the ᶜAbbāsiyya that is now extinct, the youthful days that are now in the distant past and the human relationships that time or death has severed appears to grow ever more agonizing – an agony that he has given expression to in his latest novel to date, *Qushtumur* (1988) and in a powerful short story entitled 'Half a Day',[39] both of which are desperate and pained attempts at capturing again through feats of memory times and places past.

But above all Mahfouz owes to ᶜAbbāsiyya one of the most powerful and mystifying experiences of his life which was to be recreated with corresponding intensity in the story of Kamāl's unrequited love for ᶜĀyda Shaddād in *The Trilogy*. The germination of this key experience in the novel was apparently a quite brief and uneventful encounter in Mahfouz's early youth, but one which has in an inscrutable, almost mystical, way had a strong hold on the author's consciousness for the rest of his life. In his memoirs he tries to rationalize the experience in the following terms:

> In ᶜAbbāsiyya I experienced true love for the first time. It was an abstract relationship because of age and class differences. There was actually no form of communication

whatsoever [between the two parties]. Had this happened, the experience would perhaps have not acquired much of [the halo] that I bequeathed on it. The effects of this relationship were later to appear in the experience of Kamāl ᶜAbd al-Jawwād's love for ᶜĀyda Shaddād in *The Trilogy*.[40]

Mahfouz's rendering of this personal experience in *The Trilogy* was not, however, his first. His attempts at domesticating this wildly painful experience in art form go as far back as the 1940s. I refer here to a short story with the title 'A Moment's Dream' included in the writer's first collection.[41] The story is naively written and structurally weak, but the circumstantial evidence in it leaves us with no doubt that it probably was the author's earliest attempt at achieving catharsis through art. The story is an account of a fleeting encounter between a young scientist and a beautiful young woman – an encounter that consisted in nothing more than the exchange of glances, but one which left the protagonist desperately and obsessively in love and without hope of fulfilment.

Even after the later, maturer and more complex rendition of the experience in *The Trilogy*, Mahfouz's feelings still apparently needed further purgation, for he comes back to the subject in the episode entitled 'Ṣafā' al-Kātib' in *Mirrors*. This episode, written when the author was nearly 60 years old and more than forty years removed from the experience, shows him still haunted by it and still unable to explain it. Written in intense, poetic language, the account must, however, be seen as the most factual and least fictionalized of his renderings of this key experience of his life. He often describes the encounter in near-mystical terms: 'As soon as my eyes caught sight of the girl's face, I embraced one of life's bursting secrets.' And again:

> I saw her in the carriage for a few seconds no more but that was enough for me to lose all will-power and to find myself flung in a new phase of evolution. . . . I knew how a man could wander away while being there and be wide awake in his sleep, how he could be lost in solitude amidst the crowd and make a companion of pain. I [also knew] how a man could penetrate to the roots of plants and the waves of light.[42]

The episode ends with the narrator in his old age wondering what had become of his love. His words echo with a pain that has not quite subsided:

> Whatever might have become of her and whatever others might have thought of her, did she not have the right to know that she had been worshipped like a goddess in a temple? And that she had once unleashed in a certain heart a life that still throbbed from time to time with her memory?[43]

EDUCATION AND INTELLECTUAL INFLUENCES

Mahfouz's education, in common with his generation, began at the *kuttāb* (Qur'ān School) where he learnt religion and the principles of literacy before he joined the primary school.[44] The novelist recalls briefly his experience at the *Kuttāb* in *Fountain and Tomb*, but rather than telling us about the educational system, he seems more interested in tracing the beginnings of his nascent sexuality through describing his feelings towards one of the girls there.[45] (In fact, the evolution of the young protagonist's sexuality is a central theme in the book.)[46] About Mahfouz's primary and secondary school education, however, we face a dearth of information concerning the nature of the educational system and its effects on him. Apart from two anecdotal episodes in *Fountain and Tomb* (Tales 21 and 22) and a substantial number in *Mirrors* of sketches of school friends and teachers, and recollections of sit-ins and anti-government demonstrations during the 1920s, there is not much else to know. Significant additional enlightenment, however, can be obtained from the author's account of Kamāl's childhood and adolescence in *The Trilogy* (Parts I and II).

In *Fountain and Tomb* the author tells us how he discovered 'reading' at the primary school when a friend lent him a detective story to read. From that time on he became addicted to reading.[47] During the primary stage and the early years of secondary education he moved on from detective stories to historical and adventure novels, all read in translation. He mentions the names of Sir Walter Scott and Sir Henry Rider Haggard in this connection. He started writing during school holidays while he was still at the primary school. His method was to rewrite a novel he had read, adding in some details from his own life. As he advanced through his teens he discovered Muṣṭafā al-Manfalūṭī (1876–1924), the Egyptian sentimentalist whose prose style influenced whole generations of educated Egyptians during the early decades of the century.[48] After Manfalūṭī comes what he terms 'the period of the awakening'. During that period he came to read what he calls 'the innovators'. Among these he enumerates the names of Ṭāhā Ḥusayn (1889–1973), ᶜAbbās Maḥmūd al-ᶜAqqād (1889–1964), Salāma Mūsā (1888–1958), Ibrāhīm al-Māzinī (1889–1949), Muḥammad Ḥusayn Haykal (1888–1956), and (at a slightly later stage) Maḥmūd Taymūr (1894–1973), Tawfīq al-Ḥakīm (1898–1987) and Yaḥyā Ḥaqqī (1905–92). To these writers he admits his indebtedness for his 'emancipation from the traditional way of thinking . . . the attraction of [his] attention to world literature, [providing] a new outlook on classical Arabic literature', as well as offering him models of the short story, the novel and drama.[49] Ṭāhā Ḥusayn's famous book *Fī al-Shiᶜr al-Jāhilī* (On Pre-Islamic Poetry) (1926), which questioned the validity of received opinion on both Islam and literature associated with it, and caused a literary and political uproar at the time, is described by Mahfouz as the book that had the greatest influence on his intellectual development. To him the book was 'an intellectual revolution which elevated reason, giving it priority above tradition'.[50] The enthusiasm with which Mahfouz speaks about this book should come as no surprise, as his own work was later to reveal a strong rationalist sense, consistently 'elevating reason above tradition'.

Apart from Ṭāhā Ḥusayn, there are two other Egyptian writers whose ideas appear to have appealed to and influenced the intellect of Mahfouz during its formative years. The first is Salāma Mūsā whose secularist, socialist and evolutionist outlook on life can be found in almost every book that Mahfouz has written during more than sixty years of his creative life, and whose passion for Ancient (as opposed to Islamic) Egypt can be traced in the novelist's early Pharaonic short stories and novels. Some of Mahfouz's very early writings were printed during the 1930s in *Al-Majalla al-Jadīda* (The New Review) published by Salāma Mūsā. Also published by Mūsā was Mahfouz's first novel, *The Game of Fates*, and prior to that his translation from English of a book on Ancient Egypt. In his memoirs Mahfouz recalls his brief personal acquaintance[51] with Mūsā during his undergraduate years and recreates their encounter in chapter 13 of *The Trilogy* III relegating his own part to Aḥmad Shawkat rather than Kamāl (his usual persona in the novel) and changing the title of the magazine published by Mūsā to *'Al-Insān al-Jadīd'* (The New Human Being). Elsewhere, Mahfouz admits, 'From Salāma Mūsā I have learnt to believe in science, socialism and tolerance.'[52]

The second writer is ᶜAbbās Maḥmūd al-ᶜAqqād whose enquiries into the principles of aestheticism and other philosophical issues appear to have helped push Mahfouz in the direction of selecting philosophy as the subject to study for his first degree. He tells us that during his secondary education he excelled in mathematics and the sciences and that the assumption had always been that at university he was going to study either medicine or engineering. That was until he started to read the philosophical articles by ᶜAqqād and others, then:

> Philosophical questions began to stir deep inside me . . . and I imagined that by studying philosophy I would find the right answers for the questions which tormented me . . . that I would unravel the mysteries of existence and man's fate.[53]

Thus he joined King Fu'ād I University (now Cairo University) as a philosophy student between the years 1930 and 1934. The agony which his final choice caused to his father is briefly remembered in Mahfouz's memoirs[54] and unforgettably recreated in the famous scene involving Kamāl and his father in chapter 4 of *The Trilogy II*.[55]

During his secondary school years he started also reading classical Arabic literature. He mentions by way of example *Al-Bayān wa al-Tabyīn* by al-Jāḥiẓ, *Al-Amālī* by al-Qālī, *Al-ᶜIqd al-Farīd* by Ibn ᶜAbd Rabbih and *Al-Kāmil* by al-Mubarrad. He mentions also how he used to imitate the style of these sources in his compositions at school, much to the delight of his 'turbanned' Arabic teachers. The effect of these classical readings has in fact survived his school days and can be observed in the propensity in his early short stories and novels towards cliché and flowery outdated style. More positively, the effect of this early (and thenceforth 'intermittent', as he puts it) contact with classical Arabic has been to endow his Arabic style throughout his career with a purity of phrase and a correctness of grammar and structure which evaded many later outstanding writers (e.g. Yūsuf Idrīs (1927–91)). He tells us that as he matured he turned more towards classical poetry and mentions in particular the names of al-Maᶜarrī, al-Mutanabbī and Ibn al-Rūmī.[56] It must have been much later that he indulged in reading *ṣūfī* (mystical) poetry, the effects of which can be spotted in his fiction from the 1960s onwards. In a later interview he gives indeed the names of Ḥāfiẓ Shīrāzī and Rabindranath Tagore as his two favourite poets.[57]

After graduation in 1934, Mahfouz's intensive readings in philosophy, we are informed, continued as the author started working towards an MA degree. His chosen subject, according to one statement, was 'the aesthetic theory' [sic].[58] Elsewhere, however, he contradicts himself and gives the subject as '*Ṣūfism* in Islam'.[59] His intellectual reaction to his philosophy studies has been recorded in a number of articles that he published in a variety of magazines and newspapers throughout his undergraduate years and for several years thereafter. Mahfouz has always regarded those articles (most of them written when he was in his early to mid-twenties) as juvenilia and refused to have them collected and republished, which remains the case to date. Thanks to the effort of one scholar, however, we now have a full bibliographical list of those early articles, a classification of their content, as well as an attempt at analysing them for the roots of the author's thought.[60]

The list comprises forty-seven articles written between 1930 and 1945, well over half of which deal with philosophical and psychological subjects. The late Professor Badr points out the prominent place that the thought of the French philosopher Henri Bergson occupies in those articles, and expounds briefly Bergson's ideas on the duality of body and spirit and his elevation of intuition over scientific reasoning as a way of knowing, arguing that these ideas are necessary for the understanding of Mahfouz's work.[61] While Badr fails to pursue the Bergsonian connection any further in the course of his unfinished study, his generalization will indubitably prove rewarding in a future study of influences on the author. One can think of many substantiations in Mahfouz's fiction of the duality of matter and spirit and man's struggle to evolve from the bonds of the first to the freedom of the latter (Ṣābir's schism in *The Search* between his two lovers is perhaps the most clear-cut example in Mahfouz's *œuvre*).

Bergson's influence on Mahfouz has indeed been tremendous and far exceeds Badr's suggestions. The philosopher's most telling impact on Mahfouz's thought was probably in the sphere of his ideas on time and memory. Bergson's notion of 'duration', of time as a continuum, a perpetual flux (as distinguished from the spatialized, measurable conception of time), lies at the very foundation of *The Trilogy*. There is little doubt either that Mahfouz's concept of time as 'representing the evolutionary spirit of man',[62] central again to *The Trilogy* and probably the only source of philosophical optimism in the author's entire corpus, is drawn from Bergson's notion of 'creative evolution'. Nor has Mahfouz's fascination with Bergson's thought been a transient one. Far from being limited to *The Trilogy*, it is to be found also in *Children of Gebelawi*, *Harafish* and *Nights of the Thousand Nights*; in other words, in all those works which portray the evolutionary flux of history and the perpetual tug-of-war between the forces of moral progress in life and those of the baser instincts. On the individual (as opposed to collective) level, Mahfouz's obsession with the dichotomy between the unity and perpetuity of mnemonic time and the discreteness and transience of spatialized time (such as we see in *Qushtumur* and the short story 'Half a Day')[63] is yet another manifestation of the enormous power of Bergson's influence on Mahfouz. In respect of notions of time, Bergson's influence on Mahfouz was indeed reinforced by that of Marcel Proust, whose own *A la recherche du temps perdu* (much admired by Mahfouz) was itself influenced by Bergson's ideas.

Another Bergsonian notion active in Mahfouz's creations is perhaps that of the 'two moralities'. Bergson defines two sources for morality, one based on 'intelligence' and the other on 'intuition'. It is the second one which concerns us here since it finds 'its expression not only in the creativity of art and philosophy but also in the mystical experience of the saints'.[64] The mystical (or *ṣūfī*) experience has been a key one in Mahfouz's work from Raḍwān al-Ḥusaynī in *Midaq Alley* to ᶜAlī al-Junaydī in *The Thief and the Dogs*, ᶜUmar al-Ḥamzāwī in *The Beggar*, and ᶜAbdullāh al-Balkhī in *Nights of the Thousand Nights*. Mahfouz's attitude to his mystics is, however, ambivalent, for while they are shown as humans with an impeccable superior morality, their 'sainthood' is depicted as a personal achievement of little relevance to society or humanity at large, as I hope I will show later in the discussion of the above-named and other works. Suffice it to say here that of all Bergson's notions, it is this last one that Mahfouz appears to embody in his work only in order to reject it.

Mahfouz's MA in philosophy was never to be completed and within two years of graduation his orientation towards philosophy was deflected in the direction of literature. Interestingly, this is graphically reflected in his choice of subjects for his last eight published articles between 1936 and 1945 – they all dealt with literary and artistic themes, whereas earlier, philosophical themes were dominant.[65] Thus a harrowing conflict in Mahfouz's mind between philosophy and literature which had lasted for the period of those two years was brought to an end, much to his relief, in favour of the latter.[66] Philosophy in its basic sense as the search for meaning in life remained, however, central throughout Mahfouz's work.

Having decided to abandon the study of philosophy for what was to become a lifelong devotion to literature, the novelist had much ground to make up. He drew on a general guide to world literature, namely *The Outline of Literature* by John Drinkwater[67] to help him in planning his reading and selecting material.[68] The book's method consisted in reviewing world literature down the ages and across nations, which afforded Mahfouz an overall view rather than immersing him in the literature of any one period or nation. Because he started late, as he puts it, he had to be selective, confining himself to the main figures, and then only to their best known masterpieces. He also began with the modern period, occasionally going back to earlier periods. His medium was English and, to a much lesser extent, French: he read Proust in English, but Anatole France in the original. Later in his life he came to depend on Arabic translations as they began to be more common.[69]

Mahfouz has over and again given his interviewers an account of the writers he admired and the works which most impressed him. His list is long and varied and is proof of an overriding orientation towards Western culture. I shall quote one of his accounts at length. His comments on writers and works are fascinating in their uninhibited spontaneity. Often, however, they are revealing about his own inclinations and writings:

> The writers who influenced me are the ones I liked. I liked Tolstoy and Dostoevsky, Chekhov and Maupassant. . . . Of modernist writers I liked Proust and Kakfa. As for Joyce . . . he was just a writer that you had to read . . . *Ulysses* was a terrible novel, but it created a trend. . . . In the theatre I liked Shakespeare immensely. . . . Both his grandness and ironies entered my soul and made me feel at home with him. . . . Next to Shakespeare I liked Eugene O'Neill much and also Ibsen and Strindberg. In the contemporary theatre I was truly shaken by Beckett's *Waiting for Godot*. As for Chekhov's theatre, I found it flaccid and boring. In American literature I rate Melville's *Moby Dick* among the world's greatest novels if not *the* greatest. Out of Hemingway's work I only liked *The Old Man and the Sea*. His other work left me surprised at the fame he has acquired. I did not like Faulkner; he is too complicated. I also liked Dos Passos, but none of them has written a *Moby Dick*.
>
> I very much admire the all-encompassing outlook in Conrad's *Heart of Darkness*. The novel offers a very realistic story but contains at the same time a broad universal view. This is what I have been trying to do in my latest novels [NB interview was given in 1973].
>
> As for the latest trends, the Angry Young Men etc., you could say that their influence has not gone beyond the surface of my skin. *Le roman nouveau* is rubbish. It is as if you were saying, 'life is boring therefore I will write for you an equally boring novel'. The fact is that any expression of the boredom of life must be entertaining. . . . In poetry I was fascinated by Shakespeare, Tagore and Ḥāfiẓ Shīrāzī; they are the closest poets to my soul.[70]

Elsewhere he informs us that he owes his training in the realistic tradition to its later developers rather than early masters:

> I got to know realism through contemporary writers like Galsworthy, Aldous Huxley and D. H. Lawrence. After these I was no longer able to read Dickens. Nor was I able to read Balzac having already read Flaubert and Stendhal.[71]

To the Russian masters mentioned above he adds the name of Gorky, but deems him of a lower rank. His fiction, he argues, is parochial and too dependent on the message it contains.

Asked in yet another interview on the Western writers who most influenced him he lists three names as his first choice: Tolstoy, Proust and Thomas Mann. He regrets that since reading *War and Peace* and *A la recherche du temps perdu* early on in his life he never had the time to go back to them again. His fascination with *War and Peace* is understandable in the context of his own authorship of another great novel dealing with the effect of social and political upheaval on the lives of individuals, i.e. *The Trilogy*. It is worth noting here that Mahfouz does not give another famous saga novel, viz. Galsworthy's *Forsyte Saga* (thought by many commentators to have been an influence on his own *Trilogy*), any special rating as a great novel. He lists Galsworthy, however, among the authors he has read, as we have seen in an earlier quotation. Equally interesting is Mahfouz's dismissal of Charles Dickens as an author he could not read in spite of the obvious affinity observed by many critics between a novel like *Midaq Alley* and the typical Dickensian world. On the other hand, we can understand his fascination with Proust's *A la recherche* ... in the light of his own unrelenting obsession with the theme of observable time versus time in memory. If one is to see a pattern in Mahfouz's comments on writers from whom he learnt his profession, we may be able to say that he, perhaps subconsciously, tends to play down the influence of those whose achievement has been equalled or surpassed in his own work, while he continues to hold in charmed esteem those, like Tolstoy and Proust, whose attainments are deemed unrepeatable. In another interview he describes Shakespeare, Kafka, O'Neill, Shaw, Ibsen and Strindberg as writers 'whom he liked to the point of adoration'.

Mahfouz has often repeated that when he started writing his realistic novels in the 1940s he was well aware that realism was already a spent force in Europe and that he had already read Proust, Joyce, Lawrence and other contemporary modernists. When it came to writing, however, he argues, he felt that since the novel was still a nascent form in Arabic without an established tradition in realism, he could not move straight away from romanticism to modernism: the Arabic novel and his own experience as a novelist in the making had to go through the natural stages of evolution. This contention of Mahfouz's can withstand enquiry. We can indeed see modernist influences in the heart of his realistic phase, such as the occasional use of the stream of consciousness technique and his early experiment with the psychological novel in *Mirage*. Another piece of evidence that supports this contention is the fact that the moment Mahfouz felt that he had mastered the techniques of realism and exhausted their potential, that is by writing *The Trilogy*, he was to cast realism behind him and plunge into the deep and turbulent waters of modernism.

One of the inconsistencies, however, in Mahfouz's comments on his work is his persistent denial of the influence of the naturalist school on the realistic phase of his corpus. The persistence of his denial is in fact a reaction to an equally persistent and unanimous recognition by his critics of this influence in his work. Critics often cite the characters of Nafīsa from *The Beginning and the End* and Yāsīn from *The Trilogy* (a list which can certainly be expanded) as salient examples. Mahfouz, on the other hand, admits reading a lot of Zola and his followers, but insists that in his work 'heredity' is of no consequence and that the effect of 'environment' reigns supreme. However, he seems to contradict himself when he argues in the same breath that Nafīsa's poverty (environment) in addition to her ugliness (heredity) helped shape her life. Elsewhere he proclaims that all considerations, social, psychological and *biological* (my italics), influence his characters.[72] Mahfouz's denial of naturalistic influence on his work can not therefore withstand the testimony of his own fiction or, for that matter, his own conflicting statements on the subject. His attempt at denying this influence stems, I believe, from a concern that stressing the hereditary connection in his fiction might result in overshadowing the supreme importance of social and political conditions in shaping human behaviour, a belief that lies at the heart of his work. Another significant element here is the fact that all these denials of naturalism were made by Mahfouz at a time when he had moved out of his realistic phase and when heredity had in fact stopped playing any role in his fiction. It was as if, having outgrown a particular concept, he wanted to go back and obliterate it from his literary past.

Two influences which Mahfouz is, however, happy to admit are those of James Joyce in his use of the internal monologue on the one hand and surrealism and the theatre of the absurd (whose influence can be spotted in some of his short stories and one-act plays written in the aftermath of the Arab defeat in the

1967 war with Israel) on the other hand. He insists, however, that blind imitation has never been the case with him; that all the techniques he borrows are modified to suit his purposes and clearly stamped with his own artistic insignia. With regard to his use of the internal monologue he has this to say:

> The internal monologue is a method, a vision and a way of life; and even though I use it, you cannot say that I belong to its school as such. All that happens is that I sometimes encounter a Joycean moment in my hero's life, so I render it in Joyce's manner with some modification.[73]

He also plays down the influence of the absurd on his work. He argues that the absurd outlook on life maintains that it is meaningless, whereas for him life has a meaning and a purpose, and that though his work might have given in to an absurd moment in his own or his nation's life, his was a sense of absurdity that was 'rationalized, explicable and subdued', unlike the European brand, which was total and absolute.[74] Mahfouz sums it all up in connection with the question of influence when he proclaims, 'I have not come out of the cloak of any one writer, nor can I be stood under the banner of any one technique'.[75]

On the question of the influence of earlier Egyptian novelists, Mahfouz is again conservative if not dismissive. With the exception of Jurjī Zaydān, he makes no mention of Syrian pioneers like Buṭrus al-Bustānī and Fransīs al-Marrāsh. Of Tawfīq al-Ḥakīm's *ᶜAwdat al-Rūḥ* (The Return of the Spirit, 1933), he says that he found it more akin to drama than to fiction. Ṭāhā Ḥusayn and ᶜAbbās al-ᶜAqqād, he maintains were 'thinkers' whose concern with the novel was only secondary.[76] He admits, however, that Ṭāhā Ḥusayn's novel *Shajarat al-Bu's* (Tree of Misery, 1944) was instrumental in focusing his attention on writing a saga novel. It was after reading it, he tells us, that he went on to read more of the same, namely Galsworthy's *The Forsyte Saga*, Tolstoy's *War and Peace* and Thomas Mann's *Buddenbrooks* before he wrote his own *Trilogy*.[77] Asked on one occasion to clarify a statement he had made earlier in which he said that he had been influenced by the Egyptian novelists Ibrāhīm al-Māzinī and Yaḥyā Ḥaqqī, he gave this rather loose definition of influence: 'When I say that I was influenced [by a certain writer] what I mean is that I liked [his work]. My assumption is that I am influenced by the writers I like.'[78] His attitude towards the question of influence on himself by earlier Arab novelists is eloquently summed up in his pronouncement: 'There was no legacy of the novel [in Arabic] that I could depend on. . . . I arrived on a scene that was nearly empty. It was incumbent on me to discover things and to lay the ground by myself.'[79]

Finally, no review of the intellectual influences that helped formulate the thought and art of Mahfouz is complete without mention of science. Belief in science, in conjunction with socialism, as a major force in shaping modern society and the future of mankind is at the very centre of the novelist's work. His preoccupation with science was demonstrated as early as his first two realistic novels, *Khan al-Khalili* and *New Cairo*, to reach a climax in *Children of Gebelawi*, where science is shown to inherit the traditional role of religion in reforming human society. His readings in science for the layman go back, he tells us, to his early youth. He mentions such subjects as biology, physics, anthropology and the origin of matter, and admits that his readings in science have had a tremendous effect on his thinking.[80]

Mahfouz, as we have seen, is careful to fight off any suggestion of influence in the sense of imitation, especially in connection with Western writers and schools. He is nevertheless happy to articulate his admiration for European culture and his belief in the inevitability of the triumph of its values. He is also at pains to establish a historic affinity between it and Arab culture. His views in this respect are indeed reminiscent of those expressed earlier by Ṭāhā Ḥusayn in his controversial book *Mustaqbal al-Thaqāfa fī Miṣr* (The Future of Culture in Egypt), published in 1938. Mahfouz argues that:

> Our culture is very close to European culture. This is because they both are based on common foundations. For its part, European culture is based on both the moral principles of the Bible and the modern science inherited from the Greeks. The same is also true of Arabic culture, the difference between the Bible and the Qur'ān being here of no consequence as the latter maintains that it embraces both the Bible and the Gospels. The moral values are thus the same. As for the Greeks, we know that the Arabs

translated the Greeks and studied them. . . . Both our culture and that of the West belong in fact to one family.[81]

Again in a reference to European culture in the context of a discussion of the permanently hot issue of foreign influence and cultural identity, he announces unequivocally, 'I believe that there is no escape from the supremacy of the more efficient culture, and this can only be for the good of mankind, and not otherwise.'[82] These relatively recent and overtly expressed views have their testimony in the totality of Mahfouz's work where the traditional values of modern Europe such as secularism, social liberalism, parliamentary democracy, socialism and belief in science are glorified.

More recently, however, the author's intellectual stance *vis-à-vis* this question seems to have shifted. In an interview given in 1987, he argues that in the past he used to believe that modern (European) civilization was the only viable one by dint of its being an assimilation of all past civilizations – Egyptian, Mesopotamian, Greek, Roman and Arab; and that as such it ought to be the universal civilization of mankind. More recently, he goes on to say, he came to believe that different civilizations upheld essentially different world views. He feels this has caused his enthusiasm for Western civilization to shift towards an enthusiasm for a universal human need such as science, which in turn can be used in the service of the world view of one's own culture. Mahfouz concludes by describing his present position as an eclectic one which seeks to benefit from the entire human legacy.[83] This shift in his thinking remains, however, at the theoretical level. It probably has come too late in his life to be able to be substantiated in his work. One may argue nevertheless that his movement in the last fifteen years or so away from the European mould of the novel towards a more indigenously inspired form is a mark of his waning fascination with all things Western, but one would have to make the reservation here that the divergence is more in form than substance.

POLITICAL BELIEFS AND SYMPATHIES

Politics has been a major concern of Mahfouz throughout his creative career, a fact he himself emphasizes: 'In all my writing, you will find politics. You may find a story which ignores love, or any other subject, but not politics; it is the very axis of our thinking.'[84] Highly politicized in his thinking and writing though he is, he has never been politically active in the formal sense of joining a political party or occupying a political office under any of the many regimes that his life has spanned. His political awareness started blossoming, as we have seen, at the rather early age of 7 with the eruption of the 1919 revolution. This awareness must have matured during his high school and university years in the late 1920s and early 1930s. The national struggle during that period had two objectives which were closely related, namely independence from the British and the establishment of true democratic government in the face of absolutist monarchism. During the years up to the 1952 coup led by Jamāl ᶜAbd al-Nāṣir (Nasser) (1918–70), this national struggle was led by the Wafd Party which had arisen from the ashes of 1919. The Wafd was, by and large, the conscience of the nation and the focus of its political hopes. Mahfouz evinces great sympathy for the party and its leaders in his novels dealing with that period (especially *The Trilogy)*. His sympathy for the Wafd, however, never took an official form. According to him, he only participated as an individual in 'general popular actions like demonstrations and strikes . . . no matter how dangerous these were'.[85]

Another political movement active at the time was socialism, whose ideas were attractive to intellectuals though it lacked both a popular base and a recognized political organ. It cannot be doubted that socialist ideals must have claimed Mahfouz's soul from very early on in his youth.[86] The influence of socialist thought figures very strongly in his first two social novels (*Khan al-Khalili* and *New Cairo*) and has continued ever since. Parallel to this sympathy for socialism was an antipathy towards Islamic fundamentalism as expressed by the Muslim Brotherhood, a considerable political force in the 1930s and 1940s with a strong organization and a not insignificant power base among the people. Unlike socialism, which is idealized in Mahfouz's work, Islamism is critically delineated and finally rejected as unsuitable for modern times. The two models are revealingly contrasted in the two novels mentioned above and again in *The Trilogy*.[87] Mahfouz's distaste for religious fundamentalism has not waned with time. In his memoirs he does not mince his words when he proclaims in the course of reviewing political forces active on the scene during his youth: 'the ones I hated from the beginning were the Moslem Brothers.'[88] In his semi-autobiographical work, *Mirrors*, he draws a very negative portrait of a prominent leader of the movement, viz. Sayyid Quṭb (1906–66),[89] whom he knew personally in his youth at a time when Quṭb had shown more interest in literary criticism than in active religious fundamentalism (Quṭb was in fact among the first critics to draw attention to the budding talent of Mahfouz in the mid-1940s).[90]

It must, however, be emphasized that in spite of Mahfouz's firm belief, amply demonstrated in the corpus of his work, in socialism as the only way forward for his society, he cannot be pigeon-holed as a Marxist in any tight definition of the word. He asserts that he does not consider himself a Marxist despite his immense sympathy for Marxism. He admits that he has his doubts about the Marxist theory as a philosophical system, but goes on to list aspects of Marxism which he would like to see applied in human society. His words amount to a political credo and merit quoting in full.

> I believe:
> 1 that man should be freed from the class system and what it entails of privileges such as inheritance. . . etc;
> 2 that man should be freed from all forms of exploitation;
> 3 that an individual's position [in society] should be determined according to both his natural and acquired qualifications;
> 4 that recompense should be equal to need;
> 5 that the individual should enjoy freedom of thought and belief under protection of law to which both governor and governed should be subject;
> 6 in the realization of democracy in the fullest sense;
> 7 in the reduction of the power of central government so that it should be restricted to [internal?] security and defence.[91]

Central to the understanding of the bulk of Mahfouz's work from the beginning of the 1960s to the present day is an adequate grasp of his attitude to the 1952 revolution, a subject on which he has spoken outside the scope of his fiction with a profuseness which is only paralleled by his extensive preoccupation with it in his creative writing. 1952, the year when

Mahfouz had completed the writing of *The Trilogy*,[92] heralded an uncharacteristic stalemate in his creative life: he was to stop writing until 1957, when he started work on *Children of Gebelawi*. Since that time he has had to explain many times the reason for those five silent years. In answer to untiring critics he argued that he felt that the society he had been writing about for years had changed overnight and that many of the social ills which had moved him to write were remedied by the new regime.[93] There is no reason to doubt the truthfulness of this remark in so far as it applied to the early years of the revolution. But as the years went by and the shortcomings of the Nasser era began to make themselves felt, one critic's remark that Mahfouz, 'rather than finding nothing to say . . . was unable to say what he wanted to' rings true.[94] This seems even more the case when we look at the content of what the novelist began to say when he had recovered and summoned to his assistance the tools of his art. His first novel after the silent period, viz. *Children of Gebelawi*, was an allegorical lamentation on the failure of mankind to achieve social justice and to harness the potential of science for the service of man, rather than his destruction. Masked in allegory though it was, the novel could hardly be seen as the offspring of an intellect basking in a sense of revolutionary fulfilment. The publication of his next novel, *The Thief and the Dogs* in 1961, shows in unequivocal terms that his disillusionment with the revolution was complete. Almost all the novels of the 1960s can in fact be seen as a barrage of bitter criticism aimed at a revolution that has abjectly failed to deliver the goods.[95]

Such, then, was the extent of Mahfouz's disillusionment with the 1952 revolution during its heyday in the 1960s and even before its crowning failure in the shape of the 1967 defeat in the war with Israel. His criticisms were unsweetened and often hit the mark and it is common knowledge now that some of his novels written during that period would not have seen the light if it were not for the influence of Muḥammad Ḥasanayn Haykal, confidant of Nasser and editor at the time of the Cairo daily *Al-Ahrām* (where Mahfouz serialized his novels). The publication of his work and that of others of a similar critical nature may indeed have been a calculated attempt to use it as a safety valve and to give a semblance of tolerance towards criticism.[96]

It must be stressed, however, that Mahfouz's quarrel with the

1952 revolution has never been over principles; it was rather over its practices which failed to live up to its principles. He proclaims in an interview given in the relatively freer climate of 1973 (three years into the era of Anwar al-Sādāt (1918–81)):

> There is no doubt that the declared aims of the 23 July [1952] revolution would have been to me and to my entire generation very satisfactory only if they had been carried out in the spirit in which they were declared. . . . I wanted nothing more than true socialism and true democracy. This has not been achieved.[97]

Following the military debacle of 1967 and Nasser's death in 1970 Mahfouz's onslaught on the revolution rose to a crescendo in *The Karnak* (1974), a bitter condemnation of the repressive techniques of the police state and their destructive effect on the dignity of the individual and hence the nation as a whole.[98]

The novelist's ambivalent attitude towards the 1952 revolution can perhaps be best illustrated by two separate passages from *Mirrors*. Here is the first passage (from the sketch titled 'ᶜAdlī al-Mu'dhdhin') in which the narrator/protagonist of the novel (a persona for Mahfouz) expresses his early enthusiasm for the revolution:

> I felt for the first time in my life that a wave of justice was sweeping away without a let up the deep-rooted rot and I wished that it would stay on its course without hesitation or aberration, and for ever remaining pure.
>
> (p. 250)

Further on in the book in the sketch entitled 'Qadrī Rizq', the narrator draws a portrait of a member of his group of friends who belonged to the Free Officers' Movement which carried out the 1952 coup. The character, which is obviously meant to be representative of the top echelons of the revolution, is portrayed critically but with unmistakable affection. Here are the closing lines of the episode:

> Qadrī Rizq is counted among the sincere and respected men of the revolution. He may be difficult to classify in accordance with universal principles, but he can be described accurately in the light of the Charter.[99] He believes in social justice as much as private ownership and individual incentives, in scientific socialism as much as reli-

> gion, in nationalism as much as pan-Arabism, in the legacy of the past as much as science, and in a popular base as much as absolute government. Nevertheless, whenever I see him walking in with his limp and his remaining eye, my heart beats with affection and admiration.
>
> (p. 345)

The revolution here is ridiculed as a mixture of conflicting social and political principles, while the officer's deformities (dating from the Suez War) are obvious symbols of the revolution's shortcomings. The evident affection is, however, proof of the ambivalence in Mahfouz's attitude towards the rule of Nasser: consistently he has shown himself to be equally aware of both the positive and negative sides of the experiment.

Apart from his fiction and interviews there is another major source for the novelist's views on the Nasser period and indeed on his political, economic and social views generally. By this I mean the current affairs column he has been writing weekly in *Al-Ahrām* ever since the mid-1970s. A large selection of these short articles has appeared recently in three volumes under the titles: *Of Religion and Democracy, Of Culture and Education* and *Of Youth and Freedom*. In this weekly column and for the past fifteen years or so not a single anniversary of 23 July 1952 has passed without remembrance of the many horrors together with the many achievements of the revolution.[100] There we can also catch glimpses of Mahfouz's nostalgia for the glorious days of the Wafd Party in his repeated celebrations of the anniversaries of its leaders Saᶜd Zaghlūl and Muṣṭafā al-Naḥḥās (1879?-1965).[101] In those columns we can again trace his support for the democratization process begun by Sādāt and his wholehearted espousal of the establishment of peace with Israel[102] and the normalization of relations between the two states.[103] The volumes make tedious reading on the whole but are priceless for the direct insights they afford us into those ideas of the writer which are usually more carefully disguised in his fiction.

Mahfouz, as we have seen, was born into a lower-middle-class Cairene family and his work has remained very much the product of this fact. The background for his fiction is always urban: mainly Cairo and occasionally Alexandria; the countryside has no place in his world. His fiction, on the other hand, is inhabited by members of his own class; their progress within society, their loves and hates, ambitions and frustrations, both private and public, are vividly recreated there. The aristocracy, the upper middle class, the working class and the peasantry form no part of his customary scene and when individuals from those groups make an occasional appearance in his fiction, they are usually portrayed from outside and through the eyes of the petit-bourgeois protagonist, their importance being drawn solely from their relationship with him (a striking example is to be found in *Miramar* where the peasant heroine Zahra is at the centre of the action, yet the novel is told from four points of view, of which not one is hers).

Thus Mahfouz has been labelled by critics (and perhaps rightly so) as the novelist of the small bourgeoisie.[104] It is a label that he appeared to resent at first, but has since become resigned to. In recent interviews he has professed his 'bias' for the small bourgeoisie, which he views as 'the candidate for the salvation of humanity'. The upper bourgeoisie, he explains, is arrogant and seeks to control and exploit the people. The proletariat, on the other hand, is equally intent on usurping power from its exploiters. Only the small bourgeoisie with its middle stance between the extreme positions of the classes above and below itself is capable of recognizing the advantages and faults of both sides and evolving an order viable for everyone. Mahfouz goes on to illustrate his point in interesting, if somewhat eccentric, terms:

> A good small bourgeois rejects the shortcomings of the upper bourgeoisie such as exploitation and love of power at the same time as he admires its inclination towards knowledge, art and refinement of manners. On the other hand he is also aware of the vices of the proletariat forced upon them by poverty, but he is equally aware of their genuine mettle and the fact that they represent the majority. No wonder then that the small bourgeoisie produced Socialist Democracy which combines the best in Liberalism and Communism. Such was the case in history too. For religions whose prophets were kings or princes like Akhenatunism and Judaism failed to spread widely, contrary to Christianity and Islam whose prophets belonged to the small bourgeoisie – a carpenter and a small merchant respectively.[105]

THE NOVELIST AS CIVIL SERVANT

Like many of his characters Mahfouz was a civil servant.[106] From the year of his graduation (1934) to his retirement (1971), he served in a wide variety of government departments in various capacities and under different political regimes. Thus Mahfouz was not able to devote himself entirely to literature until he retired from service at the age of 60. 'What a waste!' is one's first impulse, but in fact it was quite the opposite. Mahfouz's fiction is profoundly indebted to his civil servant career for an infinite variety of types, individuals, plots, settings, images, symbols, atmospheres – he has admirably succeeded in finding a metaphor for the human condition in the drab world of the small Egyptian civil servant.[107]

In 1934 he joined the administration of King Fu'ād I University (now Cairo University) as a clerk (there, for instance, he picked up the model for Aḥmad ᶜĀkif, the eccentric hero of *Khan al-Khalili*). In 1938 he moved to the Ministry of Religious Endowments, where he worked as parliamentary secretary to the minister. The variety of claimants there that he came in contact with in his official capacity ranged, according to him, from descendants of the Ottoman Sultan, ᶜAbd al-Ḥamīd, to poor Egyptian peasants. Those claimants of *waqf* (religious endowment money) and their stories were later to provide his fiction with a great many characters and situations, most notably the eccentric protagonist of *Heart of the Night*. In 1945 he was transferred to al-Ghūrī Library in Jamāliyya at his own request, thereby returning to work in his birthplace, which was to remain a permanent spiritual refuge for him and a fathomless source of inspiration for his art. His duties at the library appear to have been so scant as to allow him, on the one hand, to wander in the area and spend time in its cafés, watching human types and imprinting pictures of places on his memory and, on the other hand, to indulge in major reading projects – it was at that time, he tells us, that he read Proust's *A la recherche du temps perdu* (in English translation). From there he moved on, still in the service of the Ministry of Endowments and still in Jamāliyya, to manage the Good Loan Project – apparently an interest-free loan scheme for the destitute. It was a period of his life that he enjoyed fully – he spent whole mornings, he informs us, chatting with lower-class women who came to apply for loans. But it was not totally idle chatter; many of those women have later come to populate his fiction, especially in the realistic phase.

The early 1950s brought Mahfouz's connection with the Endowments to an end and saw him move to the seemingly more appropriate sphere of information and culture. For the next twenty years or so of his civil servant's career (all served under the regime of Nasser's revolution) he was to occupy fairly influential cultural posts: secretary to the Minister of National Guidance (i.e. information); director of the Film Censorship Office; director-general of the Film Support Organization; adviser to the General Organization for Film Industry, Broadcasting and Television; chairman of the board of directors of the same; and finally, adviser to the Minister of Culture. When he retired in 1971 at the age of 60, he was invited to join the host of distinguished 'writers emeriti', as it were, at *Al-Ahrām* newspaper, which systematically attracted to its exclusive pages the cream of Egyptian writers as and when they became free from their official occupations. The last novel he serialized in *Al-Ahrām* was *Qushtumur* in 1988. He has also contributed a short weekly column on topical, mostly non-literary issues for the last fifteen years or so. It is an observation worth making that human models drawn from the milieu of the first half of his career have mostly populated the corresponding half of his output, i.e. from *Khan al-Khalili* up to *Children of Gebelawi*. Novels written after that seem to have drawn mainly on the environment of the second half of his career. Here we meet many intellectuals, professionals and high government officials in contrast with the lower and lower-middle classes of his earlier work. However, this division is by no means rigid, for models of the earlier half have continued to cross this imaginary barrier all the time, and increasingly so since the mid-1970s when, with works like *Fountain and Tomb* and *Harafish*, it became apparent that Mahfouz was experiencing nostalgia for his old world.

From the late 1940s and up to the early 1980s Mahfouz worked as an occasional freelance film scenarist. Altogether he has written the scenarios for twenty-five films, many of which are today counted among the classics of the Egyptian cinema industry.[108] Significantly though, there are to date some thirty-four films based on his own work, for none of which did he write the scenario himself: he would not interfere with the adaptation of his own work for the cinema.[109] Though he originally started writing scenarios as a way of supplementing his income, the experience was to have an influence on his literary style, particularly in his use of the montage technique and flashbacks which began to feature noticeably in his work from the 1960s onwards.

Mahfouz is a prolific writer. To date he has published thirty-five novels and fourteen collections of short stories and plays, in addition to three collections of his journalism and one translation.[110] Though his first novel was published in 1939, his fame and esteem were to grow slowly and it was not until the publication of *The Trilogy* in the late 1950s that he was hailed as the unrivalled master of fiction in the Arabic tongue. In 1970 he was awarded the State Prize for Literature. Though Mahfouz was first translated into the main languages of the world in the 1960s, interest in him in the West remained largely confined to orientalists and students of Arabic, while publication of translations of his work was mainly in the hands of academic and small-circulation publishers. Nevertheless, by the late 1980s the strength of his reputation among learned circles in the West as a writer with a universal human appeal and a lifetime's achievement was such that he was awarded the Nobel prize for literature in 1988, thereby becoming the first Arab writer to win this international seal of literary approval.

A PERSONAL SKETCH

Mahfouz remained a bachelor until the age of 43 – for many years he laboured under the conviction that marriage with its restrictions and commitments would hamper his literary future (compare Kamāl's bachelorhood in *The Trilogy*!). His prolonged bachelorhood gave him the opportunity to know many women, all of whom, he tells us, were later to appear in his fiction. In 1954, however, his defences against marriage collapsed and he has since enjoyed a happy and stable marriage which has produced two girls. Mahfouz has always jealously defended his privacy against the curiosity of the media. The onslaught in the wake of the Nobel prize was, however, too fierce to resist and it was only then that journalists and cameras were admitted to his house and the public were allowed a glimpse of his family life.

When he got married he moved from the family house in ᶜAbbāsiya to an apartment overlooking the Nile in Jīza where he still lives. It is worth noting that the Nile did not play a major role in his fiction until some time after his move to the neighbourhood of the old river. Full recognition of the effect of this change of habitat on the creative imagination of Mahfouz appeared in his 1966 novel, *Chatter on the Nile*.

In all his life Mahfouz has been out of Egypt only twice: once to Yemen[111] and once to Yugoslavia – both visits being on short, official missions. He had very much wished to travel to Europe and study in France in his youth in the manner of Tawfīq al-Ḥakīm and other Egyptian writers, but there was no opportunity.[112] European literature as well as European social and political thought have had a tremendous influence on his intellect, as we have seen. One wonders how this influence would have been tempered or, for that matter, enhanced through direct, prolonged contact with Western culture. As he grew older and more established and opportunities became available, he had become too set in his ways, too enslaved by a routine of work and life to care to disrupt it.[113] This was so much the case that when he was awarded the Nobel prize he refused to travel to receive it in person.

No account of Mahfouz is complete without mention of the *maqhā* (café) and the important role it played both in his life and in his fiction. In his youth, in common with men of his generation, the café acted as a social club – much like a public house in Britain. There personal and literary friendships were forged and many intellectual, heart-searching discussions took place; proof of which we find in the many café scenes involving Kamāl in *The Trilogy*, to give but one example. In maturer years, Mahfouz used the cafés of Cairo (and Alexandria in the summer) as literary salons where he met his literary peers and where scores of young aspiring writers came to listen to him and debate intellectual issues with him. There is hardly a novel by Mahfouz in which the café does not represent a significant part of the scene, and there are several in which the café is the most important element in the setting. Two of them actually have as their titles the names of the cafés where the action unfolds: *The Karnak* and *Qushtumur*. At least the first of these is known to be closely based on Maqhā ᶜUrābī[114], a favourite haunt of Mahfouz in ᶜAbbāsiyya.

Critics of Mahfouz agree that he is a skilful literary architect with a great feeling for structure and the almost geometric organization of material. This literary quality reflects his personal temperament, the daily fabric of his life over many decades having been as tightly structured and the details of its pattern as carefully organized as if it had been one of his own novels. In fact, Mahfouz's legendary reputation for self-discipline, ruthless control over his time and total subservience to the force of habit all make a mockery of the conventional image of the artist as a bohemian animal.

Mahfouz habitually sought to alleviate the sense of horror that interviewers confronted him with over this matter by simply explaining it as a by-product of the necessity of combining a civil servant's life with a creative writer's: he had to organize the second half of the day so carefully to have the time to read and write. This was even more the case as a chronic allergy in the eyes rendered him incapable of writing from April to the end of the summer, so that he only had the winter months for his creative pursuits. He also makes little of what he calls 'the luxury of inspiration' and confesses that once an idea was past the thinking stage (which could go on for years, as in the case of *The Trilogy*), nothing would stop him from sitting at his desk for two or three hours every evening until the work was completed. He writes the first draft quickly and spends a longer time over revision and rewriting. He maintains that the revised text is often substantially different from the first one, though the central idea usually hardly changes.

Rigorously disciplined and readily dismissive of romantic ideas about the creative process though he is, he still happily describes his first conception of a work in terms of a 'tremor' that may be triggered by a place, a person, a relationship or some form of meditation. He then goes on to add that 'the embryo then begins to grow and evolve, governed only by irrational laws (or so it seems) – laws of the imagination, of the aesthetic sense and of emotion'. He goes so far in this mystical denial of conscious intent on the writer's part as to say that it is to his critics that he owes most of his knowledge about the aims and ideas of his work.[115] Asked what he wanted to say in the totality of his work, he answered:

It may be that I did not mean to say anything, but only

drew comfort from making certain motions and emitting certain noises in a certain order which gave a semblance of purpose and signified, as it should of necessity, certain things. But if those things had been firm and clear, I would have preferred to present them in a different manner. Believe me – art is but the creation of life.[116]

2

LOOKING BACKWARD TO THE PRESENT: THE HISTORICAL NOVELS

Mahfouz's career as novelist began with three novels set in Ancient Egypt, the first of which was published in 1939. His preoccupation with the history of Ancient Egypt goes back, however, several years to 1931 when, still a student, he published a translation of an English text with the title *Ancient Egypt*[1] by one James Baikie. The original was published in London in 1912 as part of a series entitled 'Peeps at Many Lands'[2] aimed apparently at young readers in English. The translation, on the other hand, with the title *Miṣr al-Qadīma* appeared in the 'Publications of *Al-Majalla al-Jadīda*' (The New Review) published by Salāma Mūsā,[3] who, as we have seen, encouraged Mahfouz at the beginning of his career.

The book describes in a simple, narrative style the various aspects of Ancient Egyptian life. It remains Mahfouz's first and only translation and one is tempted to believe that he did not think much of it as he had not allowed it to be reprinted in nearly sixty years – he lifted the ban only in 1988, probably under the pressure of increased interest in him after the Nobel prize award. Why did he translate the book? The answer he gives is that it was an exercise undertaken to improve his English.[4] But this does not explain why he chose a book with this subject-matter in particular – it is obvious the choice must have been dictated by a growing interest in the history of Ancient Egypt which was only a few years later to be expressed more extensively. This interest must also be placed within the context of a main intellectual current at the time which found in the face of foreign rule a sense of national and cultural pride in Ancient Egyptian history.[5]

Elementary as the translated book is, there is no doubt that it had an influence on Mahfouz's early historical novels. Some of the details of daily life described in those books can easily be traced back to this source.[6] In fact the entire plot of Mahfouz's first novel *The Game of Fates* is taken from chapter 7 in the book which gives an account of some Ancient Egyptian legends.

All three historical novels bear the marks of an apprentice artist who, even when he finished the third of them, had not yet completely mastered the tools of his craft. Had Mahfouz stopped writing then, these novels would not have earned his name a lasting place in the annals of modern Arabic letters and would themselves have long been forgotten today. The fact, however, remains that these novels provide a valuable glimpse into the mind of the young Mahfouz. Thus, while their consideration from an aesthetic viewpoint is bound to be a largely futile practice, it may prove immensely rewarding to look in them for the germination of his later themes, characters and, to a lesser extent, techniques. This is what I will try to do here.

THE GAME OF FATES

The Game of Fates (1939) is set during the reign of Khūfū (Cheops), builder of the Great Pyramid and second king of the Fourth Dynasty in the time of the Old Kingdom.[7] The action begins when one day Khūfū asks a soothsayer how long his posterity was to reign over Egypt. The soothsayer answers that though the king himself was to rule undisturbed until the last day of his life, none of his descendants would sit on the throne after him, but rather a boy just born to a priest of the god Ra^{c}. Immediately the king sets out at the head of a military campaign to protect his throne against the young would-be usurper. Thus he is set on a collision course with the fates, and Mahfouz has his first opportunity in fiction to demonstrate to his readers a tenet that was to remain central to his work, namely that man's rationalized world is never secure from the haphazard and destructive interference of some mysterious force or law of existence. This force or law will take many forms and names in Mahfouz's work. It could be called fate, accident, chance, coincidence, time or death, but will always have the same effect – to upset man's plans and shake the foundation of his rational calculations for his life and the world. This does not necessarily imply belief in the supernatural on the part of Mahfouz. What he seems generally interested in is merely to record that the failure of human endeavour is not always comprehensible in the simple terms of cause and effect.

Needless to say Khūfū, in the novel under discussion, rather than thwarting the designs of fate by killing the newborn babe is, by a supreme act of irony, made the very tool for the accomplishment of the prophecy: he kills the wrong baby and unwittingly saves the right one from further danger. Eventually, the young man whom Khūfū would have murdered many years before saves him from murder at the hands of his own son and heir-apparent in an attempted *coup d'état*. In recognition of his loyalty and distinguished services, the king, who finally learns on his death-bed the identity of his saviour, appoints him successor to the throne. Thus the prophecy is fulfilled by the very man who once thought in his vanity that he could avert the preordained.

RHODOPIS

Rhodopis, Mahfouz's second novel, appeared in 1943. It is set during the short reign of Mirinra[c] (Mercnrē) towards the end of the Sixth Dynasty of the Old Kingdom.[8] The young Pharaoh of the novel is engaged in a power conflict with the clergy over their enormous land possessions. Meanwhile, accident (or should we say fate?) brings the king in contact with Rhodopis, the courtesan at whose feet the cream of the city's men lie prostrate. It is love at first sight – love which takes possession of the king to the detriment of the affairs of the state and the feelings and pride of the queen, his sister and wife. More tragically, the affair gives the clergy a moral weapon to use against their opponent, who is finally killed in a popular uprising which he bravely faces without protection. True to romantic form, Rhodopis commits suicide with poison.

Rhodopis, like *The Game of Fates*, is centrally built on coincidence. Life here is again shown to be a frolic of fate, now assuming the form of an eagle which carries away Rhodopis' sandal and drops it in Pharaoh's lap, thus offering him the bait of love and eventually death. The central role that Mahfouz assigns to coincidence in life is eloquently explained by one of his characters in *Rhodopis*: 'coincidence is an abused word, [wrongly] confused with randomness. . . . Yet, all fortunes, both good and ill, are attributed to it, and seldom do the gods rely on logic' (p. 31). Elsewhere in the novel, coincidence is described as 'fate in disguise' (p. 79). The unfolding of the action to its tragic end comes as a testimony to this fatalistic thread that runs through the book. One difference, though, between this novel and the previous one is that in *The Game of Fates* the conflict between man and fate is direct and brutal. There is a divine prophecy and a man setting out to circumvent it (in a manner much reminiscent of Sophocles' *Oedipus Rex*), whereas in *Rhodopis* fate acts by proxy using circumstantial elements (such as the conflict between king and clergy and the king's weakness before his passions) to accelerate the inevitable end. Thus the sense of predestination in the latter novel is somewhat reduced by allowing action, once it was set in motion by the initial coincidence or act of fate, to be developed by character to its predestined end. In this sense there are perhaps grounds for saying that *Rhodopis* is conceptually and structurally less defective than the earlier novel. It is already a step in the direction of upgrading coincidence from a mechanical device to a discreetly used philosophical conviction. One thing is certain though, that this early appearance of fate in the work of Mahfouz would prove, if one may say so, a genetic quality: it would persist in his work, only gaining in subtlety with time.

THE STRUGGLE OF THEBES

The Struggle of Thebes, Mahfouz's third novel, appeared in 1944. It deals with the struggle of the Egyptians against the foreign rule of the Hyksos, the invaders from Asia, who ruled Lower Egypt for around a hundred years in the sixteenth century BC. The action of the novel spans some twelve years and the reign of three Pharaohs until Egypt is finally and fully liberated under the leadership of King Aḥmus (Amose), later known in history as the founder of the Eighteenth Dynasty.[9] The heroic, nationalistic line of the plot is further complicated by a love story between the victorious King Aḥmus and the captive daughter of the vanquished Hyksos king Abūfīs, a love which he will have to renounce in favour of duty.

Structurally it is a better novel than its predecessors in that the action does not depend on coincidence, and conflict between human wills takes precedence over conflict between man and fate. Altogether *The Struggle of Thebes* represents a considerable movement forward for Mahfouz as a novelist. It is the maturest and most balanced of his early historical trio. On the other hand, the fact that it was to be his last venture into history for a very long time should come as no surprise: his obvious preoccupation with the present through his treatment of the past seems in retrospect to have been a natural step on the road to realism, which he adopted in the next novel.[10]

The novel which deals with the Egyptians' struggle to liberate their country from foreign rule at a certain period in the past was written at a time when Egypt was under combined foreign rule: the British on the one hand, and an aristocracy of Turkish stock on the other. Throughout, the novel contrasts the brown-skinned Egyptian *fallāḥīn* (peasants) with the white-skinned Hyksos shepherds. The old Hyksos held the Egyptian *fallāḥīn* in contempt just as their modern Turkish counterparts did. Egyptians in the novel are equally contemptuous of the Hyksos who are portrayed as uncouth shepherds coming from the north Asian desert. In modern terms this corresponds to the nomadic origins of the Ottoman Turks. In the novel again the Hyksos are consistently described as arrogant and quick-tempered 'tyrants without minds' (p. 25), epithets which correspond neatly to the modern Egyptians' popular image of the Turk.[11] All of which leaves us with no doubt that Mahfouz had in mind the contemporary scene as he was writing this novel – history offered both parallel and hope.

The Struggle of Thebes did not only herald the beginning of Mahfouz's involvement in the political reality of modern Egypt, but also in the social and economic structures dictated by it. The socio-economic pattern regulating the relationship between governor and governed in the novel is summed up by these two respective statements by two characters, the first a Hyksos, the second an Egyptian: 'If you want to make use of a *fallāḥ*, first make him poor and then whip him!' (p. 113), and 'The rule followed in Egypt is for the rich to rob the poor while the poor are not allowed to steal from the rich' (p. 95). The modernity of the very phraseology used here cannot be missed.[12] In fact, so preoccupied was Mahfouz with the injustices of the present that he ascribed to Aḥmus, at the expense of anachronism, the economic and social reforms that he wished for modern Egypt. He puts the following words in the mouth of the Pharaoh:

> The land belongs to Pharaoh [i.e. the state] and the peasants deputize for him in investing it. They shall have what is sufficient to guarantee them a life of welfare, and he shall have the surplus to spend on public interests. Egyptians shall be equal before the law; only merit shall raise one above the other.
>
> (p. 173)

Mahfouz is happy to admit to this historical untruth: he was trying to mix history with the social utopia he had been dreaming of, as he puts it.[13]

SOME CONSIDERATIONS OF FORM IN THE EARLY HISTORICAL NOVELS

Characters in all three historical novels are flat and lacking in individuality. There are no shades of grey in their portrayal: they are either totally good or wholly evil. The nearest we get to a moral conflict is near the end in *The Struggle of Thebes* when King Aḥmus is faced with the choice between keeping his beloved captive, the daughter of the Hyksos king, and releasing her in return for 30,000 Egyptian captives and a peaceful retreat into the desert by the Hyksos. The Hyksos princess reminds Aḥmus that though 'Kings enjoy the best in life, they also shoulder the heaviest duties' (p. 259). Nor was she prepared to forget her duty towards her vanquished father. Both Aḥmus and Aminrīdis are shown here as Mahfouz's counterparts to Mirinraᶜ and Rhodopis in the previous novel where love triumphed over duty. There, 'the heaviest duties' are forgotten, while 'the best in life' is enjoyed to the full. This is not permissible in Mahfouz's moral code, which is why Mirinraᶜ and Rhodopis end tragically, whereas Aḥmus and Aminrīdis go their separate ways, unhappy but ennobled and made wiser by the pain of their sacrifice. From this point on this moral code is always observed in the novelist's world: slaves of passion and self-interest will always fall, and those who uphold duty will always survive and prosper.

An important character type first presented in *The Struggle of Thebes* is that of Tūtīshīrī, the queen mother, who survives three generations and appears to be above the afflictions of age. She is in fact a symbol for the timeless soul of Egypt – the continuity of the nation in the face of all hardships. She was the blueprint for a type that the novelist was to use time and again. Notable examples are ᶜAmm ᶜAbduh, the guard of the boathouse in *Chatter on the Nile*; the grandmother in *There Only Remains an Hour*; and the grandfather in *The Day the Leader was Killed*. In *The Struggle of Thebes*, however, Tūtīshīrī is a symbol floating on the surface; later Mahfouz was to learn how to weave his symbols more convincingly into the texture of the work. The author's lifetime fascination with the civil servant in all his transformations also gets an early showing in these novels. Bishārū, the inspector at the building site of the pyramid in *The Game of Fates*, will only need to change his costume to appear in one of the author's latest novels. Even the archives section described there has nothing to distinguish it from this favourite haunt of Mahfouz except that the files are in the shape of papyrus scrolls.

All three novels are narrated by an omniscient author moving freely from scene to scene and from character to character. The author's presence is felt in the books and intrusive comments on the actions and speeches of characters are not withheld.[14] By the time we reach *The Struggle of Thebes*, however, such crudeness had been expurgated. In these novels we can also see the roots of the realism to come, represented in a proclivity for detailed accurate description of character and setting. On the other hand, description of nature, when it occurs, is stylized and not functional. In later years, however, natural description would only be used to underline character mood. The prose in which the novels are written is generally flowery, oscillating between the grandiloquent and the sentimental. It is full of archaisms and clichés of classical Arabic which can only sound grotesque to today's readers[15] (on first publication of the novels, they would have been less so, as a modern Arabic style was still in the process of evolving). What is worse is that the same prose was used for dialogue, which made it sound twice as incongruous. The irony is that Mahfouz insisted on using this heightened form of Arabic at a time when older masters than himself like Muḥammad Ḥusayn Haykal and Tawfīq al-Ḥakīm were happy to use colloquial or even rural dialects in dialogue. This, however, has remained a point of principle with him – he was never to write dialogue in the vernacular. He was nevertheless to struggle hard (and not without success) to draw the two languages nearer each other.

One puzzling question, though, is that Mahfouz's translation of *Ancient Egypt* which pre-dates his historical novels by several years was written in a modern simple prose that we can read today, sixty years later, without feeling the time gap. This in addition was at a time when the flowery style of the Egyptian bellettrist al-Manfalūṭī was the model to emulate for every young writer. How can we explain, then, that when the young Mahfouz came to write *The Game of Fates* years later, he gave up that important achievement and reverted to a hackneyed style? Could it be that the translator worked independently of the creator – in the sense that as translator he was influenced by the simplicity of the English text, while as absolute creator he was more prone to the pressures of the conventional style in which he had grown up? This may well be the case, aided and abetted by the historical-cum-romantic content of the novels, alien both to the reality and the idiom of the day. Whatever the reason, with the end of Mahfouz's short historical phase, his prose style was to make a quantum leap into modernity.

HISTORY REVISITED: *BEFORE THE THRONE*

When Mahfouz published *The Struggle of Thebes* in 1944, he was to leave behind the history of Ancient Egypt for the next forty years or so. Indeed, both he and his critics thought that he had done with it for good. According to the novelist, before he started writing his historical novels, he had spent several years researching Ancient Egyptian history and had prepared the plans of up to forty novels on the subject. After the first three, however, the whole project was to be abandoned and contemporary society was to claim the undivided attention of Mahfouz. The impulse had been lost and he came, as he puts it, to realize that history was no longer able to offer a medium for what he wanted to say in his fiction.[16] This proved to be the case for the next thirty-nine years, which encompassed some twenty-five novels and ten short story collections. Then in 1983 Mahfouz surprised his readers (and presumably himself as well) by rediscovering the usefulness of history as a medium for expressing himself on the present: he published a book entitled *Before the Throne* with the subtitle 'A debate with Egypt's men from Menes to Anwar Sādāt'.

The book is a consideration of Egypt's political history. It stretches back in time some 5,000 years and starts at the beginning with Menes, the great king of the First Dynasty who united Upper and Lower Egypt into one kingdom, and thence works its way up to the assassination of Sādāt. The 'throne' of the title is that of Osiris, god of the underworld, before whom are brought all past rulers of Egypt for judgement according to their national deeds. It is a difficult book to classify, being unlike anything previously or since written by Mahfouz. It certainly is not a historical novel, nor is it a scholarly book of history in spite of its strict adherence to historical fact. Based mainly on dialogue rather than narration, it uses a fictitious dramatic situation (i.e. the underworld trial) to bring into focus a certain vision of Egyptian history in its entirety. This, however, does not make the book into a play as it consists of independent scenes held together only by the unities of space, action and theme without either plot or character development.

Whatever the form of the book, its content is invaluable as the writer's pronouncement on his age placed in historical perspective. Mahfouz's division of eternity follows the Dantesque paradigm: hell, purgatory and heaven. Viewing the book as a whole, it is not difficult to determine the author's yardstick (for he is the real judge here rather than Osiris) in judging Egypt's rulers throughout history. Those who go to heaven are the strong rulers who maintained the country's independence and national unity, their personal shortcomings forgiven in return. Those who go to hell are selfish and weak rulers who favoured their personal interests over their country's and put at risk its unity and security through bad policy and neglect. As for those who go to purgatory, they are rulers who were well-meaning but were faced with circumstances beyond their power or ability. The spectrum of the book is as vast as the period it purports to cover, but throughout, the past is continuously interpreted in terms of the present and vice versa with the result that there emerges in the end a sense of the unity of history and a unique failure to learn from it.

I will limit myself here to the trial of Nasser, for whom Mahfouz evidently has more rebuke than praise. According to the regulations of Osiris's court, rulers accorded a place in heaven automatically occupy a seat as members of the jury, as it were, and are involved in trying subsequent rulers. Thus we have the great Pharaoh Tuthmosis III railing at Nasser's military defeats: 'in spite of your military training, you have shown yourself to be adept at many things except those military; indeed you were a general of no consequence whatsoever' (p. 194). This reproach comes naturally from a great Ancient military victor. Equally natural is an accusation of despotism from a modern democratic leader, viz. Saᶜd Zaghlūl (pp. 195–6). The most bitter attack on Nasser, however, is reserved for Muṣṭafā al-Naḥḥās, the great Wafdist leader thrown into oblivion by Nasser after a quarter of a century of heading the Egyptian national struggle before 1952. Al-Naḥḥās's impassioned tirade deserves to be quoted at length:

> You did away with freedom and human rights. I do not deny that you brought security for the poor, but you were the destruction of the intellectuals – the vanguard of the nation. They were detained, imprisoned and killed indiscriminately until they lost their sense of human dignity and initiative. . . . If you were only more moderate in your ambitions! Developing the Egyptian village was more important than adopting the revolutions of the world; sponsoring scientific research was more important than the Yemen campaign; fighting illiteracy was more important than fighting international imperialism. Alas! You have lost the country an opportunity which it had never had before.
>
> (pp. 197, 198)

This outburst is evidently Mahfouz's final dictum on the Nasser era; it is the culmination of all the hints and lesser pronouncements he had been making in his fiction since the early 1960s, and as such it comes as no surprise. It is the pained lamentation of a liberal, socially committed writer who witnessed the demise of freedom and hopes of progress at the very hands of the regime that initially promised to achieve them. Nasser is eventually admitted to heaven, but significantly not before some hesitation on the part of Osiris who tells him: 'Few people have served their country as you have and fewer still have damaged it as you have' (p. 198). By comparison Sādāt's trial is a 'whitewash'. He is quickly acquitted and recommended to be sent to heaven on the claim that his reign was mainly devoted to the task of trying to put right the mess he inherited from Nasser.[17]

(It was in a later novel, viz. *The Day the Leader was Killed* (1985), that Mahfouz was to give his studied evaluation of the Sādāt period; of which more later in this book.)

HE WHO LIVES IN THE TRUTH

Mahfouz's next novel was to show him still in a historical mood. In an interview given in 1973 he listed some subjects which were abandoned when he decided to switch from history to the modern social scene. One of these subjects which he considered to be 'very important' was Akhenaton,[18] the Eighteenth Dynasty monarch who ruled Egypt some fourteen centuries before Christ and preached a new religious cult based on the worship of the one god, Aten, symbolized by the sun disc. Little did Mahfouz know then that some twenty years later this subject was to reach out from the dark recesses of the past and claim its primary right to be written and its secondary right to be useful in elucidating the present.

The novel, whose title evokes the king-prophet, is *He Who Lives in the Truth* (1985). It takes the form of a quest for the truth about Akhenaton. The narrator is a young historian from the generation born after the fall of Akhenaton. In his boyhood he was taught that the king had been an 'infidel' (*māriq)*, whose policies had brought division and destruction to the country. Now he wants to discover the truth for himself and thus he embarks on a series of interviews with important men and women who were contemporaries of Akhenaton and who either supported or opposed him at the time. Through these interviews there emerges a picture of Akhenaton which oscillates between holiness and madness, wilfulness and effeminacy, tolerance and fanaticism according to the point of view. The High Priest of Amūn, the god ousted by Akhenaton, accuses him of having been weak 'to the point of hating the strong. He invented a god in his own image, weak and effeminate with only one function – love. . . . He sank in the marshes of folly neglecting his royal duties . . . until the empire was lost and Egypt laid waste' (pp. 11–12). On the other hand, we see Nefertiti, Akhenaton's wife, question the integrity of the High Priest who, according to her, pretended to worry about the empire whereas all he cared for was the clergy's share of the wealth (pp. 35–6) (some echoes here of the theme of the conflict between king and clergy first treated in *Rhodopis*).

Mahfouz portrays Akhenaton in idealistic terms – he is at once a sensitive poet, a mystic who experienced a moment of divine revelation and a prophet who calls his people to a faith based on love and peace. On the other hand he is also pictured as a ruler guilty of the neglect of the affairs of the state and striking division among his people through his fanaticism and persecution of religious non-conformists. Faced with a situation which has deteriorated, Akhenaton asks the advice of his chief general, who recommends a 'declaration of the freedom of worship' (p. 58). This liberal call falls, however, on deaf ears and the king persists in imposing his religious dogma on the affairs of the state until the sad end.[19]

Written in the 1980s at a time of worldwide Islamic resurgence when the influence of the Islamic Republic in Iran was at its highest, and when religious fundamentalism in Egypt was calling for *jihād* (holy war) against the 'infidel' State and the adoption of *sharīᶜa* (religious law) in a society which, on the one hand, is largely secularized, and which, on the other, has a sizeable Christian minority, the ancient message of the tragedy of Akhenaton could not have sounded more contemporary. Once more Mahfouz had harnessed history in the service of the present, but this time he did it with the maturity and craft of an artist at the height of his career: not a trace here of the aesthetic blemishes of his early historical novels.[20]

3

PAINS OF REBIRTH: THE CONFLICT BETWEEN PAST AND PRESENT

In 1945 Mahfouz published *Khan al-Khalili*[1] thereby marking a shift of interest from ancient history to contemporary social reality. *Khan al-Khalili* was to be the first of a series of novels dealing, in the best traditions of realism and naturalism, with contemporary Egyptian society before the 1952 revolution. Throughout this phase of his writing, which culminated in the publication of *The Trilogy* in 1956–7, Mahfouz appeared to have (amidst the immense diversity of character, situation and idea that are the hallmark of these works) one particular theme which ran through all of them, sometimes obviously, sometimes not so obviously, but always there. By this I mean the conflict between old and new, or past and present: in other words, the conflict between two value systems; one wallowing in the security of age-old tradition, and the other attracted to Western modernity with all its attendant perils. In all these novels Mahfouz appears highly sensitive to the tragic potential of such conflict to both individual and society and sets out to explore it with varying degrees of emphasis and from different angles. This I hope will become apparent in the course of the present chapter.

KHAN AL-KHALILI

Khan al-Khalili spans one year in the life of a Cairene family during World War II: from September 1941 to August 1942 during the height of German air-raids on Cairo. The family decide to escape from the modern quarter of al-Sakākīnī where they have lived for a long time to the old religious quarter of Khān al-Khalīlī in the neighbourhood of the shrine of al-Husayn, grandson of the prophet Muḥammad. They believe that al-Ḥusayn will protect the area and that the Germans should know better than unnecessarily invoke the wrath of Moslems by bombing their holy places. The symbolic aspect of the family's flight can hardly be missed: it is a flight from the dangers of the new to the safety of the old, and one which the course of events will prove to have been futile.

Mahfouz uses two of his characters to advocate respectively the old and the new (a technique that he used again in *New Cairo* as well as *The Trilogy* III). The old is represented by Aḥmad ᶜĀkif, the eldest son and provider for the family, while the new is represented by Aḥmad Rāshid, a lawyer who frequents the same local café as ᶜĀkif, where they engage in endless conversations. The lawyer is a well-read socialist who believes that modern society has no place for religion and that social progress can only be achieved through dependence on science: 'Just as religion had saved us from idolatry, science must save us from religion,' he declares (p. 91). He also argues that modern times have their own prophets and names Freud and Karl Marx as two examples. He quotes with admiration the achievements of modern science, such as the discovery of the composition of the atom and of the existence of endless worlds beyond our solar system, at the same time as he dismisses religion as 'myth' and casts doubt on 'the use of pondering insoluble questions, while we faced innumerable questions which can and must be solved' (pp. 61–2).

Unlike the case in *New Cairo* (as we will soon see), the advocate of religion in *Khan al-Khalili* is no intellectual match for the secularist. He is a frustrated and introverted government clerk with little formal education. He has, however, read extensively, if not perceptively, in traditional religious literature. In contrast to the secularist's belief in science, he believes in magic and the possibility of harnessing the jinn in the service of human beings. But when it comes to modern thought, he is so ignorant he has not even heard of Marx, Freud or Nietzsche. He is portrayed as suffering from an inferiority complex whose symptoms are displayed in a misplaced intellectual haughtiness and a sense of having been wronged by the world verging on megalomania.[2]

Taken at its face value, the juxtaposition of the old and the new, represented respectively by Aḥmad ᶜĀkif and Aḥmad

Rāshid, might appear to be forced on the book since neither advocate is a political activist nor, indeed, does the book have a political theme as such. This would not, however, be so if (as suggested earlier) we read the family's move from Sakākīnī to Khān al-Khalīlī in symbolic terms, i.e. in terms of an escape from the uncertainty and dangers of modernity symbolized by modern warfare to the familiarity and safety of the past symbolized by the old religious quarter of Khān al-Khalīlī. There is much indeed in the presentation to support such a reading. The old quarter is described in the text as having 'resisted modern civilization, countering its madness with wisdom, complexity with simplicity and realism with dreaminess' (p. 8). These qualities of the old quarter seem to match those of Aḥmad ᶜĀkif, the advocate of the old, who lives in a world of his own making, steeped in the wisdom of the past and totally ignorant of the complex thought of the present, as we have seen. By contrast and true to his role in the novel, Aḥmad Rāshid, the advocate of change, sees in the old quarter nothing but 'derelict remnants . . . only filth . . . that ought to be razed to the ground to give people the chance to live healthily and happily' (p. 55).

Within this symbolic framework we can understand better Aḥmad ᶜĀkif's shyness before women, his chronic clumsiness and cowardice in the face of love that have left him a resentful bachelor at the age of 40. His inability to approach the 16-year-old living across the road from him in spite of her encouragement is symptomatic of the malaise and reticence of a whole society enticed by a new and attractive culture but unable to summon up the courage necessary to embrace it. The whole situation is summed up by the motif of the window – the protagonist's window overlooking the girl's balcony. In his perpetual hesitation between his love of life and his fear of it, he keeps wondering whether he should open the window (allowing communication and possibly consequent pain), or keep it closed: 'Isn't death in safety', he wonders, 'better than an anxious and tormenting life?' (p. 103).

Mahfouz's answer to the dilemma posed by the situation is unequivocal: the past is no adequate refuge; there is no escape from the hazards of modernity and the pain attendant thereon, for the family who run away from death in Sakākīnī find it lurking patiently for their arrival in Khān al-Khalīlī to snatch away Rushdī, the younger son, who dies of tuberculosis contracted during their year in Khān al-Khalīlī. Rushdī is the extreme opposite of his brother: extroverted and totally without fear or worry. He is given to a hedonistic way of life (gambling, drinking, womanizing, etc.) and is able to conquer overnight the heart of the girl across the road whom his elder brother has had weeks to win over without avail (he does this, however, unaware of his brother's interest in the girl). One might be tempted to argue that Rushdī's death should not be read in symbolic terms since it did not result from an air-raid. But it must be remembered that Rushdī's hedonism, which kills him and which is the opposite of all the traditional values that the old quarter stands for, is part of the cultural package symbolized by modern, Western warfare from which they had tried to escape. The seed of modernity, i.e. destruction, has already been sown in the modern Egyptian and until he knows how to strike a balance between old and new, self and other, he is going to pay the price.

I have shown that the advocate of the old is negatively portrayed in certain ways. It must be observed now that the socialist advocate is also presented in less than attractive terms. He is a dry, lifeless character as bigoted and tunnel-visioned as any Moslem revivalist to be portrayed later by Mahfouz,[3] and although he is free from Aḥmad ᶜĀkif's shyness and clumsiness, he is shown to be equally incapable of love in spite of his access to the same girl as her private tutor. Is this a defect in portrayal or is it a rejection by Mahfouz of a totally socialist solution? If the novel is examined in isolation, the case would seem to be the second, but looked at in the context of *New Cairo* and *The Trilogy* III (in both of which novels the famous duo is recreated), one may be tempted to go for the first option. The issue, however, is far from clear, and it may well be that the tension in characterization reflects the tension in the novelist's soul before the stark choices available to the modern Egyptian.

Nor is the portrayal of Aḥmad ᶜĀkif free from trouble. The author seems indeed to have an ambivalent attitude towards him, at once showing him as a hollow, laughable character and a man with a sublime sense of duty who sacrifices his career and personal happiness for the sake of his parents and younger brother. As such he is in fact the prototype of a character type that will always command the respect of the author and will be traditionally saved from the harshness of his poetic justice.[4]

Indeed, he survives here and is left at the end with the authorial reward of a promised job promotion and the prospect of a suitable marriage. If this is the case, why the insistence throughout on the negative side of his character? The answer to this question must lie solely with the imperfections of the young artist's craft.[5] Aḥmad thus survives on moralistic grounds, the same grounds on which his brother Rushdī is condemned to death: Mahfouz wants to say that life is not about pleasure-seeking but commitment and the performance of duty – a lesson that he is never tired of reiterating.[6]

NEW CAIRO

In *Khan al-Khalili* the cases for the old and the new appeared largely to be presented in a social vacuum since the novel lacked a socio-political theme, while the arguments for each case were confined to the idle talk of two unevenly portrayed characters sitting at a café. *New Cairo*, published a year later in 1946,[7] was an improvement. A socio-political theme was introduced so that the choice between different systems is made a matter of relevance and vital importance.

New Cairo is indeed about moral choices, on both the individual and the social levels. In fact, in Mahfouz's world individual morality and social morality are indivisible; they are the two sides of one coin. Thus an individual who is solely concerned with his own personal salvation, showing no regard for other individuals in his immediate environment or in society at large, is an accursed self-seeker who can hope for no place in Mahfouz's heaven. Maḥjūb ᶜAbd al-Dā'im, the main protagonist of the novel, is the unrivalled archetype of this kind of character which was to figure again and again in Mahfouz's social panorama.[8] His philosophy, as defined by the omniscient author, is 'to liberate oneself from everything, from values, ideals, beliefs and principles: from the social heritage altogether' (p. 25). True to naturalistic form, the author tells us that Maḥjūb owed his philosophy to his own disposition, emphasized by his poor background, which meant that he virtually grew up 'in the street' (p. 26). These, then, are the effects of temperament and the environment, though temperament is not shown here to be the product of heredity.

It is against a backdrop of extreme poverty and widespread

unemployment and political and official corruption in the Cairo of the 1930s that we are made to witness Maḥjūb's moral disintegration, which turns him, as it were, into a private pimp who trades his wife in return for a government post that would otherwise have been difficult to attain. Here we are faced with a problem. On the one hand, Mahfouz seems very concerned with the question of social evil and its corrupting influence on the individual. On the other hand, however, he insists in his portrayal of Maḥjūb on his utter depravity and complete moral nihilism from the outset – a fact which detracts from the force of the author's blaming of society for the downfall of the individual.[9] This problem originates in my view in an inherent dichotomy in the novelist's moral outlook. While he strongly condemns the corrupt social system, he seems equally unwilling to exempt, on this account, the individual from the responsibility for his own fall.[10] Thus we find ourselves in the end faced with a fallen individual in a corrupt society, yet the one does not seem to follow from the other. The method of presentation would have us think that the individual would have fallen anyway regardless of the social condition. In later novels Mahfouz solved this problem through more balanced portrayals of his protagonists and tighter linkage between social injustice and the individual's fall.

The novel, however, presents us with two more protagonists who are equally pure, equally altruistic and equally desirous of being instrumental in the reform of their society: one a Muslim fundamentalist and the other a socialist.[11] While they are both foils to the amoral character of Maḥjūb, they are themselves at odds, with no hope of reconciliation. They both agree on the importance of moral principles for man, but they radically differ on the nature and source of these principles. The fundamentalist is content with the principles of Islam 'laid down by God Almighty', as he puts it, whereas the socialist's principles consist in 'belief in science instead of superstition, society instead of heaven, and socialism instead of competition' (p. 9) – words which echo those of Aḥmad Rāshid in the previous novel.

Which, then, of the two opposed social visions does the author favour? To argue that the novelist is merely a neutral recorder, portraying the different socio-political forces at work in Egypt at the time is to fail to interpret the first signs of

Mahfouz's social philosophy, which was to be expressed again and again more elaborately and more subtly in later works. Indeed, one may enlist here the support of Mahfouz himself who has argued that 'neutrality between ideas [in his novels] is only technical', and that beneath the crust of neutrality lies his own stance: 'I am not neutral to the end,' he proclaims.[12]

Let us then establish without further ado that the social creed which the novelist adopts is that of the secularist and the one he discards is that of the revivalist Islamist. The evidence for this conclusion can be found in the terms in which each character is portrayed. The Islamist is described as being 'not devoid of fanaticism and a sharpness of temper', and as being occasionally capable of 'demented cruelty'. He is also described as 'given to loneliness', 'socially clumsy', 'without a sense of humour' and 'scathingly frank'. We are also told that he had an abnormal childhood, having been afflicted by a nervous disease which kept him from school until the age of 14 (pp. 12–13). Against this gruesome portrait is juxtaposed the abundantly more human and benign one of the socialist who is shown as possessed of a sociable and genial nature, with his time fairly divided among activities such as reading, sports, intellectual debate, travel, and meeting his girl friend.[13] We are also told that when he cast aside religious faith, the question which most agonized him was to find a new foundation for personal morality. The answer came through the philosophy of Auguste Comte, who 'preached a new god called society and a new faith called science'. The omniscient author goes on to tell us about his character that

> he came to believe that atheists, like believers, had their principles and ideals . . . and that good was deeper in the human nature than religion; it was human goodness which first created religion, and not the other way round as he had used to think.
>
> (pp. 22–3)

The ideas about individual morality and social progress expounded in *New Cairo* are seminal ones that would grow and flourish in subsequent novels.[14]

MIDAQ ALLEY

Mahfouz's next novel, *Midaq Alley* (1947), takes us back to the streets and folk of old Cairo that he introduced us to earlier in *Khan al-Khalili*. The country is still in the grip of World War II, though at a more developed stage than that shown in *Khan al-Khalili*. Textual evidence suggests late 1944 or early 1945.[15] The war actually ends during the course of the action of the novel.

Midaq Alley is in a sense the inversion of the metaphor created by *Khan al-Khalili*. The latter showed us the vanity of seeking refuge in the past from the threat of the new. *Midaq Alley*, in contrast, reveals to us the horrors attendant on the flight from the past to the present. The outcome of both is shown to be calamitous. Torn between past and present, the modern Egyptian seems to stand paralysed without a future, and the pessimism expressed in *Khan al-Khalili* is enlarged to the point of desperation in *Midaq Alley*.

Midaq Alley is a novel with many protagonists, all enjoying the almost equal attention of their creator with the exception of the heroine, Ḥamīda, who is perhaps somewhat more central to the book than the rest. The book is episodic in structure lacking a central plot and held together mainly through the unities of place and theme.[16] The place is of course the old alley of the title and the theme is that of change, of the painful conflict between old and new whose theatre is the soul of man. This theme is introduced soon after the opening lines of the novel and sets the pace of the entire work from that moment on. We see the old poet, who has entertained his audience at the café in the alley for many years by singing for them the exploits of traditional Arab folk heroes, being mercilessly ousted by an act of rejection of the past, an act of modernization: a radio set is being fitted in the café which cannot accommodate both. An important factor is thus symbolically established from the outset: the old and the new cannot coexist. Choices must be made, sides must be taken and loyalty should be undivided. By dint of this yardstick the fates of characters in the novel faced with the necessity of choosing will be decided: those who sell their souls to modernity without a moment's hesitation and pay the price with unflinching eyes, like Ḥamīda and Ḥusayn Kirsha will be spared, but those who waver and stop to look behind, like ᶜAbbās al-Ḥulw, will perish. As in *Khan al-Khalili*, modernity here is represented by the war. There people fled from the destruction of modernity to the illusory safety of the past. Here people escape from the poverty, filth and death-in-life of the old alley to the promise of a new life offered by employment in the camps of the British army.

Ḥamīda, however, enters the service of the army in a somewhat different and unofficial capacity: she joins the whore industry catering for the needs of British and allied soldiers.[17] Long before she makes her final choice, her contempt for and rejection of the alley with all it stands for is total and complete.[18] Her initial acceptance of ᶜAbbās' offer of love and marriage was made out of circumstantial necessity, the barber being the best the alley could offer. Even so, it was only made after the young man had decided to make the sacrificial journey to the British camps to bring back money and the promise of life out of the alley. Thus when the wealthy old merchant, Salīm ᶜAlwān, who does not belong to the alley (either by class or means) but only has his storehouse in it, asks her hand in marriage to satisfy a nagging lust, she drops the barber without so much as a moment's thought. The immediacy and ease with which she does this illustrates her total disdain for the value system of the alley, which stands in the way of her aspiration for material success.[19] The project, however, comes to nothing as fate strikes the merchant with a heart attack that leaves him nearly dead. But there is no going back to ᶜAbbās: Ḥamīda now understands herself better and knows that her fulfilment lies in a different world, well outside the scope of the alley. Thus when Faraj Ibrāhīm, suave pimp and emissary of that world to her, makes his appearance and utters his seductive words: 'This place is not where you belong and these people are not your people. You are different – you are a stranger here' (p. 178), he is only voicing her own conviction. The novelist makes clear beyond doubt both in his direct probings of her psyche and in his omniscient author's comments that there was no question of deception – she leaves the alley of her own free will and in the full knowledge that she is going to embark on a whore's career.

The symbolism of Ḥamīda's parting with the alley is brought out through the narrative's harping on the motif of past and present in chapter 24 where she makes up her mind to run away from the alley for ever:

> She did not feel very much the burden of the tug-of-war between her past and her present.
>
> (p. 214)
>
> Is there a way to escape the fetters of the past except through that man who lit the fire of her imagination?
>
> (p. 215)
>
> She turned her back on the past and no longer thought of anything but the future.
>
> (p. 216)
>
> Her body gave in to the feel of the car as it sped away from the whole past.
>
> (p. 221)

She conceives of her journey as one towards 'light, wealth and power'[20] and in her imagination addresses her 'seducer' in these words: 'I'm coming unto you. Let my strength meet yours and let us forever wrestle happily together' (p. 215). So fraught are the words with meaning and so dense is the texture of the narrative with suggestion that Ḥamīda and her escape cross in the reader's mind the demarcation line between realism and symbolism and a whole new world of meaning erupts into existence: this is not merely a novel about a poor girl dazzled into a life of sin by her ambition and her lust for life – it is as much a novel about a nation at the crossroads, torn between a cultural past that is her very identity but no longer viable, and a modern world which will not accommodate her unless she is ready to shed all vestiges of the past.

Ḥamīda, with all her shocking qualities, appears indeed to be Mahfouz's answer, *malgré lui*, to the dilemma of past and present, old and new, East and West, religion and secularism or any other name that it might be called by. In the novel she is the only character who succeeds in ripping herself irrevocably apart from the alley. She thrives on it without regrets – even after an attempt is made on her life by the past (in the person of her ex-fiancé, ᶜAbbās), the author allows her to live unscathed and to continue to thrive, while her poor attacker is crushed to death under the feet of drunken and enraged soldiers. She succeeds because she is ready to pay the price in full – her old soul, her old *honour*, the quintessential symbol of the old morality and the entire cultural fabric behind it. Ḥamīda, with her ambition, adventurism, individualism, entrepreneurialism, solipsism, shamelessness, bellicosity, freedom from emotionalism, practical (if not philosophical) atheism, etc., symbolizes in fact many of the intellectual values which made the modern West. The very fact that Ḥamīda can only free herself from the past at the expense of becoming a prostitute in the service of Western soldiers is not without significance on the symbolic level: for is not the renunciation by a culture of its traditional and historic identity in return for the 'light, wealth and power' of modernity an act of prostitution *in extremis*?[21]

In addition to Ḥamīda, two more characters leave the alley, Ḥusayn Kirsha, the belligerent and unprincipled son of the café owner and, as previously mentioned, ᶜAbbās al-Ḥulw, the barber. In a sense they too are prostitutes, the difference between them and Ḥamīda being only cosmetic. They sell their physical effort in the service of the army of occupation, while she hires her body to the soldiers of that army. Thus while all three engage in basically the same practice, they are allotted different fates by the author: Ḥamīda and Ḥusayn survive whereas ᶜAbbās perishes. I have explained why Ḥamīda survives, and it is for the same reason that Ḥusayn does. He shares Ḥamīda's traits (which is the significance of his being her foster-brother) and his contempt for the alley is also total and unqualified. When he is made redundant by the army towards the end of the war, he has no choice but to return to the alley, but only physically; his rebellious spirit is forever lost to the old. ᶜAbbās, on the other hand, is a foil to both Ḥamīda and Ḥusayn.[22] He leaves the alley reluctantly and only under pressure from his friend Ḥusayn and his own desire to make himself worthy of his ambitious fiancée. His spirit is desperately attached to the alley, to the old, to death – and therefore die he must. Nor is the revulsion that Ḥamīda feels towards ᶜAbbās without meaning on the symbolic level; it is the revulsion between opposed cultures, the old and the new, that which is destined to die and that which has the promise of life.

Despite its episodic form, it is nevertheless difficult to imagine a novel more cohesive than *Midaq Alley*: a cohesion which emerges from the powerful evocation of a sense of place and a relentless subjugation of all episodes to one ultimate thematic significance. All this is done with such sleight of hand that one could imagine, as indeed many critics have done, that one were simply reading a latter-day piece of naturalistic fiction. There is no doubt in fact that *Midaq Alley* exists comfortably at this level, but there is no doubt either that it exists equally as a symbolic novel. All the main characters and their stories (which may or may not tie in with the central story of Ḥamīda) contribute, while forming part of the social fabric and realistic detail of the alley, to the theme of the book, i.e. the inevitability of the clash between old and new and the human pain attendant on the process.

Let us begin with Shaykh Darwīsh, the half-mad dervish or holy man who sits all the time at the entrance of the café, lost permanently in his thoughts except for his occasional and timely eruptions into insightful or prophetic utterances (Mahfouz in fact assigns him the function of the chorus in a Greek tragedy). Shaykh Darwīsh used to be in his younger and saner days, we are told by the omniscient author, a teacher of English at a charitable school run by the Department of Religious Endowments. In addition he was a happy family man. Then, through an act of modernization, the Endowment schools were appropriated by the Department of Education. Lacking the qualifications required by the more stringent standards of the new employer, he was demoted to a clerical job and his salary accordingly reduced. The change was too much for his pride and his nerves. Thus he gradually drifted away from his job and his family and ended up the way we meet him in the alley – an accomplished victim of *modernization*.[23] His prophetic utterances are partly made in English, which of course is an intrusive language in the context of the alley, but then the whole novel is about the intrusion of the new and Western on the old and traditional.

Another minor but functionally important character in the alley is ᶜAmm Kāmil, the confectioner. He is middle-aged, without a family, and corpulent almost to the point of immobility. He dozes off in the chair in front of his shop all day. His excessive girth, perpetual slumber and childish naiveté make him the laughing-stock of the alley. He is caricatured by the author in such a way as to make him appear practically a living corpse. This is endorsed by his obsession with securing a shroud for himself before his death. The author actually wonders in one of his comments: 'What harm will death bring him when his life has been an act of continuous sleep?' (p. 6). Thus ᶜAmm Kāmil becomes a symbol of death-in-life, of a past that has overstayed its time, a past that is only clinically alive.[24] In fact, images of death and decay permeate the texture of the book, preparing the atmosphere for the tragic end of ᶜAbbās and creating an association in the mind of the reader between life in the alley and death. Two examples will do. In his attempt to convince ᶜAbbās to leave the alley, his friend Ḥusayn argues that 'this alley contains only death. As long as you are living here, you will never need to be buried' (p. 39). Later on, Faraj Ibrāhīm, the pimp, pursues the same line of argument towards the same end with Ḥamīda: 'It is an act of blasphemy that a beauty like you should live in a grave full of decayed bones' (p. 208).

Another variation on the theme of death is played through the character of Salīm ᶜAlwān, a man of excessive wealth and with an equally excessive sexual appetite, who wanted to take Ḥamīda as a second wife in spite of the huge gaps in age and class between them. The author, however, will have none of that and fate (ever ready in the service of Mahfouz's sublime motives) steps in to smite him with a heart attack that does not quite kill him but leaves him hanging perpetually over the grave: he becomes another image of death-in-life, like ᶜAmm Kāmil. Once more the author illustrates that old age cannot be refurbished by borrowed youth, that the only right place for the past is the grave. Salīm ᶜAlwān, not being one of the poor alley people, has a higher symbolic value in the book. He extends the metaphor beyond the scope of the destitute class and gives it a wider social context: the problem is thus shown to pertain to a whole society.

Kirsha, the café-owner, is yet another apparition of the living dead in the alley. He leads a sub-animal existence constantly under the effect of hashish and constantly chasing one homosexual partner or another. Nor should the significance of his homosexuality be lost on us; it is a symbol of sterility adding to the sense of stagnation and death in the alley. Ironically, Kirsha's perversion is condoned in the alley whereas Ḥamīda's behaviour is condemned. This discrepancy in the social code of the alley is a gratuitous indication of its inherent inadequacy.

Equally sterile is the marriage of Saniyya ᶜAfīfī, the well-to-do widow of the alley. Fifty years of age, her relative wealth enables her to buy a husband twenty years younger. This episode obviously runs in parallel with the episode of Salīm ᶜAlwān-Ḥamīda. Although in this case the marriage does take place, its link with death is established in a masterly stroke when the woman discovers that the golden dentures she had fitted in her attempts to refurbish her image before her wedding had actually been pulled out of an exhumed corpse. Again, the past is shown to be decayed beyond restoration.

Standing apart from all the other characters of *Midaq Alley* is that of Raḍwān al-Ḥusaynī. He is portrayed as a saintly figure – a man beyond good and evil and beyond common human suffering. He has had more than his fair share of suffering though, before we meet him in the novel: 'he had lost all his sons . . . then out of the darkness of sorrow, his faith brought him to the light of love' (p. 12), so the author tells us. He is in fact Mahfouz's prototype of the many *ṣūfīs* or mystics who will later play important parts in his fiction, and who probably have their philosophical origin in Bergson's notion of the two moralities, referred to in chapter 1 of this study. The people of the alley revere him and seek his counsel in their trouble, but there is little that he can do to save them beyond preaching his transcendental philosophy of faith and love. His philosophy can bring comfort only to himself since *ṣūfism* is essentially a formula for personal rather than communal salvation. The way Mahfouz portrays him shows him as an exalted version of individualism. The individualism may be spiritual, but it is ultimately a self-saving attitude with no genuine social value. Towards the end of the book Raḍwān al-Ḥusaynī travels to Makka to perform the *hajj* (pilgrimage). Ironically, this is the only journey out of the alley without calamitous consequences. Might one suggest that this is so because it is the one journey not made to the new world? It is a journey to the past, to the quintessentially old – a journey outside time and therefore outside the scope of pain.

If Raḍwān al-Ḥusaynī is all good, then Zayṭa, the deformity-maker, is all evil. Mahfouz portrays him as the devil incarnate, a social outcast by choice and a man who delights in the sorrows of others and enjoys inflicting pain on them when he has a chance. His evil is motiveless, and as such he is unique in the work of Mahfouz. As such, too, he is the counterpart to Raḍwān al-Ḥusaynī: they both live intrepidly in a world of absolutes, far beyond the human lot.

The beggars who flock under cover of night to the 'wasteland' where Zayṭa lives to have themselves deformed by his 'devilish' art (deformity being a necessary qualification for a successful begging career) are all sons of the old world – the world of poverty, ignorance and sickness. They do not belong to Midaq Alley itself, but they come from similar *old* alleys all over the city to the al-Ḥusayn area, the heart of the *old* city where the prospects for begging are greatest. Begging is their only means of survival and within the symbolic framework of the book their condition is symptomatic of a whole nation whose survival is dependent on cultural begging from the West. Just as they are unable to practise begging without acquiring a deformity, so cultural transition or begging is also not possible without pain and deformity. Zayṭa thus stands as a symbol of the evils of cultural transition. Raḍwān Ḥusaynī and he are the two polarities of the book: the one stands for the absolute past stretching all the way back to Makka, the point where it begins in time, and the other stands for the absolute present stretching all the way forward to the farthest point of pain and loss that modernization can lead to.

Between these two polarities Mahfouz's answer seems to be the one offered by Ḥamīda's example: leap into modernity with all your will and might and you could survive like Ḥamīda or waver and look back and perdition will be your certain fate like ᶜAbbās! It is a brutal vision emanating from the deepest wells of despair in the novelist's subconscious and to date none of his works has evinced anything half as ferocious.

MIRAGE

In *Mirage* (1948)[25] Mahfouz takes a momentary break from old Cairo with its seedy streets to pay a visit to al-Manyal, a decent middle-class area in the south-west of the capital. With the change of habitat there comes naturally a change in the inhabitants: none of the poor company of Midaq Alley here, but a wealthy family of Turkish descent. Unlike in *Khan al-Khalili* and *Midaq Alley*, the war has no part here to play and we are back at some undefined point in the 1930s.[26] But above all our attention is diverted (or so it seems) from society to psyche – Mahfouz here appears to be concerned with the representation of psychological rather than physical or naturalistic reality. In the process of doing so he vacates his hitherto habitual position of omniscient narrator and hands us over to his protagonist,

Kāmil Ru'ba Lāẓ, to tell his own story and to reveal to us other characters from his solitary point of view.

The novel is a cathartic journey into the past by the protagonist-narrator.[27] It is a long and probing look inward to understand the make-up of his perturbed soul and the composition of the mesh of events and relationships that led to catastrophe. The catastrophe consists in the tragic death within hours of each other of both his wife and his mother: Kāmil believes that he was instrumental in both deaths. About 28 years of age, he traces the tragedy back to its beginnings in his infancy. He was the youngest child of a divorced mother already deprived of seeing her two other children by their father, who has legal custody of them. She thus concentrates all her affection on him. The child grows up in an abnormal atmosphere completely isolated from the outside world by his over-loving, over-protective mother. She also instils in him a hatred of his father, whom he does not meet until he is 17. The boy grows up a social misfit without self-confidence, without friends, and a failure at school. He has no relationships with girls and his only sexual outlet until he is married at the age of 26 is masturbation. Marriage, however, suggests that he is sexually impotent, but later an affair with an ugly, middle-aged woman proves the opposite (an ugly maidservant had initiated him into sex as a young boy, but they were found out by the mother and he was left with a guilt complex). It turns out that he associated his beautiful wife with his mother and was thus unable to 'defile' her sexually – only an ugly and earthy woman (like the servant of his childhood) could trigger sexual response in him. His frustrated wife finally has an affair and dies during an abortion performed on her by her cousin, a doctor, the very man with whom she had the affair. Kāmil knows the truth only after her death. In his despair he blames everything on his mother, whose weak heart collapses under the pressure of the shocking news and the sudden barrage of hatred from her son.

All critics have seen the book for the one thing that it certainly is: a psychological novel offering a study of an acute case of the Oedipus complex and following the techniques of psychoanalysis used by Freud.[28] Those who read it as such and no more see it as an unclassifiable oddity in the work of Mahfouz.[29] Others, however, insist that the novel, read at a deeper level, is well within the mainstream of Mahfouz's social and intellectual concerns.[30]

The present writer subscribes to the second school of thought and reads in Kāmil's psychological case a metaphor for a society fixated on its cultural past and too *impotent* to free itself from it. As such *Mirage* comes as a natural thematic sequel to *Khan al-Khalili* and *Midaq Alley* and a forerunner of *The Trilogy.* That the novel is obsessed with the past is beyond doubt. It is a long act of retrospection – an attempt by the protagonist at reconstructing the past in memory and on paper in order to comprehend it and by so doing liberate himself from it. The mother is established from the beginning as a symbol of a haunting past, a figure that is dead but will not lie down. 'She is dead to this world,' writes Kāmil of her, 'but she still resides in my depths . . . always behind my hopes and pains, my loves and hates' (p. 8). This ambivalence in the protagonist's attitude towards his mother is sustained throughout the narrative. Kāmil explains how she instilled fear in his childish heart to curb his aspirations towards freedom (p. 22) and how her over-protectiveness cut him off from the outside world leaving him friendless, extremely shy, seeking solitude, inarticulate and distrustful of strangers (p. 43). These shortcomings are shown to have a very negative influence on his life. His shyness and inarticulateness, for instance, result in his giving up his university studies at the School of Law because he cannot face colleagues and deliver a speech (a requirement for a course on oratorical skills) (chapter 17). He describes the life structured for him by his mother in terms of a prison which contained both 'his pleasure and his pain', but in which he was also 'secure from fear' (p. 64). This abnormal upbringing retards his intellectual growth and impedes his progress in education so that he does not finish his secondary schooling until he is 25. His mother's cure for his educational problems consists in amulets and visits to the shrine of 'Umm Hāshim, grand-daugther of the prophet Muḥammad (p. 90).

All these details and myriads more will fit neatly in a metaphorical reading of the book. Kāmil's subconscious fixation on his mother which renders him sexually impotent with his young and beautiful wife is symbolic of a culture fixated on its past and therefore powerless to embrace modernity. The very fabric of the long book (over 400 pages) is made up of words and images and situations all denoting bafflement and lack of fulfilment on the intellectual, emotional, sexual and social levels. The motif of masturbation, with its suggestions of sterility and loneliness (accruing enhanced significance when it continues to be the protagonist's method of sexual satisfaction even after marriage), is only one example. His fears, inhibitions and mental retardation are all symptomatic of an introverted culture escaping from modern reality into illusions of the past, into a 'mirage' – to invoke the suggestive title of the novel. Kāmil's ambivalent attitude towards his mother is also indicative of the mixed feelings of attraction and repulsion that a culture in transition feels towards its past, which is at once seen as a shackle and a safe haven from the perils of change. This ambivalence is further strengthened on the symbolic level by another dichotomy in the protagonist's psyche, namely the one between soul and body or, to put it in terms of conflicting cultures, spiritualism and materialism (Bergson again!). On the realistic level this dichotomy is expressed through his simultaneous attraction to both his young and beautiful wife and his ugly, middle-aged mistress who cures him of the impotence he suffers from in his relationship with the former. He admits that he 'needs them both' and that his 'agony is but the agony of a man who cannot achieve an inter-marriage between his soul and his body' (p. 356).[31] Here we face again the age-old duality of spirit and matter and the opposition of cultures based on the one or the other. While Kāmil is entirely in the grip of the past (i.e. the spiritual culture), he continues to be impotent but when he escapes the hold of the past into the carnal, 'materialistic' arms of the ugly and lustful ᶜInāyāt, he regains his potency. Once again Mahfouz seems to be saying, as he has done through Ḥamīda in *Midaq Alley*, that the way out of the cultural stalemate of his nation is through embracing Western materialism. This message seems to be confirmed by the almost simultaneous death of both mother and wife, the two symbols of spiritualism in the book. The metaphorical power of the deaths is augmented by the fact that in the case of the mother the death is virtually caused by Kāmil – as if it were a ritualistic killing of the past. Against this symbolic banishment of spiritualism, the book ends on a final note of welcome to materialism when ᶜInāyāt, with characteristic daring, goes to visit the convalescing Kāmil in his home.

If Kāmil with his isolationism and total attachment to an illusory past represents a complete negation of *the other*, then Amīn Riḍā, the doctor, represents the complete negation of *the self*, other and self being used here in the cultural sense. The doctor is indeed presented in the novel as a foil to the character of the protagonist, but interestingly, as we will see, his type is equally rejected by the author. He is shown as an outgoing, socially and politically involved character. During his student days, we come to know, he was active in the nationalist cause to the point of imprisonment; obviously the extreme opposite of Kāmil, who did not know the name of the prime minister of the day (p. 66). After graduation he travels to England to complete his studies. He returns a totally changed person, full of admiration for the English way of life, paralleled only by an unmitigated disdain for his own country's (pp. 292–4). Ironically he speaks of the Egyptians as 'all living in a big prison', which poignantly coincides with Kāmil's description of his own life as a prison, quoted earlier. This total rejection of his own culture by the doctor, juxtaposed with Kāmil's symbolic apotheosis of it, is, however, not benignly looked upon by the author. Having completely dropped the traditions of his culture, the doctor is shown as if he is acting in a moral vacuum. He shows little regard for the ethical code of his profession as the physician treating Kāmil for his impotence. He seduces Kāmil's wife and then performs an illegal abortion on her, which furthermore he is not professionally qualified to do. When she dies as a result of the operation, he shows no emotion at all and his only concern is to save his skin through the falsification of facts – not a pleasant character at all. No wonder the author happily sends him to prison.[32]

The question, however, remains: if Kāmil as the epitome of the past or spiritualism is rejected and the doctor as the epitome of modernity or Western materialism is also rejected, where is the model favoured by the author? What further complicates the issue is that when Kāmil shakes the burden of the past from his shoulders and faces up to reality in the shape of his mistress, it is again a very materialistic reality that he embraces. It is much like replacing one bondage with another. Nevertheless, the novelist allows him to survive at the same time as he destroys the doctor. The result is a blurred vision: the author obviously does not approve of either of the two extremes of spiritualism and materialism. He wants the best of both worlds and, like his nation, he has not found it. The tension in the vision is reflected in the narrative, which appears to transmit conflicting signals.

THE BEGINNING AND THE END

The Beginning and the End (1949) is set in the Cairo of the mid-1930s,[33] and more particularly in the poor parts of the old suburb of Shubra.[34] The novel brings a depth of vision and a mastery of technique, hitherto lacking in the work of Mahfouz, to concerns already familiar from his four previous novels. Fate, whose supreme role in the world of Mahfouz has been established, if somewhat crudely, in his first novel, *The Game of Fates*, and whose deadly blows have afflicted Rushdī ᶜĀkif in *Khan al-Khalili* and ᶜAbbās al-Ḥulw in *Midaq Alley*, is here crowned as unrivalled lord over the life and aspirations of mankind, a force which, in the words of one character, 'grinds and devours' its victims (p. 184). The whimsical acts of fate start just before the beginning of the action by snatching away the life of the head of the lower-middle-class family whose fortunes (or rather misfortunes) constitute the subject-matter of the book. Already of limited means, the family of a widow, three sons and a daughter, is now reduced to measures of extreme austerity in order barely to survive on the meagre pension left by the deceased father. The death of the father, however, was only fate's opening skirmish and the narrative maintains an atmosphere of bleakness and a sense of impending doom that leaves the reader in no doubt that more disasters are to come. Fate, however, is in no hurry; it likes to do a good job. Thus the action of the novel spans some four years, during which the proud daughter of a professional family is reduced first to seamstress and then whore; the eldest son to a night-club bouncer and drug-trafficker; and the second son to giving up his hopes of higher education to become a petty clerk. The youngest, however, seems, thanks to the help and sacrifices of the rest of the family, set to escape misfortune – or does he? He graduates as an army officer and just as he prepares to begin a new life, fate smiles its knowing smile and deals the final blow for which the scene has long been set. With alarming speed the young aspirant's world falls to pieces: a marriage proposal from him is rejected by an upper-class family on account of his humble origins; his eldest brother is being chased by the police as a wanted criminal; and his sister is arrested in a brothel. Unable to face the shame and the scandal, he forces her to commit suicide before he follows suit.[35]

In the novel fate as a supernatural power has only a limited role to play, namely through the death of the father at the beginning. But the rest of the tragedy does not simply follow from this supernatural and inescapable interference in the life of humans. After this initial act, fate actually chooses to work through perfectly reasonable means, namely individual temperament and, to a much lesser extent, society. Ḥusayn, the middle brother, explains to his younger brother, Ḥasanayn, that while God 'may be responsible for the death of our father, he can by no means be responsible for the inadequacy of the pension he left' (p. 32). What is at issue here is the question of social justice; death may be a supernatural evil, but social injustice is entirely man-made and therefore curable.[36] It is a form of fate that can be fought and vanquished. Many critics have been misguided by the poverty of the family as well as the words just quoted above into blaming the subsequent tragedies on society or, as it were, social fate.[37] Mahfouz himself has indeed misleadingly argued that the real villain of the novel is Ismāᶜīl Ṣidqī, the despotic prime minister of Egypt at the time.[38] In fact Ṣidqī is not even mentioned in the novel, nor does the plot have a political background in any significant measure, such as was the case in *New Cairo*, for example. All that is there are marginal references to demonstrations against the British and to the signing of the treaty of independence in 1936.[39]

The novel in fact is an indictment of human nature, of the way we are made: character is fate. The insistence throughout on Nafīsa's physical ugliness and passionate sexuality leave little room for the possibility of blaming her fall on society. Even in a social utopia, she would still be ugly, without a husband, and with a sexual urge demanding satisfaction. The same goes for Ḥasanayn, to whom society gives ample leeway by allowing him to rise against considerable odds to an officer's position. It is his own egoism, excessive ambition, impatient nature and denial of his own class that bring about his downfall. By contrast, Ḥusayn is optimistic, patient and self-denying, and is thus a foil to the character of his brother. These qualities save him from destruction, even though society has been much less kind to him than to his brother, forcing him to sacrifice his higher education in order to support his family. Fate in *The Beginning and the End* is thus first and foremost temperament. As Ḥasanayn puts it in his final moment of revelation before jumping into the Nile, 'There is something fundamentally wrong with our nature – I don't know what it is but it has destroyed me' (p. 381). Mahfouz is undoubtedly also concerned with the shortcomings of society which make such conditions as his characters live in possible, but his insistence on their own hereditary weaknesses, both physical and temperamental, largely neutralizes his condemnation of society: what we have here is a lopsided version of naturalism. Three novels later, his vision of society and the individual is still as uncomfortable as it was in *New Cairo*.[40]

Ḥasanayn is by far Mahfouz's most sophisticated rendering of the ultimate egoist. Unlike his prototype, Maḥjūb of *New Cairo*, and his temperamental peers, Rushdī ᶜĀkif in *Khan al-Khalili* and Ḥamīda in *Midaq Alley*, he is a tragic hero who commands our full sympathy in his heroic and fatal struggle against the past. Painfully class-conscious and aspiring to mobility across the social strata, once he becomes an army officer he wants to reshape his life as if the past had never existed. He wants 'a new past, a new house, a new grave [for his dead father], a new family, plenty of money and a glamorous life' (p. 283). The past, however, haunts him[41] in the shape of his own gnawing fears and worries, his incurable insecurity and most palpably through his fallen brother and sister. The past clings to him like a leech, while the new life symbolized by the upper class rejects him with contempt. In his final moment of truth, his thoughts run like this: 'I have always wanted to erase the past, but the past has swallowed the present – the past has been none else but me' (p. 381).

Mahfouz is obviously still agonizing over the theme of past and present. Ḥasanayn's conflict with the past here is yet another episode in the series of novels which began in *New Cairo* with Maḥjūb ᶜAbd al-Dā'im's wholesale jettisoning of the values of the past.[42] Through metaphor after metaphor, the novelist's belief in the non-viability of a total rejection of the past is reaffirmed. His best compromise so far appears to be the character of Ḥusayn in the present novel. He is a composite of the Islamist and the socialist models of *New Cairo*, believing in 'a socialist system which does not conflict with religion, family or morality' (p. 302). Unlike his brother, he is also a pragmatist who realizes that 'if we could economize in our dreams or take our inspiration from reality in creating those dreams, we would not be sorry or disappointed' (p. 180). He is a man of integrity, duty, persistence, moderation and gradual progress – he is no rebel, and with him the status quo could go on indefinitely. But the book is not about him. It is about Ḥasanayn, the fire that feeds upon itself. He lacks his vivacity and lustre and he fails to strike a spark in our imagination. It is with only half a heart that Mahfouz offers him as an alternative.

4

TIME AND THE MAN: FOUR EGYPTIAN SAGAS

A preoccupation with time is at the centre of Mahfouz's work. A thought that has been uppermost in his writings has been how time affects the individual and the community and how human memory relates to external time. In this chapter I have grouped together some novels in which time is a prime concern. The first three novels treated here are all *romans fleuves* in the sense that they are concerned with the examination of the changing conditions of life for individuals and society across a succession of generations in a given family. However, of the three it is only *The Cairo Trilogy* which is written on the grand scale associated with this type of novel, as established by such European masters as Balzac, Zola and Mann. The other two are *romans fleuves* of a lesser order, cramming too many events and characters into what are very short novels, and more inclined towards the quick reportage of change than in its detailed representation and the creation of a real sense of the passage of time. *Qushtumur*, the fourth and last novel dealt with in this chapter, is not technically a *roman fleuve*. The reasons for including it here notwithstanding will be explained in the course of discussion of it.

Mahfouz has been explicit about his philosophy of time, which, as we have seen in chapter 1 of this volume, has been considerably influenced by the ideas of Henri Bergson. In the course of discussing techniques of dealing with time in the novel, he contrasts 'logical time' with 'psychological time' and comes out mostly in favour of the first. He insists on the historicity of time and argues that 'time represents the evolutionary spirit of man; it perpetuates the human experience of life. Therefore, while it may mean extinction to the individual, it means eternity for the species.'[1] In another statement he reaffirms the same point:

> My contemplation of time and death has taught me to regard them with the eye of collective man and not [that of] the individual. To the individual they are calamitous, but to collective man a mere illusion. . . . What can death do to human society? Nothing. At any moment you will find society bustling with millions [of lives].[2]

But if Mahfouz views the relation between man and time as inevitably a tragic one on the individual level, he makes it amply clear that he believes it need not be so on the social level. Indeed, so optimistic is he about human progress that he does not preclude the possibility of a final human victory over time and death as the following extract suggests towards the end:

> As long as life ends in disability and death, it is a tragedy. . . . Even those who see it as a crossroad to the hereafter will have to accept that the first part of it is a tragedy. . . . But the tragedy of life is a complex one. . . . For when we think of life as merely existence, we tend to see it only in the abstract terms of existence and non-existence. But when we think of it in terms of existence in society, we discover in it many artificial tragedies of man's own making, such as ignorance, poverty, exploitation, violence. . . . This justifies our emphasis on the tragedies of society, because these are ones that can be remedied, and because in the act of remedying them we create civilization and progress. Indeed, progress might ameliorate the original tragedy [i.e. death] and might even conquer it altogether.[3]

All the novels discussed in the following pages are metaphors of varying complexity and accomplishment embodying the author's view of time in relation to the individual and to society.

THE CAIRO TRILOGY

Having explored both the physical and social environments of Cairene society over a period of some fifteen years (1930–45 roughly) and having examined the tragic struggles of the individual against the trials imposed by that society on its aspiring but largely powerless children, Mahfouz wanted, as it were, to put the fragments together and trace the social tension between past and present back to a clear and definable point when it can be said to have started in earnest and which led to the situations in which we have seen his heroes faced with the necessity of a stark choice between two irreconcilable value systems. He thus came to write *The Trilogy*,[4] going back in time to 1917, to the years leading up to the popular revolution of 1919 and continuing through three generations of the protagonist-family to stop at 1944, the temporal watershed which none of his novels up to *The Trilogy* had crossed. The symbolic power of the dates is self-evident. The novel begins in the middle of a world war and terminates with the end of another. The world is in the process of convulsive change and so is Egyptian society. Change is painful but inevitable. And change occurs in time which may be favourable to society, its benignity being embedded in the infinite hope attendant on its own infiniteness. Not so, alas, is time to the individual because here it is hopelessly finite and, as it inexorably advances, it can only hold the promise of death and decay. This novel is about time and man and the myriad nameless things that such a story would entail.

The 1,500 pages or so which constitute the three parts of *The Trilogy* are a powerful embodiment of Mahfouz's concept of time expounded above. At the end of the 28-year period spanned by the novel, the members of the ᶜAbd al-Jawwād family are in a poor state indeed, their fortunes ranging from shattered hopes (Kamāl) and death-in-life (ᶜĀ'isha) to actual death (Fahmī). Conversely, the society to which these victims of time belong is seen at the end to be in much better shape than it was at the beginning: Egypt has survived two world wars partly fought on its soil and a revolution brutally put down by a great colonial power, has gained partial independence, and the national struggle which in Fahmī's generation had been limited to the issues of independence and constitutional government has been widened in Aḥmad Shawkat's generation to include the issue of social justice as well. Thus while Fahmī, who was killed in the revolution, has been decaying in his grave for twenty-six years, Egypt has been steadily progressing on the course he and many other individuals died for.

Mahfouz allocates the first forty-seven chapters of *Palace Walk* (henceforth *PW*), roughly two-thirds of the book, to a description of the homely and the quotidian. We get to know all the members of the ᶜAbd al-Jawwād family in no inconsiderable detail as we become familiar with the routine of their daily life. We see all the morning rituals: waking up, baking the bread, breakfast, the men going out to work or school and the women doing housework. We are also taken to the afternoon coffee gathering shared by all the family except the father. We see Fahmī on the roof professing his love to their next-door neighbour, Maryam; the father in his shop and in his rowdy gatherings at night with his friends and their singing mistresses; Yāsīn in his obsessive pursuit of Zannūba; the little adventures of the young Kamāl on his way back from school; the weddings of ᶜĀ'isha, Yāsīn and Khadīja in succession. All this we see and much more. And it is this descriptive quality that gives the book, among other things, its documentary value. There is no other source, literary or otherwise, that records with such detail and liveliness the habits, sentiments and living environment of Cairene Egyptians at the beginning of the century.[5] Without the novelist's loving and observant eye much about that period that no longer exists would have gone unrecorded forever.[6]

Interesting in itself as this detailed record of the homely and the quotidian is, it has another function, namely to prepare the scene for the shattering impact of the approaching revolution. The sheer space devoted initially in the book to this account of the quotidian creates a sense of timelessness about the protagonist family. We feel as if they have existed with their little happinesses and miseries since time immemorial and that they could go on like that endlessly. They probably feel the same. But they are wrong and so are we. They will soon learn, and we through them, that no human condition can go on immune from the transgression of time and that when history convulses, the lives of individuals crack and crumble.

When the British authorities exile Saᶜd Zaghlūl, having refused him permission to travel to Paris to air the nation's demand for independence before the peace conference at Versailles in 1919, the revolution erupts and martial law is enforced. From that moment the life of the family, like that of the whole nation, is never the same again. The novel reveals to us gradually the build-up of public events, and as the pace of action is stepped up, the inevitable convergence of public and private reaches its tragic conclusion. The afternoon coffee gathering formerly reserved for innocent chat and the usual bickerings among brothers and sisters is now dominated by talk of politics and accounts of demonstrations and violent confrontations with soldiers. Everyone has something to tell whether it is the 10-year-old schoolboy Kamāl, or the 19-year-old university student Fahmī, who is actively involved in distributing handbills and organizing demonstrations and strikes. Even the nightly pleasure gathering of the father and his friends is affected. On the night when Zaghlūl was exiled we are told that for the first time in twenty-five years their gathering 'was mirthless and reigned over by silence' (*PW*, p. 403). As the revolution escalates, the British decide to occupy the old quarter of al-Ḥusayn (a focal point for revolutionary agitation) where the family lives. They camp right outside the family house. The household is thrown into confusion and for some time the family impose house-arrest on themselves because they do not know the intentions of the occupying force. ᶜAbd al-Jawwād's family is thus made to embody the condition of the entire nation and historical danger is seen to be as close to the individual as the front door of his own house. The consequences of such menacing proximity materialize without delay when we see the fearsome and much-respected patriarch, ᶜAbd al-Jawwād, arrested at gunpoint on his way home one night and forced most ignominiously to take part in refilling a trench dug earlier by rebels. Another consequence is the courtship of Maryam by a soldier. Her favourable response is witnessed and innocently publicized by the young Kamāl, a fact which breaks the heart of Fahmī, who loves the girl and would have been engaged to her but for his father's objection. Yet another consequence is the near-lynching of Yāsīn at al-Ḥusayn Mosque when he is wrongly suspected by worshippers of being a spy for the British. These and many other small incidents bring home to the reader the true meaning of history (one not to be found in the annals of historians) as little units of time filled up by little units of people, the amalgamation of whose sufferings and deaths is what we later come to call a revolution or a war.

We all live through time, cataclysmic or ordinary, labouring under the illusion that its afflictions are things which befall others and not ourselves. Thus when the father learns of Fahmī's involvement in the revolution, he is shaken to the foundation: 'Had the flood reached his doorstep?' The revolution has had his support, financial and emotional, but when it comes to the involvement of one of his own sons, that is a different matter: 'It was as if they were a race unto themselves, standing outside the domain of history. He alone was the one to draw the limits for them, not the revolution, not the times and not other people' (*PW*, p. 483). But alas! Such pride, such heroic defiance can only be in vain. Fahmī is killed in a demonstration: 'The times, the revolution and other people' pushed him far beyond the limits set for him by his father. He has become an *individual* brick in the edifice of *history*.

Fahmī may die as an individual and his death may bring infinite grief to his father and mother, causing the first to relinquish for five long years his night life of pleasure and the latter to age beyond her years, but this is not his end. Not quite, according to Mahfouz's philosophy of time. When a person has exhausted his units of individual time, he must depart from the scene and allow his inexhaustible stock of social or collective time to be used on his behalf *in absentia*. Thus Fahmī dies, but the national struggle does not cease and society benefits from his death and that of other individuals. The novelist underlines this meaning by resurrecting Fahmī in the image of another revolutionary in the next generation of the family, namely Aḥmad Shawkat, his nephew, born years after his death. Some twenty-five years after the death of Fahmī, his incarnation is sent to prison on account of his socialist views and active involvement in spreading them. Collective time has obviously carried the national struggle a step forward: the issue now is no longer just political freedom, but also social justice, and Aḥmad Shawkat, like his old incarnation, is prepared to pay out of his *individual* time for the *public* cause. This is a moralistic view of the relationship between man and time and is at the very heart of Mahfouz's vision. There is no doubt that on the existential level he sees time as man's worst enemy and as such the battle against it becomes his first moral duty.[7] The battle, however, is bound to be lost on the individual level since death is ineluctable. Our only hope in victory, then, is social or collective. Aḥmad Shawkat sums it up neatly: 'The common duty of humanity is perpetual revolution which consists in the persistent endeavour to realize the will of life as represented in its evolution towards the highest ideal' (*Sugar Street*, p. 393; henceforth *SS*).

Time, however, does not need to call up revolutions, wars or any other form of historical cataclysm in order to inflict death and destruction on the lives of individuals. Cataclysmic time is only a heightened form of quotidian time, which is equally destructive. Cataclysmic time sees to those individuals who die in violent demonstrations, warlike actions, earthquakes, floods, etc., whereas quotidian time looks after those who die of old age, prolonged illness, accidents or for no comprehensible reason at all. Death, however, is only time's final and, ironically, merciful blow. What is really tragic is the time process in its daily unfolding as it leads up to death, i.e. the consciousness of the changing self and circumstances in time – ultimately, the consciousness that life is but death in progress. Aḥmad ᶜAbd al-Jawwād is a good example. He is portrayed in almost superhuman terms. Physically a giant resplendent with health and beauty; an authoritarian patriarch at home, as much feared as loved; a successful merchant; an adored friend and lover; at once a libertine and a devout worshipper – a bundle of contradictions fused together in a harmonious and admirable whole that by just existing seemed temporarily to mock the very idea of Time. *Temporarily*, I said, because so things appear, until time claims its due. After a long process of gradual deterioration begun after the death of his son Fahmī and extending over a period of some twenty years (amply illustrated in the book), this paragon of strength and vitality is reduced to a disabled bundle carried home like a child from an air-raid shelter by his son Kamāl. The cycle is completed and the man has become child again: that night after this final humiliation, he dies.

Unlike cataclysmic time, which has no pattern and can kill someone like Fahmī at the age of 19 without overtaxing human comprehension,[8] quotidian time seems to work according to some sort of pattern, or so embattled humans imagine. People usually expect, despite their awareness of the inevitable end, a reasonable allowance of time in which to grow up, mature and fulfil themselves in life up to a point, within their means and circumstances before the laws of mutation and decay claim them. But time does not always oblige. A pattern it may have, but patterns have exceptions, and time patterns are no exception. Thus ᶜĀ'isha loses her youthful husband and her two young sons at one stroke. Typhoid does it. A few years later she loses her remaining daughter, who dies in childbirth within one year of her marriage. ᶜĀ'isha's sanity, which barely withstood the first breach of the pattern, collapses at the second. Grief gnaws at her heart, and, still in her thirties, she becomes the living remnants of what not too long ago was an image of beauty and the love of life.

In real life death can seem quite accidental and totally without meaning except for the mundane affirmation of the fragility and transience of human existence. In Mahfouz, however, and contrary to received critical opinion, death is rarely so.[9] Even when it looks most irrational, at closer view it will transpire that the author has imbued it with a subtle moral point. We have already seen examples of this in the deaths of Rushdī ᶜĀkif in *Khan al-Khalili* and ᶜAbbās al-Ḥulw in *Midaq Alley.* The tragedy of ᶜĀ'isha and her family here is yet another example. In the expository sections there is an insistence (which is sustained at intervals throughout the novel) on her beauty on the one hand, and her uselessness on the other: 'She appeared in the midst of the family like a beautiful but useless symbol' (*PW*, p. 24). She is also shown to be narcissistically obsessed with her beauty, always admiring her reflection in the mirror. She has a carefree temperament, singing or humming all the time in her beautiful voice and showing little interest in housework – all of which may appear to the ordinary eye to be sins of a venial nature. But not according to the stern ethics of Mahfouz. What makes matters worse is that she gets married to one of the Shawkat brothers. The two brothers are portrayed by the novelist as the epitome of idleness. Of Turkish descent, they are without education and without jobs (in fact they profess their contempt for work), but with enough income from property to provide for a decent standard of living. Their days and nights are spent at home in sleep or useless activities (such as playing music in the case of Khalīl, ᶜĀ'isha's husband). Even the look in their eyes is repeatedly described by the author as 'languid'. Naturally, they display no interest whatsoever in the turmoil of public life. As they advance in age, they continue to possess good health and young looks: they are described as 'the two amazing men who do not seem to change with time as though they stood outside its stream' (*Palace of Desire*, p. 34; henceforth *PD*). Considering her natural tendencies, it is no wonder that ᶜĀ'isha, after marriage, 'was submerged in Shawkatism up to her neck' (*PD*, p. 183). Naᶜīma, ᶜĀ'isha's daughter, is depicted as a replica of her mother. Her beauty is that of a 'pin-up girl' (*PD*, p. 45), and her eyes 'reflect a gentle and dreamy look washed in purity, a naivety and a sense of foreignness to this world' (*SS*, p. 6). Like her mother, she is given, from her infancy, to singing and dancing and 'uselessness'. Now 'standing outside the stream of time' watching life go by and enjoying oneself no matter what, is an indulgence that real time might occasionally overlook, but, harnessed in the service of Mahfuzian morality, it would seldom pardon. Therefore the entire Khalīl branch of the Shawkat family is wiped from the face of the earth, while ᶜĀ'isha, as a further punishment, is spared to muse upon her loss and die a slow death.[10]

One might wonder why not as well kill off Ibrāhīm Shawkat, Khalīl's elder brother who got married to Khadīja, ᶜĀ'isha's elder sister. He is every bit as useless and as aloof from the 'stream of time' as his unfortunate brother. Is there a flaw, a measure of double standards in the Mahfuzian time-morality? Far from it. The system is exemplarily fair and the fact of the matter is that Khadīja redeems Ibrāhīm and his branch. Ugly, energetic, responsible, totally committed to her family and above all 'useful', she is a foil to her sister. Being the stronger party in the marriage, she imposes 'Jawwādism' in the heartland of 'Shawkatism' and she brings into the world two sons, ᶜAbd al-Munᶜim and Aḥmad, who are completely like her and unlike their father. She pulls her family back into 'the stream of time' and therefore survives and saves them.

We have seen that Mahfouz views time as 'representing the evolutionary spirit of man' and as 'perpetuating human experience'.[11] This of course is time only as conceived by collective or social man. On the social level Mahfouz has demonstrated to us how the death of the individual Fahmī was redeemed in time through the evolution of the social cause he had died for. It would appear then that collectively we are able to steal from time the victory we are deprived of as individuals. On closer inspection, it would appear also that Mahfouz thinks a measure of victory is possible even on the individual plane: through heredity, that is. Now much has been said about the influence of naturalism on the work of Mahfouz from *Khan al-Khalili* and up to the novel under discussion.[12] And much of this is doubtless true despite the novelist's own denials.[13] It appears to me though, that by the time he reached *The Trilogy*, the author had forged a special brand of naturalism to suit his own scheme of things. Heredity in this novel is not merely a scientific factor that predetermines the fate of character, as would be the case in a naturalistic novel proper. Heredity here is also seen as a human defence mechanism against the ravages of time. It is a means of perpetuating the individual, if not in person then at least in character. Thus Khadīja with her combination of physical ugliness and redoubtable spirit is a perpetuation (after realignment: her father's strength of personality and sense of humour, but his enormous nose; her mother's agility and devotion to family duties, but not her delicate features) of what is best in her parents, ᶜAbd al-Jawwād and Amīna. Yāsīn too (the most obvious example of naturalist influence in Mahfouz's entire output), with his physical beauty, lasciviousness and insatiable lust for life, is a perpetuation of his parents, ᶜAbd al-Jawwād and his first wife, Haniyya. True, he inherits only the negative side of his legendary father's character, just as Khadīja inherits the positive qualities of her parents' characters without their physical beauty, but this is immaterial. Let the law of heredity wreak what havoc it will with noses and eyes and weaknesses of character and strengths! Let it produce the most motley combinations across generations! What matters is that it sustains us against the law of extinction. It allows us, as individuals, to perpetuate our lives from beyond the grave and in spite of time. The novel ends with the death of the matriarch Amīna and the birth almost at the same time of Yāsīn's first grandchild: sorrow over the end of individual time is assuaged, if not neutralized, by hope in collective and hereditary continuation.[14]

Are the mutations of time totally against man as an individual then? Perhaps not. But this depends on perspective. One example is that of Fu'ād al-Ḥamzāwī, the son of ᶜAbd al-Jawwād's assistant at the shop. He is the same age as ᶜAbd al-Jawwād's son, Kamāl. They are classmates at school and friends outside, though Kamāl is the stronger party in the relationship as a reflection of the social gap between their two fathers. As schoolboys, Fu'ād used to have Kamāl's old clothes as his father could not afford new ones, and when his studiousness qualifies him to join the respectable School of Law, ᶜAbd al-Jawwād, always generous, undertakes to finance his education. Fu'ād ends up in the influential office of attorney for the prosecution and Kamāl as a primary school teacher. The family are hopeful that he will ask for ᶜĀ'isha's daughter's hand in marriage and decide that they will in this case overlook his humble origins and condescend to accept. But *he* does not condescend. His high office and promising career have moved him up the social ladder and he can now hope for a more advantageous marriage than into the family of his old benefactor. He has done well, then, by the mutations of time. But of course the view from the other end of the perspective, i.e. that of ᶜAbd al-Jawwād's family, is quite different. They seem to have done quite badly, and it is through their perspective that Mahfouz shows us the view. Similarly the fall from wealth and grace of the aristocratic Shaddāds – to such a point that Kamāl, whose love was once scorned by their daughter ᶜĀyda, is later considered more than a match for her younger sister Budūr – can be seen in one sense as a positive mutation of time. But this is not the aspect from which the situation is viewed. Rather, Kamāl's meditations are centred on the tragic meaning of the fall. Mahfouz is obviously not blind to the fact that time's mutations can bring about positive results too in the life of individuals, but it is not this aspect that interests him. He wants to tell us about the ultimate horror of time, not its ephemeral kindnesses.

There is another aspect to the relationship between time and man, namely the relationship between past and present, which transfers us from the realm of metaphysical time to that of value-impregnated time. In other words the past-present duality is about what man does with the life quota allocated him by metaphysical time. The life quota assigned to individual man is naturally finite and all too short for significant achievement, but that assigned to man socially or collectively (i.e. as a species) is infinite and carries equally infinite possibilities for improvement. It is the duty of each individual to use his share of time to the best of his ability towards this objective, i.e. the betterment of the human lot. This moral concept of time is central to Mahfouz's vision as I have indicated before. It would be no exaggeration, indeed, to argue that the only source of hope in his work emanates from his view of man as a force endlessly active in a time continuum across individuals, generations, ages and cultures.[15] Wherever he portrays man as an isolated human unit wrestling against the odds of time and space, the consequence is always tragic. 'Tragic' is indeed the word he uses to describe his view of life which ends in death for the individual. But, as we have seen, he stresses that while death is inevitable, it is incumbent on us (while we live) to fight social evils which are perfectly avoidable and which indirectly aid death in its perpetual victory over humanity.[16] Now social evils can of course be remedied only in time. Not static time, but changing time. And change is about the tension between past and present – a tension whose arena extends from the soul of the individual to the full spectrum of society. This tension, of which we have seen various manifestations in previous works by the author, is much more profoundly explored in this novel.

The extension of *The Trilogy* across three generations provided the novelist with an excellent opportunity to explore this favourite theme of his through observing the mutation of values across generations, the time gap between different contemporaneous social classes, and the changing lifestyle concomitant with the changing value system. Through an intricate, multi-layered, multi-directional symbolic system so well woven into the robustly realistic texture of the novel, Mahfouz renders in artistic terms that have yet to be surpassed the dichotomy that his nation still lives today and will probably do so for a long time to come. The generation of the parents stands for the past. The father, as mentioned before, is a bundle of contradictions: a stern, authoritarian, much-feared patriarch at home, but a cheerful, witty, much-loved friend and businessman outside; a true believer and pious worshipper in daytime, but at night a devoted libertine given to drink, women and merrymaking. Yet, all these contradictions live inside him in a harmony worthy only of a god. The phrase is actually Mahfouz's own comment on his character.[17] Nor should we think that he used the word 'god' lightly, for ᶜAbd al-Jawwād is portrayed as in every way a god in his home. This is not only shown through the supreme, unquestionable and irrevocable authority that he wields over the fates of the members of his household, and through episodes like the banishment of his wife from his home after twenty-five years of total obedience, for once going out without his permission (a banishment which evokes the Fall and expulsion from Heaven). Not only through this, but also the narrative prose which persistently attributes to him epithets and qualities appropriate to Allah.[18] In this context we should perhaps call to the mind *al-Asmā' al-Ḥusnā* or the divine attributes of God in

Islam whose contradictions are as wide as is the distance between 'the Merciful' and 'the Compassionate' on the one hand, and 'the Tyrant' and 'the Vengeful' on the other – compassion and tyranny both being attributes of ᶜAbd al-Jawwād, incidentally. This supreme harmony, this peaceful coexistence of opposites in the character of the father is a masterly rendition of a culture at peace with itself, a protected and isolated culture with neither external influence nor inner conflict. Needless to say, the father has little education beyond reading and writing and the basic book-keeping necessary for his trade. A merchant and the son of one, he was born in the old quarter of Jamāliyya and was to die in it. Practically intelligent, witty and socially accomplished, his ignorance of life beyond his small world is endearingly illustrated when he asks his son Kamāl whether Charles Darwin (about whom the latter had published an article in a newspaper) was a teacher at his school (*PD*, chapter 33, *passim*). His generation represented the last bastion of the past in Egypt, the past when it reigned supreme, unchallenged and, like God, infallible. The harmony and freedom from conflict that he enjoyed is something that none of his children or their children will ever experience. Represented by Kamāl in the second generation, and his nephews Aḥmad and ᶜAbd al-Munᶜim in the third, they are the ones to live through a duality of values, through the schizophrenia created by the encroachment of the present on the past and of the 'other' on the 'self'.

When the children discover the duality of their father's nature, i.e. that the 'Divine' is also human, that 'God' can laugh and drink and play the tambourine as well as fornicate, the discovery shakes them to the foundations. Yāsīn was the first to make the discovery and the scene where he peeps through the partly open door with unbelieving eyes at the unknown side of his father is rendered in epiphanic terms which strengthen the view of the father as symbolic of God.[19] Years later, when Kamāl was grown up, Yāsīn let him in on his secret knowledge. This shocking revelation coincides with many other disturbing revelations that Kamāl has had. It was as if his world had been deprived of the last gravitational force that held it in place. From that moment on his soul was to wander lost in the infinite space of doubt and disbelief. His father now is just 'another illusion' (*PD*, p. 410), no longer possessing 'the divine attributes that [his] bewitched eyes had seen in him in the past' (*PD*,

p. 412). At this point the symbolism almost comes up to the surface of the text as Kamāl addresses his father in his mind with these words: 'But it is not you alone whose image has changed. God himself is no longer God as I worshipped Him in the past. I am sifting through His attributes to clean them from tyranny, despotism, coercion, dictatorship and the whole gamut of human instincts' (*PD*, p. 412). Thus Kamāl discards his veneration for his father in the same breath as he discards the conventional, religious image of God. In his drunken delirium, he condemns parenthood and the family, 'that hole in which stagnant water collects', and prays for 'a homeland without history and a life without past'(*PD*, p. 413).[20] The father dies (years after this revelation) following an air-raid that his frail heart could not withstand. Minutes before his death, Kamāl had said by way of commenting on the effect of the air-raids on the old houses of Jamāliyya: 'If our houses are destroyed, they will at least have the honour of being destroyed by the latest devices of modern science' (*SS*, p. 264). What is really destroyed is not the old houses, but the old values of their occupants. The death of the father as a result of an act of modern warfare is a symbolic ending for a symbolic character. He is the once secure past ousted by Western modernity. His death in this manner is a forerunner of the death of another father/God figure and also at the hands of modern science, namely Gebelawi (correctly Jabalāwī) of the author's next novel, *Children of Gebelawi*.

Amīna, the mother, is also an emblem of the past. The nuances of her portrait strengthen the symbolic dimension to her husband's, so that together they represent the past in its last secure days, the past as it will never be again. Her relationship with her husband, characterized by total and unquestioning acceptance of his authority, is itself an image of the stability of the value system that is the frame for this relationship. The imperturbable serenity of her temperament (much stressed by the author), like her husband's unique ability to accommodate his contradictions in a state of harmony, should be seen as another manifestation of the stability of the world-view behind it. By the time we reach the second generation, this stability is already shaken. This is conveyed by the completely different relationships that her daughters have with their husbands: in the case of ᶜĀ'isha a relationship of equality, and in the case of Khadīja one where the woman seems to have the upper hand. In the third generation the values of the old world become almost unrecognizable as one of the grandchildren, Aḥmad Shawkat, brings as wife into the family a working woman as much in contact with the reality outside the home as himself.

Illiterate, without any education except for an oral religious one steeped in superstition and received from her father (himself a man of religion), Amīna is obviously the representative of a culture that at the beginning of the century was not only almost totally religiously oriented, but happy to be so and unaware of an alternative. Like the culture she represents, she lived in complete isolation from the outside world, cocooned inside the *old* Cairo, or more accurately inside the walls of her home in old Cairo, where all she could see of the outside world was the view from the roof, which consisted of nothing but 'the minarets of mosques and the roofs of adjacent houses' (*PW*, p. 43). She believed in the jinn and did all she could to placate those of their species that lived in her home. In the author's words, 'she knew much more about the world of the jinn than she did about that of humans' (*PW*, p. 7). No wonder then that when, after twenty-five years of this protected, blindfolded life, she decides to venture out only as far as al-Ḥusayn Mosque in the immediate vicinity, the contact with outside reality is catastrophic in its consequences: she is hit by a car and has a broken collarbone which confines her to bed for three weeks. A yet more serious consequence was her temporary exile by her husband/God as a punishment for tasting of the forbidden tree-of-knowledge-of-the-extradomestic. Just as the old ᶜAbd al-Jawwād's death, many years later, was to come as a consequence of the encounter with the devices of the modern world (i.e. the bombers conducting the air-raid), the meaning of the car that hits Amīna should not be lost either. It too is a device of the modern world, its symbolic value heightened by its relative rarity on the streets of Cairo in those days.[21]

Amīna's embodiment of a past isolated from reality and the true meaning of things perhaps has its fullest expression in the scenes where we become acquainted with her political views. She finds it improper conduct that Saᶜd Zaghlūl and his colleagues should travel to London to ask the British to get out of Egypt: 'How could you go to visit someone in their house when your intention is to kick them out of yours?' she argues (*PW*, p. 371). Eventually she wishes them good luck expressing her faith that if they knew how to talk to Queen Victoria, she, being a woman and therefore tender-hearted, would oblige with the desired independence. She did not know of course that Queen Victoria had then been dead for nearly two decades. Her naiveté is as charming for us as it was painful for her son Fahmī, who was involved with all his being in the national cause and dreamed of 'a new world, a new homeland, and a new family' (*PW*, pp. 373–4). When her younger son Kamāl, very close to her in his childhood, matures, he comes to reject her too, not as a mother of course but as a past value that he has outgrown. Her rejection is part of a wholesale discarding of the past. I refer here to the previously quoted monologue in which Kamāl announces his freedom from God and father. In the selfsame monologue he labels her 'the ignorant gentleness' as opposed to his father, who is 'the ignorant roughness', and he calls himself 'a victim of those two extremes'. 'Your ignorance', he goes on, 'filled my soul with myths. You have been the link between me and prehistoric man. How I will suffer to liberate myself from your influence' (*PW*, p. 413).

Suffer he does indeed and most of the second volume of *The Trilogy*, i.e. *Palace of Desire*, is devoted to an account of his suffering. Some of the most profound soul-searching ever rendered in Arabic prose is contained in this volume. And it is written with such intensity and immediacy and with a poetic quality that must be drawn from the admitted autobiographical link between Kamāl and his creator. As Mahfouz has often repeated, Kamāl's spiritual crisis was that of an entire generation,[22] by which he meant his own generation. The crisis, as we have seen, consists in the now classic Mahfuzian conflict between old and new or past and present, that conflict which is a natural corollary inherent in the fluid state of time. Kamāl's dilemma results from his exposure to an influence that his parents' generation did not experience. This was mainly the influence of modern Western thought disseminated through the modernization of the educational system which had already taken root in the 1920s and 1930s when Kamāl was growing up. The gap between the two generations is probably best dramatized in the book in the famous scene in which Kamāl is taken to task by his awesome father for having published a newspaper article in which he expounded Darwin's theory of evolution. For the father the issue was crystal-clear: the Qur'ān says that 'God made Adam of clay and that Adam was the father of mankind', and to publicize any views to the contrary was an act of denial of the faith. Kamāl, however, was well past all that. Outwardly apologetic to his father, his inner thoughts ran like this: 'I will not open my heart again to myth and superstition. . . . Adam, my father! I have no father. Let my father be a monkey if Truth so wills' (*PD*, p. 372). Apart from scenes like the above, conversations with intellectual friends like Riyāḍ Qaldas and an endless stream of internal monologues, Kamāl's dilemma is delineated through two central relationships heightened by being endowed with a symbolic dimension. The first is his relationship with his parents, which I have already examined; the second is his unrequited love for ᶜĀyda Shaddād. As we have seen, his relationship with his parents ends in his rejection of their symbolic value, i.e. as exponents of the past, even though he continues to love and respect them as parents. ᶜĀyda, on the other hand, represents the alternative value system and lifestyle that he craves but cannot quite attain. She is the elusive present which he cannot reach far enough to embrace, and her rejection of him is as symbolic as his of his parents.

Critics have tended to regard both Kamāl's infatuation with ᶜĀyda and her rejection of him in terms of social class. This is undeniably one level on which the relationship can be perceived. Kamāl is a commoner, the son of a small merchant who lives in the *old* popular area of Jamāliyya, whereas ᶜĀyda is the daughter of ᶜAbd al-Ḥamīd Shaddād, wealthy aristocrat and friend of the exiled ex-Khedive of Egypt, who lives in a great mansion in the *new* Cairo suburb of ᶜAbbāsiyya. The unwritten social code would permit Kamāl to become Ḥusayn Shaddād's (ᶜĀyda's brother) best friend, but marriage and the union of the families was a different matter altogether (not that Kamāl ever went as far as proposing to ᶜĀyda, anyway). Another level on which the relationship can be viewed, and which is in fact an upgrading of the class level, is the cultural one. ᶜĀyda, both personally and as a member of her class, does not belong to the traditional value system that Kamāl and *his* class live in accordance with. She and *her* class are, or at least so appear to the bewildered and infatuated eyes of Kamāl, emancipated from the past. To him she means modernity, Western modernity with the full plethora of associations that the term brings. Throughout there is an insistence on her Parisian upbringing and an opposition of what this means in terms of social behaviour to Kamāl's traditional upbringing. Unlike his mother and sisters who never step out of the house (and if they do, it is from behind a *ḥijāb* (veil) that they see the world), ᶜĀyda is a model of Parisian chicness who mixes freely with her brother's friends (including Kamāl) while he watches and 'suffers the bewilderment of one steeped in the traditions of the Ḥusayn Quarter' (*PD*, p. 22). 'Has her breach of observed traditions brought scorn upon her in your eyes?' he says to himself. 'No. Rather, it has brought scorn upon observed traditions' (*PD*, p. 23). When he sees her parents walking towards their car, arm in arm, chatting casually like two equal friends, 'not master and servant', he wonders, 'Would you ever see your parents in this situation?' (*PD*, p. 184). When Kamāl goes on a picnic to the Pyramids at Jīza with Ḥusayn, ᶜĀyda and their little sister Budūr, he is shocked when they produce out of their lunch box pork sandwiches and beer, religiously forbidden food and drink that he has never tasted. Shocked as he is (as he also is when he discovers that ᶜĀyda knows more about Christianity and its ritual than about her own confession and that she attends mass at her French school and learns hymns off by heart when she cannot recite a single verse from the Qur'ān), all this only serves to increase his fascination with her. This 'light attitude towards the prohibitions of religion', sanctified by her very embracement of them, would from now on, he fears, become necessary credentials for him to admire any woman in the future (*PD*, p. 217). On that occasion he touches neither pork nor alcohol. Before long, however, his conversion completed, he would be taking pride in his atheism, announcing happily to his friends that he no longer prayed or kept the fast of Ramaḍān. Before long, too, he would be a customer at public bars and brothels. The process of his secularization was accomplished via a one-way journey from Jamāliyya to Paris via ᶜAbbāsiyya.

ᶜĀyda is idolized by Kamāl. He places her on a pedestal and worships her unconditionally and without hope of response. In his fervid monologues he refers to her as *al-Maᶜbud* (the worshipped one), and often alludes to her in words and phrases imbued with religious associations.[23] He sees her as pure spirit, is uncomfortable to see her eat and drink and unable to imagine her performing other biological functions or succumbing after marriage to such mortal changes as are brought about by pregnancy and childbirth. All this of course is in the eye of the beholder. The reader is occasionally able to see for himself through Kamāl's thick curtain of romanticization. Finally many facts are brought to the attention of the incredulous Kamāl by his more down-to-earth friend, Ismāᶜīl Laṭīf. ᶜĀyda, three years Kamāl's senior in age, generally maturer, more experienced and more sophisticated (as would be expected of a member of her class), is in reality as far as can be from Kamāl's idealized image of her. She has been looking for a suitable match among her brother's friends and when she finds one she does not hesitate to use the unwitting Kamāl to arouse his jealousy and urge him to move in the direction of marriage. She is cruel to her worshipper, carelessly hurting his feelings by mocking his rather large head and nose. Nor does she refrain from making his love for her a subject for ridicule in the family. Her realism is a foil to Kamāl's romanticism, her materialism to his idealism, her maturity to his adolescence, her arrogance to his humility, her sense of purpose to his fluidity, her exploitation to his devotion, and her indifference to his love. With her qualities, both positive and negative, and with the nature of the unbalanced relationship between her and Kamāl, she appears the perfect symbol of the ideal of modern Europe for whose sake Kamāl's generation rejected the past without succeeding, however, in attaining it. The agonizing situation is best summarized by the words of Riyāḍ Qaldas to Kamāl: 'You suggest to me the character of an Eastern man, torn between East and West, a man who has kept turning round himself until he became dizzy' (SS, p. 227).

Kamāl's infatuation with ᶜĀyda in his early youth is in my view not unrelated on the symbolic level to his infatuation with English soldiers as a child of some 10 years. When the soldiers are stationed outside the family house during the revolution, Kamāl is lured by their beauty: 'their blue eyes, gold hair and white skin' (*PW*, p. 462).[24] He becomes friends with them and every day on his way back from school, he would stop at their camp to have tea and to chat and sing with them. When the revolution is over and the soldiers evacuate the area, the child feels sorry for the end of the 'friendship which tied him to those superior masters who stood in his belief high above the rest of mankind' (*PW*, p. 559).[25] This obviously is an early manifestation of fascination with the 'other', that in Kamāl's maturer days will take the form of admiration for the 'beauty' of the culture of those soldiers rather than their good looks. It is, however, a love–hate relationship. During an anti-British demonstration that he is caught in in maturer years, Kamāl is puzzled by his own attitude: 'In the morning my heart is inflamed with rebellion against the English, while at night the common spirit of human fellowship in pain calls for co-operation in the face of the riddle of man's destiny' (*SS*, pp. 44–5). What he is referring to is his nightly readings in Western thought. The parallelism between the childhood episode referred to above and the central story of his love for ᶜĀyda is not difficult to see: in both cases there is an innocent infatuation followed by a maturer disenchantment, though never a complete rejection. When in his middle age, Kamāl walks in the funeral of ᶜĀyda without knowing, it seems a most cynical ending to a very romantic episode, all the more so because the 'goddess' of the past dies the second wife of an older man, having earlier been divorced by her aristocratic husband as well as made a pauper by her family's loss of fortune. What did Mahfouz want to say by that? Is it a tacit pronouncement on the sham of the old infatuation, on the depth of the chasm between inner illusion and outer reality? Or is it a pronouncement on the frailty of the alternative model? Or is it again just a lament over the vanity of human passion and the final mockery that Time has in store for the unwitting individual?

Kamāl's parents lived during the glorious, unassailable days of the past. By contrast, Kamāl's time was one of tension between past and present, a tension which paralysed him and served to consume his energy in contemplating life rather than living and changing it. Hence his futile celibacy, his bewilderment, his endless hesitations and doubts and his Hamlet-like inaction. The third generation, as represented by Kamāl's nephews ᶜAbd al-Munᶜim and Aḥmad, is, however, a generation of action. The two brothers are not internally torn between past and present like their uncle because the conflict is now externalized on the ground in society. ᶜAbd al-Munᶜim, a Moslem Brother, believes that the solution for the troubles of individual and society lies in the return to the fundamentals of Islam: he is the past. Aḥmad, on the other hand, sees the solution in the abandonment of old values and the adoption of science and socialism: he is the present. Both brothers are political activists taking risks for their separate causes and ending up in prison.[26]

It is Aḥmad, however, who has the sympathy of Kamāl (and indeed the implicit sympathy of the novelist).[27] I have argued earlier that Aḥmad as a nationalist is an extension across time of Fahmī, who died prematurely in the struggle. Aḥmad is also an improved version of Kamāl; he is what Kamāl could have been had he succeeded in freeing himself more radically from the past and from his romantic fixations. To prove the point, Mahfouz places Aḥmad in a similar relationship to that which Kamāl had with ᶜĀyda. His love too is directed towards the upper class, but his approach, unlike his uncle's, is daring and self-confident and when he meets with rejection, life does not stand still. His frustration is redirected towards a higher cause and is soon transcended.

THERE ONLY REMAINS AN HOUR

The Trilogy, as we have seen, begins in 1917 and stops near the end of World War II, having been completed in 1952 shortly before Nasser's revolution. After the period of silence[28] which occupied the best part of the 1950s, Mahfouz spent most of the following two decades criticizing the 1952 revolution and the new society it created – in much the same way as the novels of the 1940s had been dedicated to criticism of the old society. In 1982, however, twelve years after the death of Nasser, one year after Sādāt's and thirty years into the life of a revolution that had long spent its force, it occurred to Mahfouz, perhaps feeling the additional weight of years and the national frustrations which came with them, to review and update, through another *roman fleuve*, Egypt's relationship with time and to examine again the sorrows inflicted by the public on the private. *There Only Remains an Hour* documents the political history of twentieth-century Egypt from the time of the nationalist uprising against the British in 1919 down to the Camp David Accords and the Peace Treaty with Israel in 1979. It stops just short of the assassination of Sādāt in 1981,[29] which is dealt with in a later novel (*The Day the Leader was Killed*, 1985). Thus it can be argued that the novel is in a sense both a condensation and an updating of *The Trilogy*. Like *The Trilogy*, it is also a saga novel (though without the length associated with this type of novel), with the youngest generation reaching maturity during the Nasser era.[30]

The novel is written in simplistic symbolism, each of the characters standing for one or other of the political ideas or forces rife in Egypt during the last three-quarters of a century.[31] Most important is the character of Saniyya, the grandmother, who represents the spirit of Egypt herself. She is shown in the symbolism of the book as impervious to the ageing process. Although by the end of the book she is well into her eighties (p. 171), she is still energetic with no sign of mental or physical deterioration, unlike her own children, who seem older than her.[32] She lives in a house with a garden in the Ḥilwān suburb of Cairo, of which we are told that it had seen a few good days and suffered ages of decay (p. 6). Within a few pages of the beginning of the novel, it becomes obvious that the house and the garden stand for Egypt as a country in need of material progress and social welfare but constantly being deprived of the chance to achieve this goal. The house is shown to be in a run-down state from the outset – since Saniyya's early married years. Her thoughts run like this:

> Food and clothing eat up all our earnings. What will become of this large house? It needs repairs and redecoration. And the garden: the trees no longer bear fruit; the shrubs are withered and sand has covered most of the soil. How it wants to be revived!
>
> (p. 20)

Throughout her life, from her youth to her old age, Saniyya has had one single haunting dream: to renovate the house and garden. But generation after generation and one political era after another, her dream is shattered and her wait is indefinitely prolonged. One regime after another fails to deliver the promise of prosperity and Egypt, like the house, has to remain poor and dilapidated. Her final hope is centred on Sādāt's peace initiative which, he promised the nation, would bring prosperity with it. But this hope too is dashed, on the symbolic level in the novel as in reality. Rather than being brought back to life, the garden Saniyya is left with in the end looks like 'a target in the aftermath of an air-raid' (p. 187).

The novel is written in one long piece of continuous narrative: 190 pages without chapter divisions. It is as if the novelist wanted to delineate the history of modern Egypt as a flux of suffering and frustration, a homogeneous continuum of lost opportunities. The book ends bleakly with a family gathering in the old derelict house during a thunderstorm which underlines the tumultuous times Egypt is struggling through. As one turns over the last leaf of the book, suddenly the sense of prophetic doom implicit in the title dawns on the mind: THERE ONLY REMAINS AN HOUR. Mahfouz obviously believes that modern Egypt has wasted enough opportunities; that history's generosity is not boundless and unless something is done and done quickly, Egypt may be eternally doomed to a fate of poverty, backwardness and dependency. The sense of self-confidence in spite of difficulties and boundless hope in the future which characterized the attitude of the youngest generation at the end of *The Trilogy* has, in the intervening thirty years since its writing, been dissipated: Egypt has not been making good use of collective time.[33]

THE DAY THE LEADER WAS KILLED

Before the Throne, discussed elsewhere in this book,[34] appeared one year after *There Only Remains an Hour* and showed Mahfouz still preoccupied with the fortunes of Egypt in time. Here, in a desperate attempt at understanding his country's hapless present, he is not content to trace it back to his usual starting point, i.e. the 1919 revolution, but goes back all the way to the beginnings of Egypt in time (some 3,000 years before Christ) and retraces his steps up to the assassination of Sādāt in 1981. Unlike the two novels examined so far in this chapter, *Before the Throne* is a work more concerned with the general than the particular, with the effect of politics on the public rather than the individual level. It speaks of pharaohs and kings and presidents, of conquests and defeats and revolutions, but seldom mentions the people who are the fodder for all these cataclysms – in other words, it is about collective, historical time and not its quotidian, individual manifestations.

This extensive historical investigation seems, however, to have done little to set Mahfouz's mind at ease and so he sets off again on another journey in time: *The Day the Leader was Killed* (1985). Here Mahfouz is back within the confines of his usual period of investigation, i.e. from 1919 to the present day, the period to which he has been an eye-witness. The book is a novella of some ninety pages.[35] The day of the title is 6 October

1981 and the leader killed is, needless to say, Anwar Sādāt. The story is told through a number of alternating internal monologues divided among three characters,[36] namely Muḥtashimī (the grandfather), ᶜAlwān (his grandson) and Randa (the latter's fiancée). Although it is compact, the book can be seen as yet another *roman fleuve* where prominence is given to the first and third generations (grandfather and grandson), while the middle generation is shown only through the eyes of the other two. The monologues of the grandfather, contrary to those of the grandson and his fiancée, are rendered in poetic, evocative language and often sound like a dirge for times past and friends lost to death. But the story mainly documents the predicament of Egyptian youth during the Sādāt era, and through parallelism between the consciousnesses of the old and the young creates the sense of a continuum of national frustration across generations.

The grandfather is a kindly old man in his eighties but in good health and at peace with himself. During his long life he has been witness to the political life of the nation from the times of Saᶜd Zaghlūl to those of Sādāt. On the symbolic level he seems to play here a role not dissimilar to that of the grandmother, Saniyya, in *There Only Remains an Hour.*[37] He probably stands for the atemporal, all-encompassing character of Egypt, having survived many leaders and conflicting policies without ever being engulfed by any one current.

As for the grandson and his fiancée, they are revealed as two young people in love. They belong to the lower middle class and live with their respective families in the same block of flats. They are both graduates working in the same government office. They are both honest and morally upright, religious without fanaticism and full of the love of life. In short, together they seem to represent what Mahfouz believes to be the positive and generally moderate characteristics of the Egyptian personality. (It is interesting to note here the element of continuity between the grandfather's character and that of the new generation.) In their late twenties and having been engaged for many years, ᶜAlwān and Randa are still unable to fulfil their dream of marriage. There is no way (we are shown) that they can afford to rent and furnish a flat under Sādāt's consumer-oriented *infitāḥ* or open-door economy, wild inflation and soaring prices. Their dilemma is all the more poignant because their moral rectitude restrains them from seeking a solution by devious means. Thus the engagement is broken under pressure from the girl's family and the high ideal of love is shown to have been ditched in a society where all values have become relative. The girl is married off to her wealthy boss – a sacrifice on the altar of economic necessity. Soon after, it transpires that the man only wanted her to use her beauty in his business-brokering. The old spark of dignity flares up again and she obtains a divorce. The young man, on the other hand, is nearly tempted to marry a much older, rich widow, but he withdraws in the last minute. In the midst of all this despair, Sādāt is killed and, in an artistically naive parallel action of rebellion, ᶜAlwān attacks the corrupt executive who robbed him of his love and causes his death. Thus the simplistic parallelism of the plot serves to show the fall of the supreme head of a corrupt regime and of one of his distant satellites at the same time. However, it would be fair to say that the purpose of the novelist here (as it was in *There Only Remains an Hour*) is not so much to write good fiction as to record critically the features of an age.

Against the backdrop of this story, Sādāt's Egypt is described in scathing terms. To give a few examples, the *infitāḥ* economic policy has resulted in the Egyptians becoming 'a deprived community amidst a circus of thieves' (p. 21) and 'many nations living in one country' (p. 46). The individual, furthermore, is repressed: 'the Nile itself is no longer able to show anger' (p. 9), while the time is one of 'nauseating catchphrases . . . between which and the truth is a gulf in which we have fallen' (p. 17). 'Lies fly in the air like dust' when a presidential speech is broadcast (p. 47). Sādāt himself is 'an actor *manqué* . . . dressed up like Hitler while his actions imitate Charlie Chaplin's' (p. 47). On the other hand, a sense of nostalgia for Nasser's days seems the only comfort in an age without heroes or ideals, a nostalgia so strong it almost serves as a substitute for looking forward to the future (pp. 22, 43). The nation's initial sense of shock at the news of the assassination is shown soon to have given way to a sense of relief, almost glee. Comments among customers at a café run like this: 'This is the punishment of him who thinks the country is dead. . . . In a moment the thieves' empire has collapsed' (p. 82). Indeed, while the novella ends with the death of Sādāt, this is not at all shown as cause for gloom or despair. On the contrary, the final thoughts of the young protagonist are very positive and seem to focus, as always in Mahfouz, on the promise held by the inevitable advance of time:

> I was filled with a mysterious sense of anticipation, with unknown probabilities which promised to crush the fixity and monotony of things and to advance towards a horizon without boundaries.
>
> (p. 82)

QUSHTUMUR

Unlike the three novels already discussed in this chapter, *Qushtumur* (1988) is not a *roman fleuve* in the technical sense: there is no observation of change through the generations of a family here. This technicality excluded, much remains which binds this novel to the other three. It too is about the changes in Egyptian society and their effects on individuals over a considerable stretch of time. But rather than approach his subject through the generations of one family, Mahfouz chooses to do it here through a quick review of the lifetimes of a group of friends, representing among them a cross-section of Egyptian urban society.

In *Qushtumur* (the author's last published novel to date), Mahfouz's obsession with time seems to have reached phenomenal dimensions. His output in the 1980s can perhaps be labelled, with few exceptions, as 'a portrait of the artist battling against time'.[38] This probably has something to do with the fact that the 1980s were also the eighth decade of the novelist's life. The process of reviewing his life and times which began in the 1970s with works like *Mirrors* and *Fountain and Tomb* is accelerated in the 1980s to reach a feverish, obsessive and highly personalized pace towards the end of the decade. The author appears to be labouring under a growing awareness of the approaching end and is no longer able to write about man's old foe with the detachment he evinced in works like *The Trilogy* and *Respected Sir.* There is now a desperate attempt at the remembrance of things past, at rummaging in the memory for times lost as actual time runs out, and there is a permeating nostalgia for places, events and persons whose existence now is purely in the memory. The three works published in rapid succession over a two-year period (1987–8), namely *Tales of Mornings and Evenings*, *Good*

Morning to You and *Qushtumur*, are all set between Jamāliyya and ᶜAbbāsiyya, the two parts of Cairo that witnessed Mahfouz's childhood and early youth. They all have a strongly reminiscent tone in which the novelist's own voice can often be discerned, and characters and events appear to be largely drawn from his personal recollections of the period.[39] Together they are a homage to the past – a farewell gesture from a consciousness preparing for the final oblivion. I will deal here with *Qushtumur* and in chapter 6 with the other two.

Qushtumur,[40] which gains its title from the name of the café in ᶜAbbāsiyya where the characters of the novel habitually meet, is the latest Mahfuzian study of the space–time question. It is the outburst of an ageing consciousness horrified at the passage of time and the mutation of space, an outburst which takes the shape of a Proustian journey in the memory in search of times lost, since memory is man's only faculty capable of cheating time and arresting its continuous movement; for in life man is defeated by the alliance against him of time–space, but in the memory the more balanced battle of man versus time alone results in victory. Thus we can relive our happier and younger days at the very same time as spatial reality tells us that we are old and that our time is nearly up. The novel opens with a nostalgic, evocative passage:

> ᶜAbbāsiyya in its bygone youth: an oasis in the heart of an expansive desert. In the east stood castle-like mansions and in the west small adjacent houses which took pride in their newness and their back gardens. Surrounded by vegetable fields, palm and henna trees and groves of prickly pears, it sank in a sweet tranquillity and an all-encompassing peacefulness, interrupted from time to time by the buzz of the white tram travelling endlessly along its route between Heliopolis and al-ᶜAtaba al-Khaḍrā'. And from the desert a dry breeze would blow over it, borrowing from the fields on its way their scents, thereby stirring in the hearts their secretly cherished loves. *But*[41] in the evening a beggarly minstrel roams its streets, barefoot, goggle-eyed and wearing a threadbare *jilbāb*. He plays his *rabāb*[42] and sings in a harsh but penetrating voice: 'I put my trust in you, O Time, but you betrayed me.'
>
> (p. 5)

The first sentence of the novel is a compression of its entire meaning, the succeeding 150-odd pages being an elaboration of that sentence: ᶜAbbāsiyya was once a youthful *place* but *time* has passed and made sure that its youth is now a 'bygone' fact. ᶜAbbāsiyya of course is not an abstract place but a quarter of Cairo inhabited by many people and its 'bygone youth' is also theirs, and the whole novel is simply an act of resistance against time, undertaken by the only human faculty capable of it: memory. The memory here is that of the narrator, who is largely a persona for the novelist, and the whole tragedy lies in the *but* (*But* in the evening . . .), that *but* which is latent in the passage (as in the nature of things) from the first moment. The fact that ᶜAbbāsiyya's youth is introduced as 'bygone' implies that the description that follows of the quarter as a piece of eternity whose beauty knows no withering and tranquillity no disturbance is merely a trick of recollection. It is as if the poor minstrel, with his shabby appearance and harsh voice which belied the idyllic description of the area, was the seed of mutation and decay dormant in that ephemeral heaven.

Qushtumur is the story of four inhabitants of ᶜAbbāsiyya brought together by friendship from their primary school days, a friendship which transcended differences of temperament and class. Two of them came from the lower middle class (Ismāᶜil Qadrī and Ṣādiq Ṣafwān), while the other two (Ḥamāda al-Ḥalawānī and Ṭāhir ᶜUbayd) belonged to the aristocratic class. Their inclinations, on the other hand, varied between religiosity and doubt, capitalism and socialism, or complete nihilism. Their friendship, however, withstands all these differences and withstands too the test of time with all the changes that it brings about on both the public and private levels. The action extends over the now very familiar Mahfuzian period (give or take a couple of years): 1915 to the present day. All four characters enjoy equal attention from the novelist: there is no protagonist. We follow their growth from childhood games and the discoveries of puberty to the formation of religious consciousness and political affiliations. Later we follow their different fortunes in the arena of life: some succeed and some fail; some make families and some stay single; some get involved in political life and some stay aloof, etc.

Since the interaction of public and private is essential in Mahfouz's world-picture for producing personal tragedy, he chooses here, as he has often done, to reveal to us the fortunes of his four characters against the backdrop of Egypt's contemporary history from 1919 to the time of writing. Throughout, the novelist stresses the constant flow of time on both levels – public and private. This accounts for his avoidance of chapter or any other kind of division in the novel (just as he did in *There Only Remains an Hour* and for the same reason). He lets the prose flow from situation to situation, character to character and era to era without any formal interruption, aiming thereby at emulating the permanent flux of time both in actuality and in the memory, where time appears expansive and undivided.

There is nothing substantially new about Mahfouz's last published novel. It does not amount to much more than a variation on *There Only Remains an Hour.* All its characters are borrowed with only cosmetic changes from previous works and so are the public and private events. There is nothing new either in its view of man and society or in the author's reading of his country's socio-political history in the present century. Its value lies in none of all this, but in the gush of nostalgia which impelled Mahfouz to write it, in his desperate grip on time in the memory and in his attempt to take refuge from the inexorable flux of time in the permanence of place and human sympathy as represented by the café Qushtumur and the friendship that has held its four patrons together for so long and against many odds. This is a new and very recent note in the work of Mahfouz, which hitherto has offered no solace for the individual in his losing battle against time.

5

THE ABORTED DREAM: ON EARTH AS IN HEAVEN

The Trilogy, as we have seen, was Mahfouz's last work written before the 1952 revolution.[1] The six novels beginning with *Khan al-Khalili* and culminating with *The Trilogy* have been concerned to a large extent with a critical portrayal of Egyptian society and politics during the greater part of the first half of the twentieth century. Foremost in the author's mind has been the representation, on both the individual and social levels, of the tensions created by the conflict between past and present – the old traditional values and the new, Western-inspired ones. On the individual plane, Kamāl ᶜAbd al-Jawwād's spiritual schism was perhaps the highest expression of that conflict. On the other hand, it was Kamāl's two nephews, the fundamentalist ᶜAbd al-Munᶜim and the socialist Aḥmad, who gave that conflict its most forceful outward, social expression.

After 1952 there was the creative gap, discussed elsewhere in this book,[2] which lasted until the serialized publication of *Children of Gebelawi* in 1959. The novelist tells us that in 1952 he had as many as seven outlines of novels waiting to be written with the lines of their plots 'almost completed' and the portraits of their characters 'crystallized'. The novels were to be a continuation of the trend which peaked with *The Trilogy*. The impulse to write, however, died and the plans were abandoned for ever.[3] During the heyday of the Nasser period, Mahfouz used to answer questions on 'the period of silence' in terms of the social and political reforms brought about by the revolution, which had rid society of the kind of issues which used to provoke him to writing. In the more liberal post-Nasser era, however, he admitted that this explanation had been partly dictated by motives of self-protection against the wrath of the regime. He nevertheless remained unable to offer a satisfactory explanation in lieu of the discredited one.[4]

Perhaps Mahfouz went too far in casting doubt on the motivation behind his initial explanation of his writer's block. The revolution brought about colossal changes in both the structure and operation of Egyptian society and over a very short period at that. The result was that the society which had provided the novelist with his subject-matter for the previous decade or so virtually changed out of recognition. He needed time to observe and absorb the new society with its different ills – or even old ills in a new form. He also needed time to adapt his artist's tools to the new subject-matter. When these processes were completed he wrote *Children of Gebelawi* which, in spite of its ambitious religio-historical scope appears to have been more concerned with modern Egyptian reality than its allegorical form readily betrays. Mahfouz himself explains the whole process in a statement which deserves to be quoted at length:

> I only write when a split between society and me occurs. . . . I began to feel that the 1952 revolution which [at first] had given me assurance and peace of mind was starting to go astray. . . . Many faults and errors upset me, especially the repression and the tortures and the imprisonments. Thus I began to write my big novel, *Children of Gebelawi*, which depicts the conflict between prophets and thugs. . . . I wanted to ask the revolutionary leaders which path they wanted to choose: the prophets' or the thugs'. The stories of the prophets provided an artistic framework, but my intention was to criticize the revolution and the existing social system. At that time I had noticed a new class evolving and growing extraordinarily rich. The question which then agonized me was whether we were moving towards socialism or towards feudalism of a new kind.[5]

Mahfouz's condition for creativity (i.e. 'the split' between him and society) in place and fully operative within a few years of the revolution, his writing machine started to churn out works which embodied the split he felt between himself and the society created by Nasser's revolution. Nor was he to continue hiding behind the disguise of allegory as he had done in

Children of Gebelawi. His next novel, *The Thief and the Dogs*, was to deal directly with the new realities of Egyptian society and so were all the novels of the 1960s. His approach to the new society was, however, to be made through the employment of fresh techniques as if especially designed for it. The old keenness to describe at some length the physical and social environments and a certain way of life as seen in *The Trilogy* and earlier works was gone for ever. Gone too were the multi-threaded plots, the immense variety of characters and the omniscient author's freedom to move at will among their consciousnesses. Instead, physical and social detail was now kept to the barest functional minimum. Plots were compact and the third-person narrative used, confining the viewpoint to the protagonist alone, whose mind was fully probed through the internal monologue technique, and through whose eyes all other characters and their actions were presented and judged. Above all, the language was to become much denser and more evocative than before, using image, motif and association to depict emotional tension and to hold together in a powerful unity the entire fabric of the work. Most importantly on the thematic side, we will note a subsidence in the old pre-occupation with the clash between cultural values. This was to give way to a concern with the tragic consequences of the clash between the individual and totalitarian authority – a perfectly understandable development in view of the political realities of the day. On the face of it the State adopted socialism and science and repressed into oblivion the Moslem fundamentalist trend, an active agent in the political arena during the two decades leading up to the revolution. Society now seemed, one must stress again, only on the face of it, to be proceeding harmoniously along modernist, largely secularized tracks. But all this was achieved artificially at the expense of the political emasculation of society and the elimination of all dissent – individual or organized. Mahfouz was able to see from early on that it was not working, and could not work. When the regime faced its first real test in the 1967 war with Israel, the devastating result could not have taken by complete surprise any sensible decoder of signs in the novelist's output over the few preceding years.

THE THIEF AND THE DOGS

Fittingly, *The Thief and the Dogs* (1961), the author's first link in the chain dealing directly with the shortcomings of the 1952 revolution, is about betrayal, mainly the betrayal of revolutionary ideals once power, with the privileges that come with it, is achieved.[6] Thus the relationship between Saᶜīd Mahrān, the protagonist of the novel and the one betrayed,[7] and Ra'ūf ᶜAlwān, his fallen idol on whom he seeks to be avenged, is Mahfouz's metaphor for the rapid dissipation of revolutionary ideal and his indictment of the newly emerged establishment which inherited all too soon the privileges and complacency of the *ancien régime*.[8] Saᶜīd Mahrān, however, fails in achieving his objective. His bullets go astray, killing innocent people instead of their intended targets. Saᶜīd, who nevertheless turns into a heroic symbol for the masses of the people, is hounded down by the entire apparatus of the State – the 'dogs' of the title. Saᶜīd's failure is not of course without significance. The apparent moral is that true revolutionary action cannot originate in personal vendetta, nor is it a task for individuals on their own: organized action is essential.[9]

The Thief and the Dogs is not, however, a simple political parable – indeed none of the novels of the 1960s decade can be seen as just that. In all of them Mahfouz succeeds in transforming his probing of the predicament of the individual in his confrontation with authority into a consideration of such issues as the meaning of life, the value of human action, and the alienation of the modern individual from both society and God – themes which led critics to associate the novelist's work during that period with the existentialist movement in Europe, particularly Camus and Sartre.[10] Thus Saᶜīd's isolation and desperate loneliness are rendered in such terms as would make his story a powerful metaphor for the alienation of the non-conformist wherever he may be. Nor is his alienation only social, for in his obsession with setting right worldly reality he is unable to draw comfort from thoughts of the hereafter. This theme of modern man's alienation from God is introduced in the novel through the juxtaposition of Saᶜīd's character with that of the old *ṣūfī* (mystic) ᶜAlī al-Junaydī. Homeless and hounded, with his soul devoured by the desire to avenge himself on those who wronged him, Saᶜīd takes refuge momentarily in the house of Shaykh Junaydī, whom he has known since his childhood when he used to visit him in his father's company. They are the emblems of two worlds that cannot meet: the mystic has achieved peace with the world by completely withdrawing from its harsh reality and creating an inner invisible one for himself, while Saᶜīd is too enmeshed in the ugliness of reality to be able to see or seek a way to deal with it other than by self-condemning confrontation. The incompatibility of the two worlds and the irrelevance of transcendental escapism[11] are shown through masterful pieces of dialogue at cross-purposes, worthy of the best traditions of the Theatre of the Absurd, between Saᶜīd and the holy man. One must remark here that the *ṣūfi* character introduced in *The Thief and the Dogs* for the first time appears to be Mahfouz's heightened replacement for the Muslim fundamentalist used in earlier novels.[12] For one thing the latter had virtually disappeared from the observable social and political life of Nasser's Egypt so that it would have seemed anachronistic to allow it to play its traditional role in the author's work, set in the post-revolutionary era. On the other hand, the *ṣūfi* figure with its symbolic potential must have appeared more appropriate to a novelist who was now more concerned with the metaphoric than the lifelike recreation of reality.

In Mahfouz character is not fate – not altogether anyway. Nor is society. Although temperamental flaws, and flaws in the structure of society contribute in a major way to the defeat of his characters, his work often seems to point at something else that is wrong, something that lies at the very nature of things in the world – a contributory force that is undefinable and incomprehensible, but whose workings in our lives are undeniable.[13] Otherwise, how can Saᶜīd's stray bullets be explained? It happens twice: the first time when he tries to kill ᶜAlīsh Sidra (his one-time lackey who betrayed him to the police and robbed him of his wife and money), and the second when he tries to kill Ra'ūf ᶜAlwān, his erstwhile political mentor who betrays their revolutionary ideals. On both occasions his bullets kill innocent victims. On the first occasion, when Saᶜīd learns through the newspapers of the mistake, his thoughts run like this:

> What a waste of effort! I killed Shaᶜbān Ḥusayn! Who are you Shaᶜbān? I did not know you and you did not know

> me. Did you have children? Did you imagine one day that a man you did not know . . . would kill you? Did you imagine that you would be killed for no reason? That you would be killed because Nabawiyya Sulaymān married ʿAlīsh Sidra? That you would be killed in error, while ʿAlīsh and Nabawiyya and Ra'ūf who ought to be killed would live on? And I, the killer, understand nothing. Not even Shaykh ʿAlī al-Junaydī can understand this. I set out to solve part of the mystery only to unravel a deeper one.
>
> (pp. 89–90)

Saʿīd's career of thievery could be explained in social terms (as the novel in fact tries to do through flashbacks to his boyhood), while his determination to punish his enemies at any cost could probably be understood in terms of a temperament too obsessive, impatient and perhaps idealistic to be able to channel its personal bitterness into constructive action. But how can the stray bullets be explained? It is society and character that lead Saʿīd to his perdition – there is no doubt about that. But what is it which lays waste his effort and deprives his actions of meaning? In Saʿīd's own words, 'How absurd life would be if tomorrow I were to be executed for killing a man I did not know!' (p. 125). A mechanical explanation is of course not unavailable. In the first instance ʿAlīsh Sidra had vacated the flat in anticipation of Saʿīd's intentions, so that when the latter shoots through the door in the dark, it is the new tenant he kills, while in the second instance it is the presence of an armed guard that takes Saʿīd by surprise, causing his hand to shake and his bullet to miss its intended target. But mechanical explanations by definition only explain the mechanics of a process or an occurrence – they do not explain the cause. Nor is there a cause that is explicable. The phenomenon, however, is not short of a name: fate (also known as coincidence or the interplay of space and time) – a key concept in Mahfouz's world-picture and a prime agent in the life of his characters.[14]

AUTUMN QUAIL

In his next novel, *Autumn Quail* (1962), Mahfouz pursues his examination of the relationship between the individual and authority, and again the theme of the corrupting influence of power over the one-time revolutionary. On the face of it the novel appears to be an account of the mental agony of an old Wafdist displaced by the new revolutionary regime and unable to accept the new political reality which, though denying him a role in its power structure, appears to be achieving many of the old national objectives of his abolished Wafd Party. It is in these terms that the novel was read by contemporary critics upon its publication in the heyday of Nasserist Egypt[15] – no other public interpretation would have been possible then. Seen, however, in the context of later novels dealing with Nasser's Egypt, both in the 1960s and after, and particularly in the light of the novelist's proven Wafdist sentiments and his disapproval of many revolutionary practices, all made amply explicit in interviews given in post-Nasserist times,[16] the novel appears to call for a new reading.

Underlying the political alienation and personal resentment at loss of office and power of the protagonist, ᶜĪsā al-Dabbāgh, is a rebuke of the revolution for its banishment from public life of a vastly popular political force and the only one with a creditable national record in the generation preceding the revolution.[17] As such ᶜĪsā's displacement can be seen to sum up the political marginalization of virtually an entire society. Mahfouz, however, has no illusions about either the Wafd or his protagonist. Thus, while highlighting ᶜĪsā's patriotism, he shows him to have been personally corrupt in accepting bribes from rural dignitaries, a practice for which he is dismissed from the civil service in an early revolutionary purge. Superficially, the novelist would seem to be condemning his protagonist in portraying him thus, but this is only one side of the coin. The picture is not complete until we have heard the author's account of Ḥasan, ᶜĪsā's cousin, who is shown from the beginning as a non-Wafdist and an advocate of radical political change that would shake the very foundations of society. After the revolution, it transpires that he has been a man of the new regime. As ᶜĪsā's fortunes go down, Ḥasan's are in the ascendant, and before long, yesterday's poor man is seen driven around in a Mercedes, and when ᶜĪsā's upper-class fiancée drops her now unemployed and futureless betrothed, Ḥasan, who had hopelessly coveted the girl in the past, is quick to step in and make off with the prize. Thus as early as 1962 Mahfouz was discreetly trying to portray the revolutionary impatient to reap the forbidden fruit of power:

corruption-in-the-making replacing accomplished corruption. On the social level, the revolution is represented in terms no greater than those of a movement by a small bourgeoisie eager to inherit the privileges of the *ancien régime* even as they went about dismantling it.[18]

There is an attempt by the author here to recapitulate the *ṣūfī* theme of the previous novel when a friend of ᶜĪsā's, who suffered the same fate under the new regime, seeks comfort in religion. This solution is rejected by ᶜĪsā as it had been by Saᶜīd Mahrān. The point, however, is only touched upon and it appears that Mahfouz, having explored the theme in depth in *The Thief and the Dogs*, had, for the time being at least, nothing to add to it. There is also an attempt at depicting ᶜĪsā's predicament in terms of existential *angst*,[19] by occasionally placing his political alienation and his sense of purposelessness resulting from long unemployment in a cosmic, meaning-searching context,[20] and stressing the importance of 'work' or Sartrean *engagement*,[21] as a way out.[22] The attempt fails, however, to lift the novel from the tedious and dated political document that today it essentially is. Among Mahfouz's work in the 1960s it is his least successsful.

THE SEARCH

The Search (1964) is another metaphor of aborted dreams. Its protagonist's search for 'freedom, dignity and security'[23] is no different from the national quest of modern Egyptians, and therefore his failure must be seen as another pessimistic view, however indirectly expressed, of the state of affairs in Mahfouz's country. But one must be careful not to read too much politics into this novel.[24] In fact, of all the 1960s novels, this is the one with the least direct bearing on the political reality of the day. And while the quest of its protagonist, Ṣābir, for 'freedom, dignity and security' may seem essentially no different from that of his predecessors (Saᶜīd and ᶜĪsā in *The Thief and the Dogs* and *Autumn Quail*, respectively), it is only in *The Search* that this quest is transplanted from its habitual socio-political context to a metaphysical one. Thus Ṣābir's search for his father on the realistic level is nothing short of mankind's search for metaphysical truth (or the Father who is in Heaven) on the symbolic level.[25] Similarly, the torment his soul experiences in its division between his earthy, lustful attraction to Karīma on the one hand, and his platonic love for Ilhām on the other, is apparently meant to embody man's eternal schism between body and soul or earth and heaven.[26] The two levels of meaning coexist happily throughout the novel. The characters and events are grounded in reality with a firmness and a liveliness that grip the attention in the merciless manner of a thriller. But throughout the book are also scattered the images, the hints, the dreams, the leitmotifs, the clues[27] and the situations that point to the higher level of meaning.

But as Mahfouz's work has demonstrated before and since *The Search*, there is no metaphysical solution for man's problems on earth. 'Freedom, dignity and security' cannot come as a gift from heaven; they must be earned on earth. And they can be earned only through *work*. The supreme importance of work in the fight against existential *angst* was amply shown in the case of ᶜĪsā in *Autumn Quail*. Here the case for work is further emphasized. In lieu of God, Work (in the broad Sartrean sense of *engagement*) becomes the absolute value-giver – it is the only 'way'[28] to the tripartite human ideal of 'freedom, dignity and security'. On the realistic level, the novelist uses Ilhām as a foil to Ṣābir. She too had been denied by her father, but rather than waste her life in seeking his recognition, she discovered early on that work and self-dependence were the way to salvation.[29] In the end Ṣābir's search does not lead him to his father (physical or metaphysical) and in the futility and emptiness of the process he strays into crime. By contrast, it is Ilhām's father who eventually seeks and recognizes her – physical endeavour alone, the novel appears to be saying, is 'the way' to metaphysical truth, to meaning in life, to 'freedom, dignity and security'.

THE BEGGAR

The metaphysical search is carried on into the author's next novel, *The Beggar* (1965). The protagonist, ᶜUmar al-Ḥamzāwī, a wealthy and successful lawyer and family man, is suddenly struck by existential *angst*.[30] His work and family cease to mean anything to him and so does the rest of the universe. He is engulfed in a sense of the ultimate absurdity of all things. It all began when one day he teased a client of his on whose behalf he was fighting a case over the ownership of a plot of land: 'What if you were to win the case today and take possession of the land only for the government to come and seize it tomorrow?' ᶜUmar asks. 'Don't we live our life knowing full well that it is going to be taken away by God?' comes the dismissive answer of the client (p. 45). But it was an answer that ᶜUmar himself was never able to dismiss from his mind. As he himself puts it, 'The very foundations of existence collapsed as a result of a few questions' (p. 89).

Like Ṣābir in the previous novel, he embarks on a long and arduous search for the ultimate truth. His search leads him along many paths. A new love leaves his spiritual thirst unquenched, and so does indulgence in a 'mystical' kind of sex, in his search for, as he puts it, 'the first ecstasy of creation' (p. 64). Then one day, alone in the darkness and silence of the desert, he experiences a moment of *ṣūfi* revelation which instils in him 'a wondrous certainty infused with peace and assurance. He was filled with a confidence which promised to achieve for him anything he wanted. But he felt himself beyond all desire and saw the world a handful of dust beneath his feet' (p. 118).[31] This supreme ecstasy was, however, very short-lived and no matter how hard he tried, he never again succeeded in repeating the experience. All paths closed to him, he appeared to be progressing towards the only exit left: madness.

ᶜUmar's spiritual crisis, while it is the central preoccupation of the book, is not set in a social vacuum (unlike the case with Ṣābir in *The Search*). In his early youth he was one of a trio of friends who thought they 'had found the magical solution to all problems' (i.e. socialism), and were ready to give up their lives on the road to 'Utopia' (p. 24). Political action leads ᶜUthmān Khalīl to prison, while leaving ᶜUmar and Muṣṭafā al-Minyāwī to build up their careers and gradually succumb to the temptations of comfortable bourgeois living. In the old days ᶜUmar and Muṣṭafā were serious artists, but with the abandonment of their political idealism, they also abandoned art, the one turning to a successful lawyer's career and the other to cheap entertainment. All the time they lulled themselves into the belief that the new regime (Nasser's revolution) had taken up their old principles, thereby rendering action on their own part unnecessary: 'Since the State has embraced and is putting into practice the progressive ideals, wouldn't it be wise for us to concentrate on our own businesses?' Muṣṭafā puts it. The question they do not dare to upset their consciences with (and which haunts the novel though it is never stated) is, however, why the State continues to keep in prison the man whose principles it has applied and who was put there in the first place by the regime it has replaced.

This is the point at which the novel's spiritual obsession converges with its social concern. It was the rejection of the ideals of poetry and the perfect society for the sake of material success, we are made to feel, which finally brought ʿUmar face to face with the terrible emptiness. The full horror of his descent from youthful idealism to middle-aged satiety is emphasized through the person of his teenage daughter, Buthayna, who is a student of science with a budding poetic talent (an important symbolic combination in Mahfouz's value system, science being the way to material progress, but this should not be at the expense of poetry, i.e. spiritual values).[32] The height of ʿUmar's crisis coincides with the release from prison of ʿUthmān who, an eternal revolutionary and another foil to ʿUmar, soon resumes the fight against the new regime with the same zeal as he previously had done against the old – unlike his too old comrades he is under no illusion that 'the perfect society' is under way. Parallel to this total commitment to social action is shown ʿUmar's total withdrawal from society. His metaphysical quest leads him eventually to the complete abnegation of society. He leaves family, friends and business and retires to a solitary cottage in the countryside – 'There where your heart will never sleep, and your senses never wake' (p. 155). But the 'ecstasy' continues to elude him and a series of visions (rendered in highly symbolic terms) shows his consciousness struggling hard, but in vain, to sever itself from reality. On the other hand, ʿUthmān, hunted down by the authorities, seeks a hiding place in ʿUmar's cottage. He is soon found, however, and in the confusion of the arrest ʿUmar is injured with a bullet in the shoulder. The last scene in the book shows ʿUmar (together with ʿUthmān) in an ambulance being driven back to the city. The pain in his injured shoulder forces him out of his mystical trance and back into reality. In his semi-conscious state, he wonders, 'When would I see His face? Had I not abandoned the world for His sake?' And a line of poetry echoes clearly in his head, 'If you truly want me, why did you leave me?' (p. 170).

The ultimate truth, then, is in the reality of the world and not somewhere outside or beyond it, and the only thoroughfare to the metaphysical is a physical one, along which travellers should be committed to the well-being of each other and the maintenance of the road. Over and again Mahfouz has expressed his firm rejection of any form of transcendental escapism.[33] I have talked above about Buthayna's combining in her character the values both of poetry and science. To these Mahfouz adds a third value by marrying her off to ᶜUthmān, the indefatigable fighter for social justice. As he is rearrested, we learn that Buthayna is already bearing the fruit of the union. This is Mahfouz's hope for human society: a holy trinity of science, poetry[34] and justice.

CHATTER ON THE NILE

The relentless search for meaning in life and the despair at its apparent absence continued to drive the author's imagination into the next novel, *Chatter on the Nile* (1966). Anīs Zakī, the protagonist through whose consciousness we perceive the world of the novel, is a small middle-aged clerk in a government office (but also a well-read intellectual). He lost his wife and daughter 'to the same illness and in the same month', twenty years before the beginning of the novel's action (p. 66); he also had, for unspecified reasons, his hopes of a medical career quashed. Thus when we meet him, he is already accomplished in the art of living with life's frustrations and the sense of its meaninglessness. His answer to the harshness of social and existential reality is escape into an almost permanent narcotic stupor – a modified version within Mahfouz's world, one might say, of ᶜUmar's failed *ṣūfī* trances in *The Beggar.*

The novel is set almost entirely in an *ᶜawwāma* (boathouse) on the Nile in Cairo, where a group of men and women representing a cross-section of the well-to-do Egyptian middle class in the 1960s (they include among others a lawyer, a journalist, an actor, a literary critic and a Foreign Office official) meet every night over hashish, drink and sex. They lead a totally self-indulgent and nihilistic kind of existence: inverted mysticism, one might say, or the abnegation of the soul rather than the senses, according to Mahfouz's value system. It is through Anīs's endless stream of hashish-induced thoughts that the apathy, the purposelessness and the amorality of the group's life is placed in a historical and existential context. Here is one example:

> Had these friends met – as they do tonight – under a different guise in Roman times? And had they witnessed the fire of Rome? Why did the moon split from the earth pulling up the mountains? And which one was it of the French Revolution's men who was killed in the bathroom by the hand of a beautiful woman? And how many of his contemporaries died of chronic constipation?
>
> (p. 56)

Through this string of freely associated ideas (and scores more like it) Anīs's tragedy and by proxy that of his *ᶜawwāma* companions is shown as part of a human condition controlled by an absurdity and a randomness that has always lain at the heart of existence. Needless to say Anīs's wildest narcotic fantasies are the product of his author's most sober contemplative moments, their incoherence therefore only apparent. Thus the ancient Roman depravity is only recalled to underline current depravity which, the insinuation is, could lead to a modern disaster tantamount to the historic burning of Rome. On the one hand the painful irony inherent in the undignified manner of Marat's death (a leader of a revolution which changed the course of human history) is all too obvious. But the ultimate absurdity lies in the next thought: if death is the inevitable end for all, what difference does it make to be a Marat or a nobody; to be assassinated or to die of chronic constipation? The ultimate human indignity is death; the rest is a matter of detail. Finally, with the image of the moon separating from the earth and pulling the mountains up, the absurdity of human life and history is placed in the context of the infinite absurdity at the centre of the universe.

Against cosmic and historic absurdity are shown the social absurdities of Egypt in the 1960s where 'everyone is writing about socialism, while most dream about wealth' (p. 55). In one of Anīs's flights into history which Mahfouz uses for what then was dangerously obvious political projection,[35] the character calls up an ancient Egyptian sage and asks him to repeat the song he used to sing for Pharaoh. The song runs like this:

> Your companions have lied to you:

These are years of war and hardship.[36]
What has become of Egypt? –
The Nile still brings along its flood.
Wealthy now is he who naught had before.[37]
Would that I spoke up then!
Wise, perceptive and just are you,
But you let corruption feed on the land.
Behold how your commands are scorned!
When would you graciously desire
That someone come and tell you the truth?

(p. 126)

No fantasy of a hashish stupor this and no song by an ancient sage to an ancient Pharaoh, but the supplication of a modern sage to a modern Pharaoh. This was Mahfouz's prophetic plea to Nasser on the eve of 1967.

As always in Mahfouz, any form of escapism, isolationism, or withdrawal from society is doomed to failure – reality always reigns supreme and always eventually shocks into the recognition of its omnipresent self those who dared once deny it or closed their eyes to its circumambient glare. One night the *ᶜawwāma* companions decided to celebrate a public holiday by breaking their routine and going out for a midnight drive in the desert, south of Cairo. They cram themselves into the car of the actor, who drives at a crazy speed striking terror into his passengers' hearts. He hits and kills a peasant on the road and, with the tacit agreement of the others, fails to stop or report the accident. They all meet again at the *ᶜawwāma* on the following evening. But they are now a restless, frightened, conscience-stricken and mutually recriminating lot. The accident has shattered all their illusions and forced them out of their escapist stupor into the harshness of reality (much like the bullet which brings ᶜUmar back from the stupor of mysticism at the end of *The Beggar*). The novel ends very pessimistically in that none of the characters is able to muster enough moral courage to report the accident and bear his or her share of responsibility for it – not even Samāra, who was only a recent observer-member of the group with pretensions, unlike the rest of them, to 'seriousness', or a non-absurd view of life. In retrospect it is not difficult to understand the extent of the author's melancholy inasmuch as it is difficult not to see the *ᶜawwāma* as symbolic of a society on the verge of sinking, and the car accident in terms of an oracular vision pointing at the other catastrophic accident then awaiting the nation round the corner of history – the 1967 defeat in the war with Israel.[38]

Pessimistic as the author's vision is on the immediate level of meaning, he appears, however, to preserve his faith (maybe in a tongue-in-cheek manner) on the anthropological or evolutionary plane. The book ends with Anīs again soaring to narcotic heights and thinking along these lines:

> The origin of all trouble was the skill of a monkey, who learned to walk upright, thereby freeing his hands. He came down from the tree-top monkey paradise to the ground of the forest. They told him to climb back up before the beasts got him. But in one hand he grasped a tree branch and in the other a stone and went cautiously on, looking ahead towards an endless road.
>
> (p. 199)

What optimism is latent in these closing lines of the novel draws of course from the author's belief in collective human time – time as 'the evolutionary spirit of man'.[39]

MIRAMAR

As if exhausted by the metaphysical search which spanned the last three novels, Mahfouz drops it altogether in *Miramar* (1967). The socio-political concern which infiltrated at a steadily increasing rate all three metaphysical novels swells up in *Miramar* to shut out every other concern. The novel was also technically innovative within the framework of Mahfouz's output up to that point. The events of the story are told in the first person by four of the main characters,[40] readers thereby are made privy to each character's judgement of the others instead of being limited to the viewpoint of only one character as has been the case since *The Thief and the Dogs*. It was not Mahfouz, however, who pioneered this technique in the Egyptian novel,[41] nor did it prove a favourite with him.[42] Rather than marking a turning-point in technique, *Miramar* actually marked a shift of interest from contemplating the human condition in its timeless and universal aspects to a more mundane contemplation of the immediate manifestations of this condition in Egyptian socio-political reality. This new phase was to maintain its grip on the author until the mid-1970s.[43]

Miramar was Mahfouz's last *cri de coeur* against the aberrations of the 1952 revolution before the 1967 debacle. As in *Chatter on the Nile*, it puts together a group of different people in a confined space (the *pension* Mirāmār here stands in for the *ᶜawwāma* there) and allows the frictions arising from conflicts of temperaments and interests to escalate to a tragic climax. Each of the patrons of the *pension* represents a section of the contemporary society of Egypt[44] with Zahra the peasant maidservant standing for Egypt.[45] Significantly, the most sympathetically portrayed male character is that of the old Wafdist journalist, ᶜĀmir Wajdī, who, in a manner reminiscent of the hero of *Autumn Quail*, is shown to have been mercilessly swept aside by the new regime despite his old nationalist role. The most abhorrently depicted, on the other hand, is Sarḥān al-Buḥayrī, the representative of the lower middle class, the class empowered by the revolution to inherit the office and authority of the ousted aristocracy and upper middle class.[46] Torn between an insatiable lust for life on the one hand, and meagre means on the other, Sarḥān betrays, like his progenitor Ra'ūf ᶜAlwān in *The Thief and the Dogs*, the principles of the revolution he never ceases to pay lip service to. His moral bankruptcy and eventual suicide indicate Mahfouz's condemnation of the revolution's failure to lead by example.

Most interesting perhaps of Mahfouz's creations in this novel is the character of Manṣūr Bāhī, the socialist renegade. He is totally unlike any of the author's socialists in the pre-revolutionary novels. As we have seen in those novels, the socialist types figured as strong young men full of vigour, zeal, belief in their ideals and boundless hope in the future; they were, as the novelist portrayed them, Egypt's promise of social salvation.[47] But there is none of this in *Miramar*; the socialist type here is distorted out of recognition. Manṣūr Bāhī is an indecisive weakling who betrays his cause rather than resist pressure or go to prison. He hates himself for it and is shown as a wreck of a man, unable to enjoy life or love and verging on insanity – he is Mahfouz's elegy to the emasculation through persecution of Egypt's socialist intellectuals. Amidst all this, Zahra has to fend for herself all the time against the sexual advances of all the patrons with the exception of the old Wafdist and the psychologically unbalanced socialist, who both show concern and affection for her, though practically unable to help her. The girl, however, proves more than a match for all her attackers put together. Thus Egypt[48] emerges as strong and self-reliant; as poor but dignified, but with none of her sons sufficiently free from self-interest to do anything for her. The only flicker of hope in this deeply gloomy work is sounded by the old Wafdist when he whispers to Zahra, who has had her hopes shattered and who has a doubtful future to confront alone, armed only with her belief in herself: 'He who has known what is not good for him, will also know, in a magical kind of way, what *is*' (p. 279). Progress by exclusion – that was the extent of Mahfouz's hope for his country on the eve of June 1967. Little did he know how soon events were to justify the sombreness of his mood!

LOVE IN THE RAIN AND *THE KARNAK*

What the oracle saw in *Chatter on the Nile* and *Miramar* came to pass on 5 June 1967. The shock kept Mahfouz from writing novels for nearly five years (between 1961 and 1967 he had published one novel every year, 1963 excepted). It may be that the mood of despondency and distraction that swept the intelligentsia and the rest of the country in the aftermath of the defeat left him in no frame of mind for the elaborate, lengthy structures that novels are. His creativity, however, found a way out in an outburst of short story writing – in the three years from 1969 to 1971 he published four collections. It was in 1972 that *Mirrors* (discussed elsewhere in this study), his first novel since *Miramar*, was published, followed in rapid succession by *Love in the Rain* (1973) and *The Karnak* (1974).

Mirrors (as will be shown later in this book) was a panoramic view of Egyptian society from around the beginning of the century to the time of writing. It was in some of its episodes that Mahfouz tried for the first time in his fiction to explore the mood of the nation after the defeat. Issues like the torture of political prisoners,[49] the increasing emigration from the country of its despairing best youth,[50] and the gradual collapse of moral ideals[51] were briefly touched upon here, to be picked up again and elaborated in *Love in the Rain* and *The Karnak*. The profound sense of depression experienced earlier in *Miramar* reaches the point of suffocation in these two novels.[52] Together they evoke the national sense of loss and humiliation at the defeat, the irreparable damage to the dignity of the individual following years of repression of real and imaginary opponents, and the public apathy to events, engendered by the people's lack of trust in the regime and the habits of long years of being led from above without any measure of democratic participation in the government of their country. Inevitably these novels (both published after Nasser's death) are more candid in their criticisms, often dealing directly with issues which would have been too dangerous to address in the 1960s.

Both novels are of a documentary nature, dealing with issues topical at the time of writing and seem rather dated today. They are artistically negligible in themselves, showing no significant interest in structuring a plot, characterization, psychological probing, the heightened use of language or technical innovation[53] – all of which are qualities that the novelist had perfected in earlier work and that we have come to expect of him as a matter of course. Posterity, however, will certainly treasure these novels as a priceless source for the social and political history of the Egypt of their day. Mahfouz himself seems aware of the shortcomings of these works when he argues in the course of commenting on *The Karnak*:

> I am prepared to write a novel . . . to support a view which I respect, or in order to make a personal commentary on certain political circumstances, even if such a novel was destined to die as soon as the occasion for which it was written had elapsed.[54]

Love in the Rain is set in Cairo during the years 1967–70, dubbed at the time 'the war of attrition', referring to the continued hostilities between Egyptian and Israeli forces across the Suez Canal until Nasser accepted a temporary ceasefire shortly before his death in September 1970. The novel depicts a demoralized society with city people sunk in a bottomless pit of apathy, hardly aware of the war going on at the front,[55] with young people seeking refuge from the harsh reality by planning emigration and indulgence in sex and empty pastimes – the mood and lifestyle of the *ᶜawwāma* clique in *Chatter on the Nile* is shown to have engulfed the whole country here. The fact dawns on people that they have been living in 'a myth' (pp. 10, 15) from which the military defeat has shocked them into reality.[56] The gap between myth and reality is sardonically summarized by a nameless character in these words: 'We used to be concerned with pan-Arabism and pan-Africanism . . . and now we are concerned with the elimination of the effects of the aggression' (p. 36), quoting a phrase much used in the state media at the time. Throughout the novel we have lovers betraying each other at the first temptation, characters committing murder at the slightest provocation, sex willingly offered by respectable but needy young women in return for consumer goods – it is as if the entire fabric of society has collapsed. As though alarmed by the extent of his own despair, Mahfouz forces out of the blue and virtually on the last page of the novel a Palestinian freedom fighter with enthusiastic, forward-looking words. It does not work.[57]

Also set in Cairo, *The Karnak* extends the period covered by *Love in the Rain* by about two more years into the past, thus spanning the period 1965–70.[58] By placing *The Karnak*'s starting-point during the apogee of Nasser's era, Mahfouz's evident intention was to examine with the benefit of hindsight the seeds of decay in the regime, which caused it to disintegrate on its first real test. The novel concentrates on an issue lightly touched upon in the previous one, namely that of the repressive techniques of the police state and their destructive effect on the dignity of the individual and hence the nation as a whole. The novel is written in the first person and the narrator, who puts the pieces of the action together from encounters with the main characters over a period of some five years at the Karnak café (which gives the novel its title), is himself a writer from an older generation. Thus it is not difficult to see him as a mouthpiece for the novelist.[59] *The Karnak* is essentially a refutation of the classic argument often used by repressive regimes to justify their excesses and which consists in the so-called sacrifice of the individual for the good of the nation as a whole. Commenting on the repeated arrests, torture and lengthy detainment without charges or trial of some of the student clients of the café, the old narrator's thoughts run like this:

> I wondered at the condition of my country. In spite of its deviations, it is turning into a mighty giant. It has strength and influence. It manufactures everything from sewing needles to rockets, and sponsors the great causes of

> humanity. Why is it then that the human being in my country has become so small and trivial like a mosquito? Why is he without rights, dignity or protection?
>
> (p. 28)

In his agony he tries to provide the answer to the question:

> Does not the creation of our scientific, socialist, industrialist State; the most powerful in the Middle East – does it not deserve that we bear for its sake all those pains?
>
> (p. 20)

The narrator, however, knows in his heart of hearts that nothing can justify the sacrifice of man's humanity, for he argues, 'all the time I felt that with this kind of logic I could persuade myself of the necessity, nay, the benefit of death itself!' (p. 20). The theme here is again that of myth and reality, as we have seen in *Love in the Rain*: the myths created by the propaganda machine of the state and the reality of repression and a hollow regime which collapsed when its bluff was called. The irony becomes all the more bitter when all those sacrifices are shown to have been made for an illusion.

Towards the end of *The Karnak*, Mahfouz (who appears to have deliberately set out in the two novels under discussion to abandon every good principle of fiction writing he has learnt) forces a strange twist to the plot. Through the accounts of his victims, we come to know of Khālid Ṣafwān, Chief of Intelligence (in the novel) and sadistic torturer to the point of rape and murder. In the corrective measures taken after the military defeat of the regime, he was tried and imprisoned for three years (p. 99). Upon his release coincidence leads him to no other place than the café Karnak, where one of his victims recognizes him and reveals his identity to the narrator.[60] Rather than being lynched there and then, he is gradually accepted in the café and listened to as he outlines the new philosophy he has learnt 'in the depths of hell' and which consists in the renunciation of dictatorship and violence and the adoption of the values of freedom and science. He even goes on to express the view that peace with Israel is the way out of the stalemate: 'We have been defeated,' he argues, 'and are not ready for war. A solution must be found even if we have to pay the price. Then we should be able to spend every penny towards our progress on the course of civilization' (p. 105). This, in all probability, was Mahfouz's first voicing in print (albeit in disguise) of his later much-publicized support for an Egyptian peace with Israel.[61] Was this the reason for the bizarre twist at the end of *The Karnak* – to use the character as a mouthpiece? Whatever the reason, the ending remains unpalatable within the logic of the novel. But, as already argued, nothing appears to have been more removed from Mahfouz's mind when writing these two novels than niceties of structure and characterization.

THE HEART OF THE NIGHT

After three novels and many more short stories which dealt partly or wholly, directly or indirectly, with both the germination and the aftermath of 1967 and after a long diaspora in modern Cairo and in Alexandria, apparently too weary and too nostalgic, Mahfouz gave in again unconditionally to the combined charms of his old Jamāliyya and metaphysics. The homecoming was marked by *Fountain and Tomb* (to be discussed in chapter 6) and *Heart of the Night* (both 1975).

The author's lifelong metaphysical anguish, suppressed under immense socio-political pressure since *Chatter on the Nile*, is allowed to breathe again here. For *Heart of the Night* is nothing but a condensed allegory of the spiritual evolution of mankind. Since this was well-trodden ground for Mahfouz, it is no surprise that he found it convenient to borrow some of the symbols he had already used in his earlier allegory on the same subject, i.e. *Children of Gebelawi*. So here too we have a rich and powerful God-like father living in near seclusion in a fortress of a house standing in the middle of a paradise of a garden surrounded by high impenetrable walls. The man is a curious mixture of kindness and ruthlessness. The kindness is boundless as long as his descendants tacitly surrender their freedom of choice to him and fit happily his definition of 'the divine human being', who 'lives with God at every moment even though he may be a bandit' (p. 38). But equally boundless is his ruthlessness if they defy his will and choose to become what he calls 'the worldly human being', who 'lives *in* the world, even though he may be a man of religion' (p. 38). Thus Sayyid al-Rāwī (alias Gebelawi!) banishes from his house and mercy to destitute life and premature death his only-begotten son. Before his death, however, the son had fathered a child in a union denied the blessing of the great man. It is only when the child's mother dies too that he accepts his grandson into his care and opens unto him the long-closed gates of the great house.

If it is valid to argue that *The Search* and *The Beggar* represent modern man's remorseful quest for the God he has lost or wasted on the way to civilization, then it may be likewise valid to argue that *Heart of the Night* is the author's endeavour to retrace the course of the original journey, i.e. the flight from God. And 'flight' is indeed another appropriate word to describe the situation, for the story of the Original Sin as Mahfouz pictures it may have been an expulsion or banishment from God's point of view, but from the human point of view it was also a wilful act of escape, a conscious preference for the trials of freedom over the security of bondage – it was a mutual act of rejection between an obstinate maker and a creature too much in his image. The novel is a long act of recollection by Ja^cfar al-Rāwī, the grandson, now an old decrepit man. He recalls his early childhood (before he was adopted by his grandfather) as 'the age of myth' and describes it in terms of a primitive animistic existence (pp. 13–22). In terms of the allegory, these then must be the early days of mankind, those pre-dating the discovery of God. Then his grandfather adopts him and brings him up as a 'divine human being', 'though this', we are told, 'did not make me forget my old religion. Thus the new piled up on top of the old' (p. 39). His grandfather allowed him only a semblance of freedom, a freedom with a tether: 'You must adorn yourself with God's Revelation, then do what you will!' (p. 43). With this we have obviously come to the second phase of mankind's religious evolution according to Mahfouz: the monotheistic religions of the Middle East, with their restrictive prescriptions for the moral organization of human society and their elaborate penal codes both here and in the hereafter.

As Ja^cfar matures into manhood, his grandfather decides it is time to choose a wife for him. But Ja^cfar meanwhile has been driven out of his senses by a gypsy girl, a poor shepherdess of criminal stock. He marries her in defiance of his grandfather's will and is immediately exiled from his house and disinherited. Marwāna, the gypsy, is described as a woman of irresistible attraction, like 'a flame of fire' and 'a wild flower': 'From the first moment I felt that I was faced with a strong and ageless woman diffusing charm and defiance. I surrendered unto her, laying bare my flagrant weakness' (pp. 77–8). This, then, is Life with its infinite temptations, promise of freedom and the thrill of *knowledge*, which drew man away from the placidity, monotony and acquiescence of Heaven. Like Adam after expulsion, or Adham in *Children of Gebelawi*, Ja^{c}far is reduced to a life of poverty, toil and strife, and as Marwāna reveals the ugly side of herself to him, his passion for her subsides and she finally abandons him. But he does not regret the high price of freedom and never considers going back to ask his grandfather's forgiveness: 'It was a mad adventure of which I will remain proud for the rest of my life' (p. 91). The *Fall* from Divine Grace then was from the other end of the perspective the *ascent* to free will and therefore nothing to be repentant about.

After separation from Marwāna, Ja^{c}far, who has worked as a second-class singer since he left his grandfather's house, becomes acquainted with a respectable, educated, well-to-do and older lady who falls in love with him. He reciprocates her affection, though with a soberness which contrasts sharply with the wild passion he once had for Marwāna. They get married and he abandons his petty singing career and tramping lifestyle. During his years under his grandfather's tutelage he had only studied the religious sciences. Now, upon his wife's instigation, he turns to secular education, reading widely in history, philosophy, psychology and sociology, and finally specializing in the study of law. He learns 'to admire the scientific method' (p. 108) and to 'hold reason as sacred' (p. 112). The ideal of 'the divine human being' is replaced by that of 'the rationalist human being' (p. 113). In terms of the allegory of spiritual evolution, this phase of our protagonist's life ostensibly corresponds to the Renaissance, leading up to the Age of Reason and finally to the world of today based, as it is, on the tenets of science alone. But in such a world, is there a place for God? Here Mahfouz gives us, through the pronouncements of Ja^{c}far, his most direct and revealing statement (since Kamāl's monologues in *The Trilogy* II) on his stance *vis-à-vis* belief in God:

> It [my mind] was totally unable to perceive or imagine Him, but it found no alternative for the assumption of His existence – and this is the tragedy. And if some people argue that this is an artificial problem and that we are able

> to live without thinking about it, then everything will lose meaning however hard we try to create meaning for it through the force of imagination, will-power and courage.[62] How I envy those who can lead a great life and die satisfied without a god!
>
> (p. 116)

Ja^c^far finally sums up the ambivalence of his attitude towards God in this suggestively phrased utterance: 'I am powerless to deny God' (p. 117) – as if the denial of God was a consummation devoutly to be wished but – alas! – impossible to attain. In this, Ja^c^far probably voices his author's own attitude, an attitude which, as the totality of his work appears to communicate, consists in a rejection of all forms of institutionalized religion while retaining belief in the abstract idea of God – a version of deism, not perhaps unlike Voltaire's. This belief, however, was not a product of the 1970s; it is only being restated here. In all probability, it is a formula of faith which Mahfouz arrived at early on at some point in his youth, an assumption that is borne witness to by Kamāl's unequivocal confession in *The Trilogy* II: 'I do not deny God; I still believe in Him. As for religion – where is it? Gone!' (p. 372).

Now in Mahfouz's work, as we have seen time and again, politics is always at a stone's throw from metaphysics – and *Heart of the Night* is no exception. During Ja^c^far's early youth which he spent with his grandfather, he used to listen to political discussions between him and his friends, all of whom were members of the social élite. They used to argue that they were the ones 'with the genuine interests [in the community] – agriculture, trade and industry. As for the mob – all they need is a job to earn a living from, and some services' (p. 121). Ja^c^far tells us that in those days he did not question the validity of that theory and that he counted himself lucky that 'he was one of the élite, not the mob' (p. 121). Within the terms of the allegory this, then, must be the old traditional alliance between religion and the plutocracy. Ja^c^far's real involvement in politics does not thus begin until well into the secularized phase of his life. It was then that he came to realize that 'no intellectual system is complete until it expresses an opinion on forms of human government' (p. 122), and that 'politics is life' (p. 124). He is attracted to the principles of social justice laid down in Marxism, but sees this as no reason to believe in dialectical and historical materialism, arguing that Marxism is just another philosophy, no more entitled than any other philosophical system to turn into dogma and establish itself through dictatorship: 'To believe in materialism is intellectually no more valid than to believe in God' (pp. 129–30).[63] After prolonged and anguished research, Jaᶜfar composes an eclectic political system of his own, drawn from the best values of spiritualism, liberalism and communism. He shows the manuscript to a friend with whom he always argued about politics. His friend, who is a fanatical communist, dismisses the theory with undisguised disdain as patchwork. Jaᶜfar loses his temper and in the ensuing fight stabs the man to death with a paper-knife. As Jaᶜfar contemplates in a state of shock the corpse lying on the floor, he cries out, 'O my sacred intellect! Why have you forsaken me?' (p. 141) – words no doubt chosen to echo those of Christ on the cross: 'My God, my God, why hast thou forsaken me?' (Matthew 27: 46). Christ's reproach was naturally addressed to God, whereas Jaᶜfar's is directed at modern man's God-substitute, the human mind, as sanctified as the old God but not half as infallible, as Jaᶜfar comes to discover at a great cost.

When Jaᶜfar comes out of prison, he is a ragged and lonely old man without family or means. He learns that his grandfather died while he was in prison entrusting the whole of his enormous estate to the Ministry of Religious Endowments to manage it for the benefit of certain named religious charities. Jaᶜfar's representations to the Ministry to give him a share of the estate as the only heir to his grandfather avail him nothing: the terms of the will were specific in excluding him. One day curiosity leads him to what used to be his grandfather's house. He finds the door in the great wall half-open, he pushes it and enters, and lo and behold! 'There was no garden . . . , no sweet scents and no chirping birds, but a great wasteland, heaps of rubbish and a few tramps' (p. 146). As for the palace, a bomb had destroyed it during an air-raid. In Mahfouz's sign-strewn world, this has to be construed appropriately: bombers and their bombs are products of modern science, and so it is only appropriate that the edifice which stands for ancient, outmoded beliefs should be destroyed by them. (We will do well to remember here that in *The Trilogy* III, Aḥmad ᶜAbd al-Jawwād, father, God-figure and bulwark of tradition, also meets a symbolic end after an air-raid.)[64]

Destitute and without shelter, Jaᶜfar decides to make the wasteland his home. Thus modern man, 'the rationalist human being', his soul impoverished having done away with God, can still only seek refuge under His dead shadow. Impoverished he may have become, but proud and unbent he still is. For Jaᶜfar is advised by an official of the Ministry that if he writes a petition documented with proof of his lineage, he may be favourably considered for a small monthly allowance. Jaᶜfar, however, refuses heroically: 'Al-Rāwī has disinherited me and I decline to receive one millieme[65] from his estate' (p. 147). This is all very well, but the fact remains that he has taken shelter in God's wasteland. In Mahfouz's world-picture, the tug-of-war between man and God is an ongoing game. God is gladly fled, but no sooner is this done than He is again madly sought. It is a love–hate relationship. But one thing is certain: in the 'heart of the night' of our existence, God is wanted dead or alive.

Heart of the Night is a thesis novel through and through. Its symbolism is transparent, with each symbol exactly corresponding to its preordained meaning – no room for interpretative manoeuvring here. Characters are preconceived and coerced by the author into their tightly fitting roles. They have no margin of freedom and no semblance of independence from their creator – they are only there to illustrate ideas. Only Jaᶜfar al-Rāwī's eccentricity of phrase and action occasionally arouses our interest in him as a living character. Very often, too, the narrative is overburdened with lengthy passages of philosophical discussions. *Heart of the Night* is a work rich in thought and vision, which have not been successfully transformed into artistic metaphor – it teaches more than it delights.

THE AGE OF LOVE

The Age of Love (1980) appears to be a meaningless repetition of *Heart of the Night*. It is another simple allegory about the rebellious flight from God followed by a remorseful and painful return. The same set of symbols is used again: an opulent house and lush garden with high walls (= Paradise); a kind but domineering figure of authority – this time, a mother (= God); an essentially good-natured descendant but endowed with a rebellious and flawed personality – this time, a son (= Mankind).

The tension between the figure of authority and the rebellious descendant reaches breaking point when the latter is exposed to extra-Paradisiac temptation by a beautiful woman who stands for the pleasures of the world (compare Marwāna in the previous novel). At this point authority and Paradise are cast aside and freedom is relished in a self-imposed exile but with it also come moral loss, filth and possibly crime. Finally, after the pain and pleasure of experience comes a kind of remorse and a nostalgia for the former innocence and certainty. But they come too late. In *Heart of the Night*, the returned rebel can only take shelter amid the ruins of the old Paradise, while ᶜIzzat, his replica in *Age of Love*, returns to a mother who has lost sight and hearing in her old age and is thus unable to know of his return, let alone absolve him:[66] the impossibility of communication between modern man and God is emphasized.

The thesis is the same. The metaphor is the same. The parallelism is almost one to one. There is no innovation in technique, no change in vision, while the language sorely lacks the poetic quality we have come to expect of Mahfouz as a matter of course. *The Age of Love* bears all the marks of a work composed at a moment when the author's creativity was at a very low ebb.

WEDDING SONG

Wedding Song (1981) is a novel about a play. The four protagonists are all associated in one way or another (and so are all the minor characters) with a theatre company, and their lives are closely connected, in as well as out of the theatre. One of them, ᶜAbbās Yūnis, writes a damning play about himself and them in which their moral degradation, self-chosen or imposed by circumstance, is revealed and analysed with gruelling cruelty. In spite of this, the company director stages the play with conspicuous success. But the young playwright, an idealist with a central role in his own play, and for whom writing it was a personal cathartic act in the first place, disappears mysteriously before the première of his play, leaving behind a suicide note.

As in *Miramar* and *The Day the Leader was Killed*, the story is told from several points of view – namely those of the playwright; his father (the company prompter who turned his house into a private brothel and gambling club for its members);

his mother (the booking-office girl seduced by the company director before finally marrying the prompter); and a second-rate actor whose mistress abandons him to marry the much younger, would-be playwright. The events are basically the same in all four accounts; what changes is only the consciousness through which they are seen and the interpretation they are given. This scheme of things leads the novelist inevitably into the tedious repetition of factual details for anything up to four times within the boundaries of what is a short novel. The book touches on several themes, though none of them is sufficiently tapped or sustained long enough to become a singular focus for the story. The most persistent of them is perhaps the theme of the relationship between art and reality. All characters without exception reject their portrayals by the playwright and their own accounts show his interpretation of their actions and their motives to be false and unfair. On the other hand, the playwright's suicide after the opening of his play appears to parallel the action of his persona in the play. The moral therefore seems to be the well-established theses that art transforms reality into something else; that artistic truthfulness is not the same thing as lifelikeness; and that it is life that imitates art and not the other way round.

To have allowed this theme to take over the novel would probably have graced it with a cohesion and a sense of purpose, in both of which it appears to be wanting. But this would have represented an exercise in intellectual self-indulgence unprecedented in the work of Mahfouz. A socio-political theme must therefore be thrown in. We learn from a couple of casual remarks in the dialogue that the scene of action is Cairo some time after the '1973 victory' which did not produce the longed-for 'economic welfare' (pp. 31, 36). In addition, there is some harping in the prompter's account on the corruption of the state, which he sees as a framework for his own depravity: 'why should we go to prison in a country where the majority deserve to be locked up?' (p. 40). There is also an attempt at imbuing some symbolism into 'the old house built by the sweat of brow of the [playwright's] grandfather', to be turned into 'a brothel' (p. 148) by his father: here is Egypt – what it was and what it has come to. But the symbolism does not work; it is too fleeting and too superficial to take root in the fabric of the book.[67]

In addition to these two themes, a third is also allowed a fair amount of play in the novel. Since the four accounts are all acts of recollection, and since the author's method (in all but the last of them) is to contrast scenes and moods of the present with ones from the past, the exercise lends itself naturally to the author's most obsessive theme: the ravages of time in human life. Thus in the accounts of particularly the prompter and his wife there is some emphasis on the idea of how the years turn love into hate, hope into despair, etc. There are too many themes for a novel of well under 20,000 words. What is worse is that they remain independent of each other, leaving the work adrift in a sea of meanings, something quite uncharacteristic of the work of Mahfouz, where a strong sense of purpose is usually readily discernible. What completely defies understanding, however, is the gimmicky ending of the book. On the last two pages of the novel, which represent the end of the playwright's version of events, we discover, without any preparation, that his was the account of a dead man. The fact is never stated and all the previous accounts only mention a suicide note and the absence of a body. Through his account we know that he had retired secretly to a hotel in Ḥilwān, south of Cairo, to start a new play, only to be faced with a vast spiritual emptiness – his creativity, he finds out, is dead. Alone in the world, without money and without a future, he decides to end his life. It is here that the mostly indifferent prose of the narrative suddenly soars to poetic heights. Despondency turns into hope, and evocative words like 'rebirth', 'resurrection' and 'waking to a new age' dominate the prose, while the last sentence of the book speaks of 'a body laid bare with penury and aridity, while the will soared high up in defiant joy'. Our protagonist, no doubt, has been telling us his story from beyond the grave (albeit in the first person!).[68] What is the point of this extravagant and dazzling trick? None is apparent. It only seems to weaken further the structure of a work already overladen with themes. Here, as in the previous novel, Mahfouz's creativity seems again to have been at a low ebb.

6

FRAGMENTS OF TIME: THE EPISODIC NOVELS

Arabic literature, both classical and popular, has always abounded in forms of prose narrative. In the classical tradition, one can cite works like *Ayyām al-^{c}Arab* (the Battle-Days of [Pre-Islamic] Arabs); the eighth-century animal fables of *Kalīla wa Dimna*, which Ibn al-Muqaffa^{c} translated from Pahlavi; and the *maqāmāt*, or picaresque adventures, written by al-Hamadhānī (967–1007) and al-Ḥarīrī (1054–1122) and believed to have influenced the emergence of picaresque fiction in sixteenth-century Spain. In the popular tradition, on the other hand, mention can be made of *The Thousand and One Nights* (also known as *The Arabian Nights*) and the many medieval works of *sīra* (epic accounts of heroic exploits) such as *Sīrat Banī Hilāl* and *Sīrat ^{c}Antar*, to name but two. The above works are very different literary expressions composed over a long period of many centuries; some are classical compositions, others are folk works of oral origin; some were written by known authors at a particular time, others composed by anonymous ones over many generations and across several countries. There is, however, one element which is common to all of them: the episodic quality of their form. Some of these works, like *Kalīla wa Dimna* and *The Arabian Nights*, have their semi-independent episodes held together by a frame story, while others, such as the *maqāmāt*, enjoy no more semblance of unity than the fact that all the episodes or adventures figure the same picaroon or rogue as hero, otherwise being virtually independent of each other. Evidently none of these Arabic narrative forms conforms to the traditional Western definition of plot as laid down by Aristotle in his *Poetics*, and which has largely governed the structure of the Western novel since its evolution and until fairly recently. Late last century and early in this century, during the nascent days of modern Arabic fiction, attempts were made to revive, and adapt to the modes of the modern Arabic language and contemporary society, one of these indigenous narrative forms, namely the *maqāma*.[1] Those attempts proved, however, out of step with the times and attempts to revive the *maqāma* were quickly ousted by the growing trend to evolve modes of fiction in Arabic along the lines of Western tradition.

Thus when Mahfouz arrived on the scene in the late 1930s, the novel as a literary genre cast in a borrowed Western mould had already been established in the body of Arabic creative writing. Much of the story of Mahfouz's enormous contribution in developing this genre to full maturity, and adapting to his purposes and pushing to the limit, stage by stage, the potentials of his so-called borrowed mould, has already been told in the course of this book. One chapter of the story remains, however: the account of his own rebellion against the mould he had spent so much of his creative life in mastering and perfecting. As early as 1966, at the height of his absorption in the techniques of modernism (see pp. 99–101), Mahfouz had boldly argued: 'It is quite possible that I should come across a subject for which no form would be good enough except the *maqāma*; in which case I will write my novel in the *maqāma* style regardless.'[2] With the benefit of hindsight, this was an outburst by an adventurous and self-confident spirit rather than a declaration of intent – Mahfouz never came to write anything in the *maqāma* form. He was, however, to create an episodic mould of his own and pour into it some of the most astounding achievements of his creative imagination, such as *Harafish* and *Nights of the Thousand Nights*. It was from the early 1970s onwards that Mahfouz tended increasingly to express himself in the episodic mode (though not to the exclusion of the familiar Western form, which he continued to use sporadically). One must not forget, however, that a much earlier work, i.e. *Children of Gebelawi* (1959), is also episodic in structure. The episodic quality of *Children of Gebelawi* was nevertheless accidental rather than intentional; that is to say it was dictated by dint of its being a religio-historical allegory meant to parallel certain 'episodes' in human history. It would therefore be correct *not* to regard it as the true beginning of the author's episodic phase.

The genuine episodic phase begins tentatively with the nostalgic fifty-five character sketches of *Mirrors* in 1972, and the seventy-eight quasi-autobiographical tales of *Fountain and Tomb* in 1975. It would appear that the author was here in the business of using fragments of his life and times as the training ground for his new form. His success in transforming life matter into art and imposing order and meaning on those fragments must have strengthened his conviction that the new form was going to work. When, two years later, he published *Harafish* (a novel which today would appear on any shortlist of his most enduring achievements), it was immediately clear that the canny craftsman had mastered and pushed to the limit of its potential his newly discovered form. The enterprise which commenced with character vignettes and recollections of childhood in the first two works was extended in *Harafish* in ten lengthy tales which together evoked the human condition from creation to a millenarian future. The author sums up his experiment with the new form in these terms:

> When I started writing novels, I used to think that the European form of the novel was sacred. But as you grow older, your outlook changes; you want to free yourself from all that has been imposed on you, albeit in a natural and spontaneous way, and not just to break rules and be different. You find yourself searching for a [certain] tune deep down, inside yourself. . . . As if you were saying to yourself: 'Those forms which they [the Europeans] wrote in – were they not artistic moulds that they created? Why can't I create a mould of my own?'. . . . But I must make clear one important point: imitating the old [i.e. Arabic traditional forms] is no different from imitating the new [i.e. European form]; both are acts of bondage.[3]

Has Mahfouz indeed created 'a mould of his own' in these episodic works? My own feeling is that he has, but only in the sense that the author's imagination was the melting-pot in which the 'old' and the 'new' were fused together to produce 'his own mould'. There is no doubt in my mind that the originality of the episodic phase would not have been possible without the novelist's long experience in the arts of Western modernism, traces of whose modes of expression as well as sensibility are no less recognizable in the episodic works than are some of the qualities of the indigenous arts of storytelling. In the last analysis, it is a tribute to the author's accomplishment that the end-product can only be described as Mahfuzian.

MIRRORS

Mirrors (1972) consists of fifty-five character sketches ranging from five to fifteen pages. Each sketch carries as its title the name of the character it portrays. The portraits are presented by the narrator, who is admittedly a persona for the author. The narrator is mainly an observer recollecting in writing the lives and times of people he knew at one time or another in his life. Sometimes, however, he is an active participant in the situations delineated. He knows all the characters, though they do not necessarily know each other. He is therefore the main source of unity in the book, a gravitational centre without which all fifty-five satellites would shoot off in every direction. The sketches are arranged alphabetically, which makes cross-reference possible when a character or a related incident is mentioned in the account of another. This of course is another unifying factor though the unsuspecting first-time reader is not usually aware of the alphabetical order and the possibilities it offers. Nor is such a reader aware that the episodes do not have to be read sequentially. Certain episodes are encountered more than once when the characters involved in them tell them from their own point of view. This again helps to tie some of the many strands of the book together.

When *Mirrors* was first published, Mahfouz described it as 'a work of a special nature more akin to biography [i.e. than to fiction]',[4] by which he was referring to the fact that the portraits of which the work is made up are artistic disguises of real persons he came in contact with at various stages of his life.[5] Later, however, he changed his position and called the work 'a novel' and stressed the fact that it had 'design and structure'. He also pointed out that while the work might not have a central figure, he viewed 'time' as its 'protagonist' and 'central nerve'.[6] Elsewhere he indicates that his original intention in writing *Mirrors* was to document an age. He goes on to add that as the work evolved he was obliged to fill in the gaps created by failures of memory, with supplies from invention.[7] What Mahfouz does not say is that with public figures he had to alter facts and circumstances where a mere fictitious name for the character would not have been sufficient to disguise the real-life identity.[8] Whether or not it fits academic definitions of the word, we will have to accept *Mirrors* as a 'novel', all the more so because it proved to be the herald of a long trail of similarly structured works.

I find Mahfouz's own pronouncement (quoted above) on the novel's central preoccupation with time perfectly acceptable. The novel is a panorama of Egyptian society over a fifty-year period[9] beginning from Mahfouz's traditional point of departure (i.e. the 1919 revolution) to the late 1960s in the aftermath of the Arab defeat in the 1967 war with Israel. Appropriate pauses are made at the turbulent 1930s; the national struggle under the leadership of the Wafd Party; the emergence of the Moslem Brotherhood and other political groups; Egypt during World War II; and the 1952 revolution and the radical changes it brought about in the political, economic and social structure of society. The usual interaction of public and private is at play and as revolutions, wars and regimes come and go, individuals live or die and fortunes are made and lost. But not everything is dependent on the rationality of cause and effect for, as always with Mahfouz, there is fate, which needs no causes for its effects and whose ways pass human understanding. A striking example which poignantly sums up the author's pained incomprehension before acts of fate is given in the episode of 'Jaᶜfar Khalīl'. Jaᶜfar is a childhood friend of the narrator. An account is given of his admirable rise from poverty to a promising career as a student and practitioner of the cinematic arts. His hard work is rewarded by a scholarship to study in the United States. Four years later he returns with a doctorate and many fresh ideas for developing the film industry in Egypt. The narrator visits him on his return from America and the following morning he reads his obituary in *Al-Ahrām*. The terseness and matter-of-factness of the prose reflect the sense of paralysis of the human intellect before the enigma of fate:

> He left his flat at eight in the evening. His foot slipped on a banana skin. He lost his balance and fell. His head hit the edge of the kerb, and a few seconds later he died in front of the building.[10]
>
> (p. 83)

The fifty-five characters which throng the book represent a cross-section of Egyptian society over a number of generations. With a lifetime condensed into a few pages, potentially complex characters are, needless to say, reduced to types. Some of the portraits, however, are so vivid that they are not easily forgotten. About one-quarter of the portraits are of women and through their stories the history of female emancipation in Egypt is related and also that of changing sexual morality. In evidence also is the usual intellectual Mahfuziana: religion, science, socialism, art, philosophy, society and the individual, etc. The book is a heap of images, broken in the flux of time, each a fragment of human flotsam carried forward by the eternal current. Perhaps in the very fragmentariness of the novel is its unity.

FOUNTAIN AND TOMB

Mirrors concentrates mainly on scenes and figures from the narrator/author's adult life, all set in a faceless, generalized modern Cairo. The last episode, however, evokes a female figure from the narrator's early childhood and is set in Jamāliyya, the author's birthplace in old Cairo. Contrary to the language of the book which predominantly adopts the style of reportage, this episode is told in an evocative prose, steeped in a sense of mystery. It tells of the child-narrator's fascination with a teenage girl living across the street. The novel ends with the little boy united after many failed attempts with his enchantress. She seats him on a sofa in her room and entertains him by reading his fortune for him: 'She began to trace the lines on the palm of my hand and read the future, but I was absorbed with the whole of my consciousness in her beautiful face' (p. 413). The backward journey in time is thus completed with the narrator disembarking from his time-machine at that early station in his past: it is as if the book we have just finished was the fulfilment of the beautiful girl's prophecies.

This last episode of *Mirrors* could have been the first of *Fountain and Tomb* (1975): in both style and content it belongs there. Published three years after *Mirrors*, it proved to doubters at the time that the new episodic form was there to stay. It too is made up of seventy-eight episodes. Each is called a *ḥikāya* (i.e. tale) and given a serial number. *Ḥikāya* is a term associated with popular traditional narrative forms in Arabic, all of which are also episodic in structure. *Fountain and Tomb* carries on from where *Mirrors* broke off; that is to say, the journey into the narrator's childhood continues.[11] It can thus be seen as a sequel to its precursor though in reverse order. As in *Mirrors*, the episodes are held together by the observer/participant narrator. Unlike *Mirrors*, however, it enjoys the additional unity of place, as scene and characters are confined to the author's favourite Jamāliyya. Place is indeed evoked powerfully and poetically in this work and it is here that Mahfouz's symbolic repertoire of the *ḥāra*, the *takiyya*, the *qabw* and the *futuwwa* is born.[12]

Apart from the general unities of narrator and place, there are partial unities, as it were, where clusters of tales hold together thematically. For example there are eight tales (nos. 4–7, 10, 17, 24, 25) which relate episodes tracing the opening up of the child's sexuality; eight others (nos. 12–16, 18, 19, 23) dealing with the impressions the 1919 revolution made on the child's consciousness; and six more (nos. 50, 52–4, 56, 57) treating the role of the *futuwwa* in the *ḥāra*. On the other hand, some episodes which belong to the spirit of the book would nevertheless survive unscathed as self-contained short stories (e.g. nos. 32, 44, 45). The book is about private time rather than public time, and for once Mahfouz has written a work of reminiscences which does not get enmeshed in the politics of his country. The revolution of 1919 is there of course but only from the viewpoint of a child and as one of many factors contributing to the growth of his awareness. It is there only as are accounts of his circumcision, first days at school, childhood love and the budding sexuality, the first encounter with death, etc: the book is largely a *bildungsroman* of sorts.

Episodic as the novel is, there is yet another way in which a sense of unity can be seen in its fragments. The book opens with a tale recounting a mystical experience which the child undergoes. One day, tired of playing, he dozes off in front of the wall of the old *takiyya*, that dervish house (much like a monastery) standing aloof in the *ḥāra*, beset with mystery, its gates and windows always shut and strange hymns occasionally waft up from its garden. When the child comes to, late in the afternoon, he feels himself close to a gentle presence. He looks towards the *takiyya* and under the mulberry tree he sees a dervish standing:

> but not like those I have seen before. He was very old and very tall, his face a shining pool of light. His cloak was green and his high turban white. He was magnificent beyond description or imagination. I looked at him so intently until I became intoxicated with the light that radiated from him and I felt his presence fill the universe. A sweet thought told me that he was the owner of the place and the one in charge.
>
> (p. 4)

The child tells the dervish that he loves mulberries, but all he gets by way of reply is an incantation in a foreign tongue. The dervish then throws him a mulberry. Or so the boy imagines, for when he kneels to pick it up he finds nothing. When he stands up again, the dervish has disappeared and darkness fallen. When the boy tells the story to his father, he is reluctant to believe it as the great dervish has never been known to leave his cloister. Later in his life, the child, now an adult, keeps wondering whether he really saw the great dervish or just imagined it and, if it were true, why he had never appeared again: 'Thus I had created a myth and then shattered it. Nevertheless the alleged vision has sunk deep in my soul, a memory so sweet. Furthermore, I am still mad about mulberries' (p. 5).

The child's vision of the great dervish is of course symbolic of mankind's vision of God, just as the inscrutable *takiyya* with its garden and craved-for mulberry trees stands for Heaven.[13] The *takiyya* is used as an occasional leitmotif in the book, always associated with light and peace in contrast with another motif, i.e. the *qabw* or vault, which is associated with darkness and where evil spirits live and heinous crimes are perpetrated. The experience of the first tale is recapitulated in the last where the child, now a little more mature, discusses his vision with a well-informed friend of his father's who had himself once been obsessed with the riddle of the *takiyya*. The conversation only serves to reaffirm the child's doubts and incomprehension. Significantly, however, he stresses that, in spite of everything, he 'cannot imagine a *takiyya* without a Great Dervish' (p. 189). The two tales about the *takiyya*, one beginning the book and the other ending it, seem to encircle, with their associations of the eternal, all the other tales that occur between them, thereby giving the novel a measure of formal unity which *Mirrors* did not have. It is as if the encircled tales were instances of the temporal taking place within the framework of the eternal.

TALES OF MORNINGS AND EVENINGS

This work (1987) represents a return to the technique of alphabetically arranged character sketches first used some fifteen years earlier in *Mirrors*. It contains sixty-seven sketches of characters drawn mainly from three families whose members are all related either through blood or intermarriage. Though of moderate length (217 pages), it is to date Mahfouz's most ambitious *roman fleuve*, tracing the lives of three whole families across five generations and a period of nearly 200 years. In earlier works we have seen the author limiting himself to three generations and staying within his own lifetime, i.e. beginning at about the year 1919 with its dramatic events and continuing to the time of writing – the mid-1940s as in *The Trilogy* or the 1980s as in other works already discussed in chapter 4. It appears, however, that as he grew older and the perspective viewed from his birthpoint extended, he felt an urge to extend it at the other end too – perhaps the better to understand his own life and times in a wider time context. Thus *Tales of Mornings and Evenings* has its beginning in the late eighteenth century, namely with the arrival of Napoleon in Egypt, and concludes with occurrences from the post-Sadāt era. The French campaign in Egypt and the rule of Muḥammad ᶜAlī shortly established after its departure represent together the beginning of modern times in Egypt. The novel, concerned as ever in Mahfouz with the interplay of public time and private time, is thus a panoramic view of post-medieval Egypt to the present day.

The three main families of the novel, namely those of Yazīd al-Miṣrī, Muᶜāwiya al-Qalyūbī and ᶜAṭā al-Marākībī, represent together all sections of Egyptian urban society.[14] Significantly, the author shows all the families to have originated at the bottom of society and then accidents of time, private or public, to have raised some of them into a higher class and a different style of life. As generations pass, old links are severed and the elevated forget their former humble station. Although the novel is an account of the evolution of Egypt from medievalism to modernity, the grip of the past in the form of superstitious beliefs is shown to have remained firm throughout. This is conveyed through the portrait of Rāḍiya Muᶜāwiya al-Qalyūbī, a member of the second generation who lives for a hundred years, well into the Nasser era. She inherits her superstitions from her mother and continues to influence subsequent generations with them.

Tales of Mornings and Evenings is a sad novel. On the public level, it amounts to an elegy to the failure of the experiment of modernization in Egypt. On the private level, it is a bizarre celebration of death, of the incessant massacre by time of men's hopes and lives. Each of the sixty-seven sketches contains in a very condensed manner a whole lifetime, always beginning with birth and almost always ending with death.[15] Considering the lexicographical arrangement of the sketches, we are made to feel that individuals are no more than short, insignificant entries in the huge, ongoing lexicon of time.

GOOD MORNING TO YOU

Published in the same year as *Tales of Mornings and Evenings*, *Good Morning to You* is referred to in the author's list of publications as a *majmūᶜa* (collection), the word usually used to indicate collections of short stories. It comprises three pieces of varying lengths, and while they are structurally sufficiently independent of each other to justify calling them a 'collection', there is something about them that makes them a homogeneous, rather than a haphazard, collection.[16] All three are acts of recollection and all three are wistful contemplations of the devastating work of time in the life of the individual.

The first piece is called ''Umm Aḥmad'. It is a work which recalls, like *Fountain and Tomb*, scenes and characters from the novelist's childhood. Needless to say, the scene is Jamāliyya, the novelist's holiest shrine of the memory, to which he never ceases to make pilgrimage after pilgrimage. 'Umm Aḥmad, a matchmaker among many other things, plays in the old quarter the role that ancient bards played for their tribes: she is the memory of the place and the living register of its people and their history. On her authority, the narrator recounts the stories of four of the well-to-do families of the quarter. The accounts are strict Mahfuziana in the period they cover and in their sense of wonder at the vicissitudes of fortune. 'Umm Aḥmad herself finally becomes a relic of time too. The narrator visits her in her old age:

> Many things we remembered and many leaves of the past, both distant and near, we turned. Together we wandered about in a world inhabited by the dead. Oh, how many the departed are! As though eyes never lit up in the darkness of existence and laughs never danced over lips!
>
> (p. 22)

The profound sadness of the prose carries the tenor of the novelist's own voice. It is a personal sadness which characterizes all his recent work of reminiscence or semi-reminiscence. There is something in the writings of this phase of the nature of the flashes from a dying consciousness. Gone is the author's ability to muse upon the subject of time with any sense of detachment.

''Umm Aḥmad' is set in Jamāliyya, as has been said. The four families whose stories it tells move, however, to east ᶜAbbāsiyya in the 1920s as it was fashionable for rich families to do at the time. The second piece of the collection which gives its title to the book is, on the other hand, set entirely in ᶜAbbāsiyya. The piece is introduced by the narrator describing his family's move from Jamāliyya to west ᶜAbbāsiyya, as did many lower-middle-class families at the time, following in the footsteps of their richer neighbours who moved to the more affluent east ᶜAbbāsiyya. The factual details given in the short introduction leave no doubt that the novelist and the narrator speak with one voice, as the narrator's move to ᶜAbbāsiyya tallies perfectly with that of the young Mahfouz's own family. The story must then be read as a mixture of fact and fiction, as indeed must all these works of reminiscence.

As they are based in Jamāliyya, the four accounts in ''Umm Aḥmad' may be seen perhaps as a belated extension of *Fountain and Tomb*. 'Good Morning to You', on the other hand, based in ᶜAbbāsiyya, may be seen as an extension of *Mirrors*, many of whose accounts are drawn from the author's youthful days in that quarter. Indeed, some of the accounts in 'Good Morning to You' are re-renderings of earlier sketches from *Mirrors*.[17] 'Good Morning to You' contains fifteen episodes. Here, as in ''Umm Aḥmad', we have sketches of whole families, and not of single characters as in some of the earlier works. The episodes are independent of each other, brought together only by the unities of narrator and place: all the families lived in the same street in ᶜAbbāsiyya. But the greatest unity is thematic: victimization by the mutations of time. The story produces its total effect cumulatively as each episode leaves a certain emotional response in the reader to be built on by the following one, and so on (this is the principle relied on in all these episodic works).

The episodes are rounded off by a return to the voice of the novelist/narrator:

> When nostalgia draws me to ᶜAbbāsiyya today, there is revealed to me a strange world that I have not known. East is not east and west is not west. Gone are the fields and gardens, and vanished all things green. In their place stand rows of jampacked tower blocks without beauty or grace. Sidewalks throng with children. All means of transport seem in a crazy race. . . . Anger and violence and abuse assault the ears. I know no one and no one knows me. And I wonder, I wonder in extreme bewilderment: where are the places which saw the sweetest friendships and the most beautiful love stories?[18]
>
> (p. 98)

In *Qushtumur* the permanence of place seemed to offer some comfort against the ravages of time. But when these ravages erase features of places as well, then memory becomes the only evidence of a past that an individual has. The piece ends with this understandably paradoxical thought: 'What a curse to have a memory! But it is also the one grace left us' (p. 98).

The third and last piece of the collection is entitled 'Good Evening to You'.[19] This piece is more of a conventional short story than the other two. It consists of some fifty pages with a single line of development and, unlike the first two pieces, no subdivisions. The story is largely an extended internal monologue interspersed with pieces of dialogue. The monologue begins with a description of the protagonist's feelings on the first day of his retirement after a long and futile career in the civil service. As the past unfolds, a lifetime of misery and frustration is revealed to us. Memory again is a mixed blessing: 'Perhaps it is the good fortune of the insect creeping in the waste heap that it has no memory or imagination' (p. 99). But, on the other hand, we are also told that 'In the rubbish heap of time lie hidden, in the darkest recesses, the most beautiful memories' (p. 100).

The protagonist's life has been the epitome of lack of fulfilment.[20] Retirement finds him an old and lonely bachelor still in the room where he has lived since his childhood. He is another typical Mahfuzian victim of time's constant hostility to man as it brings about change both public and private. The protagonist muses upon his wasted life in these terms:

> I curse the mutations of time which swept over my country and the rest of the world and invaded me in my very home. Has anyone before me ever been born, grown up and retired in the same quarter and the same street, nay the same flat and the same room? Every time I try to move, events arrest me: . . . inflation, *infitāḥ*, wars and the world economic system . . . .
>
> (p. 104)

'Events arrest me' is perhaps the key phrase in this outburst, as indeed it is in the work of Mahfouz generally where the individual's will often appears powerless before the onslaught of time.

The discussion of these many works by the author, largely similar in both structure and meaning, makes this an appropriate juncture to address a particular issue occasionally raised by Mahfuzian critics. By this I mean repetition. I think an element of repetitiveness will have been readily apparent even to a reader whose only knowledge of, for example, the novels discussed in the present chapter is limited to this brief survey – much more so to one who has actually read them, and especially so to one who has read them at short intervals, rather than at the time when each was first published.

The question in fact is not limited to these relatively late works of the author, for as early as 1971 he was asked by one interviewer whether he agreed to the idea that his output consisted in 'variations on one theme'. Mahfouz refused to commit himself, but went on to confirm that the life, and so the work, of a man of letters might centre on one or two ideas.[21] Asked the same question more recently (1989), Mahfouz sounded more sensitive to the accusation:

> Every genuine artist repeats himself. An artist has but one

> receiver, one transmitter and one vision. He occupies but one station in society and is the product of one age. All of which means that repetition in his work can only be tantamount to variety and the more genuine he is, the more prone to repetition.[22]

Whatever Mahfouz might think by way of justifying repetition in his work, the fact remains that it is a phenomenon confronting any systematic reader of his output. There is repetition in period and locality, in situation, in character types and in the ideas expressed through all this. The novelist's basic ideas about man, society, God and Egypt have changed in essence very little, if at all, since he started writing. Where there has always been immense variety in his work is in style and technique – in his almost limitless ability to reorchestrate his main tunes, to find new moulds for old preoccupations. It is this ability that has seen him move comfortably among traditions of fiction as diverse as historical romanticism, realism, naturalism and modernism until finally, tired of technical borrowing and adaptation, he invented his own (to coin a word) 'episodism', as we have seen in the discussion of the last four works. It is this magical box of technical diversity which probably redeems the repetitive element in the novelist's corpus. It must be noted, however, that this element of self-repetition has reached in his more recent work, as has been shown, an obsessive pitch.

CHILDREN OF GEBELAWI

Children of Gebelawi (1959)[23] was to mark Mahfouz's return to fiction writing after the period of silence[24] which followed the completion of *The Trilogy*. Different as it is both in subject-matter and its episodic form from anything written before it, there is still a manner in which it can be seen, like its immediate predecessor, as a *roman fleuve*. The generations here, however, are those of the entire human family from Adam to modern man, and the time (totally external or public here, where there is no concern with personal tragedy) is the many millennia that it took humanity to grow out of belief in the supernatural into belief in science. Seen as such, the novel would readily present itself as a broadening of the spectrum of Kamāl's spiritual journey in *The Trilogy* discussed above, and indeed as a universalization of the theme of old and new or past and present, which Mahfouz harped on in all his realistic novels.

The novel is a panoramic view of the history of man and religion from the beginning of time to the present day. God, Satan, Adam, Moses, Jesus and Muḥammad are all there, but without the halo of religious myth: the novel is an attempt at demythologizing humanity's religious quest. It begins with an episode which parallels the Qur'ānic story of Adam's fall and his subsequent expulsion from Heaven, Heaven here being the 'Great House' of his father, Gebelawi[25] (i.e. God) with its vast garden. Adam (Adham, in the novel) is banished to the *ḥāra*[26] (i.e. the Earth) where he experiences toil and poverty after his happy life in the 'Great House'. Many years later when one of his two sons kills the other (in an episode allegorizing the story of Cain and Abel), Gebelawi finally takes pity on his disconsolate son and as a token of forgiveness bequeathes his estate to his children and their posterity (i.e. mankind) for ever and ever. Having done that, the old man retires inscrutably to his impregnable house on the border of the *ḥāra* and is seen outside no more. The Trustee of the bequest (i.e. the ruling class), however, soon turns into a thief who takes the income of the estate for himself and coerces the people of the *ḥāra* through the employment of paid *futuwwa*s or thugs. Thus social injustice began. But injustice engenders resistance; and this is exactly what Judaism, Christianity and Islam were all about according to Mahfouz. They are seen within the simplistic terms of the allegory as a succession of socio-political movements against a repressive system, aiming at establishing a just order on earth.

However, the successes of those prophets, or shall we say political rebels, were only of temporary duration, for each time the *ḥāra* lapsed again into its old evil ways. Is there no hope then? 'Yes, there is,' comes the prophetic voice of the novelist in the fifth and last book of the novel. For there we encounter ᶜArafa, the magician, who stands for modern science and inherits the role of social saviour, previously the prerogative of God-inspired prophets. Indeed, the demise of the idea of God in the modern world is paralleled in the novel by the death of the old man Gebelawi (significantly instigated by the magician's clandestine raid on his forbidden house). The role of science as the modern world's god is spelt out by ᶜArafa (note the meaningful choice of name from the root *ᶜarafa*, 'to know') in a feverish and contrite speech after the death of the old man:

> A single word from our grandfather used to drive the good ones among his grandchildren to strive until death. His death should be stronger than his words. It makes it the duty of a good son to do everything, to take his place, to be him.
>
> (p. 503)

Mahfouz goes even further in his endeavour to establish science as the legitimate heir of religion. This can be seen in the vision[27] which ᶜArafa has of a message left him by the dying old man and communicated by his maid. The text of the message is simply, 'Go to ᶜArafa, the magician, and tell him on my authority that his grandfather died pleased with him' (p. 538). This immediately establishes ᶜArafa as a recipient of revelation like his prophetic predecessors. What we have here is a gallant attempt by Mahfouz to bestow on science the spiritual power inherent in religion; it is, as we have seen in earlier novels, something that he has constantly been preoccupied with.[28] On the other hand, the limitless potential of science to bring about the Benthamite dream of the 'greatest happiness for the greatest number' is emphasized when ᶜArafa voices the hope that his magic 'may one day be able to destroy thugs, construct buildings, and provide for all the children of the quarter' (p. 483).

Despite the fact that Mahfouz's faith in science remains unqualified, he sounds, however, in *Children of Gebelawi*, a note of warning which is heard nowhere else in his earlier work. He is here for the first time aware that science in the wrong hands can be a force of suppression rather than liberation. The magician invents an explosive weapon which he uses to destroy the *futuwwa*s of the quarter, but he is then blackmailed and manipulated by the Trustee to put the invention at his service, and thus ᶜArafa becomes in effect the new super-*futuwwa*, albeit against his will. This new nightmarish vision of the author is doubtless the product of a post-nuclear world, living for the first time in history under the menace of the total destruction of human civilization – all thanks to the evil manipulation of scientific progress. The novel ends on a pessimistic note with ᶜArafa murdered at the hands of the Trustee and his *futuwwa*s. Unlike the previous prophets, he leaves the *ḥāra* worse off than it was before him. But amid the darkness there is a ray of hope:

ᶜArafa has left somewhere the notebook containing the secrets of his magic, and his brother and assistant, Ḥanash, who survives the massacre is going to find it and continue to work for the salvation of the *ḥāra*, helped by its young, who begin to disappear mysteriously, creating the belief that they are running away to join Ḥanash in his endeavours and come back one day in force to set things right.[29] Here as elsewhere Mahfouz puts his faith in the evolutionary movement of collective time.[30]

EPIC OF THE HARAFISH[31]

Separated from it by some eighteen years and written in the novelist's new-found, postmodernist episodic form, *Harafish* (1977) nevertheless recalls powerfully to the mind *Children of Gebelawi*. The locality is the same (the *ḥāra*); the power structure is the same (a pact between the well-off and the *futuwwāt*[32] to plunder the rights of Gebelawi's children, i.e. the *ḥarāfīsh*); attempts to break the power structure are also the same (strong, good individuals establish short-lived justice before the old evil pattern is restored). *Harafish* is thus in essence Gebelawi's *ḥāra* revisited. It is a fresh attempt by the author to answer in the broadest possible terms the agonizing question: why does social evil exist and how can it be eradicated? To this newer attempt Mahfouz has brought the wealth of technical and stylistic expertise accumulated since the earlier one. The result is a much more mature work. Rather than creating an allegory in which existing religious myth is deflated,[33] the novelist here creates his own myth out of a very familiar reality. Thus while *Children of Gebelawi* would be terribly impoverished if read without reference to its preconceived religio-mythological framework, *Harafish* is a self-contained work whose meaning stems solely from the sum of its parts.

Like *Children of Gebelawi*, *Harafish*, in its own way, is a *roman fleuve*. It is so, however, in a much looser sense of the term than we mean when we apply it for instance to *The Trilogy*. The novel is made up of ten tales which span the history of some sixteen generations of the Nājīs, descendants of the great ᶜĀshūr al-Nājī, founder of the family. The *ḥāra* where the action of the novel takes place is located in Mahfouz's familiar terrain in old Cairo. It is given no name, however; nor is there an attempt at creating a verifiable topography of a certain quarter, as in some of the realistic novels. Period is not defined either. There are no public events to infringe on the *ḥāra* world and by which we could determine period. True, there are references to the government, officers of the law, the police and the ministry of the interior, but these are few and made in the vaguest terms and seldom are shown to influence happenings in the *ḥāra*. The number of generations involved in the ten tales of the book would, on the other hand, easily suggest a time span of several centuries. There is, however, no attempt in the novel at defining points of beginning, end or a duration of a particular length in time. Mahfouz in fact deliberately isolates the *ḥāra* of the *ḥarāfish* from any specific framework of reference in locale or time. This device, coupled with a dense, evocative prose style which persistently infuses a subtle symbolism into such features of the *ḥāra* as the *takiyya*, the *qabw*, the adjacent *khalā'*, and the giant mosqueless minaret, universalizes the *ḥāra* into a timeless image of the human condition as the novelist perceives it (see p. 1 for the meanings of these terms). Rather than trying to interpret existing myths in terms of reality as he did in *Children of Gebelawi*, the author here condenses total reality into a tailor-made myth of his own creation the better to understand it.

In the beginning was ᶜĀshūr, who later came to be called al-Nājī (i.e. the survivor) because he was the only man to survive the plague which struck the *ḥāra*. And ᶜĀshūr was an illegitimate child abandoned in the dead of the night near the wall of the *takiyya* where he was picked up and adopted by Shaykh ᶜAfra Zaydān, an old, good-hearted, blind man with a sterile wife. In their care the child grows into a strong giant of a man with an innocent soul and a kind heart. From his young days 'his heart opened up to the joy and the light and the songs [of the *takiyya*]' (p. 11). ᶜĀshūr was content with his life and 'he thought that he would remain in paradise until the end' (p. 12), but the old man dies and the old woman is forced to return to her native village. Thus ᶜĀshūr finds himself alone in the empty *khalā'*, well out of paradise, 'but a voice rising from his heart's depth told him that though the earth may seem empty, it is filled with the mercy of the Compassionate One' (p. 12). ᶜĀshūr, however, was not quite alone on earth, for there was Darwīsh, Shaykh ᶜAfra's younger brother, who was brought up in the same house with ᶜĀshūr. But he was an evil bandit who, after the death of his godly brother, tries to recruit ᶜĀshūr's enormous strength in the service of crime. ᶜĀshūr, however, will not be corrupted and as each goes his way, Darwīsh flings in ᶜĀshūr's face the stigma that has been kept from him for many years: that he was a bastard, a child of sin.

In his despair ᶜĀshūr is drawn to the *takiyya* with its trees, birds, green lawns and singing dervishes:

> The gate beckons to him. And in his heart he hears a whisper: Knock! Ask permission! Enter! Yours will be grace and peace and joy. Turn into a mulberry![34] Let the sweet nectar fill you! Let your leaves nourish the silkworms. In the end hands that are pure will pick you in exultation.
>
> (p. 19)

but when he calls on the dervishes to offer his services:

> They hide away. They give no answer. Even the sparrows eye him with suspicion. They do not speak his language and he does not speak theirs. The stream runs no more and the grass halts its dance – no one needs his services.
>
> (p. 19)

Rejected by the *takiyya*, and alone in the *ḥāra* with evil, ᶜĀshūr learns that he will have to fight for survival (on earth) single-handedly. Mahfouz has told the story of Adam again (i.e. Adham in *Children of Gebelawi*). But while this account stands on its own merits, gaining in profundity as we gradually discover its remoter echoes, the earlier one serves mainly as a code for the Qur'ānic story, and as we decipher it, it ceases to interest us except in so far as we want to see the extent to which it follows or deviates from the original.

ᶜĀshūr obtains a job in the *ḥāra* as a cart-driver. His devotion and honesty recommend him to his employer, who gives him his daughter in marriage. He begets three sons with her. ᶜĀshūr never loses his attachment to the *takiyya*, opposite which he would always sit in the evenings listening to the dervishes' inscrutable songs and thinking about the wrongful ways of men and the frailties of the soul. He sees a lot that is unjust in the *ḥāra* but his strength remains an unused potential to set it right. Then Darwīsh, who had been serving a prison sentence, is released and returns to the *ḥāra* where he starts a bar-cum-brothel. To ᶜĀshūr's consternation, his own sons soon become patrons of the evil place. He falls out with them and they run away from home. Soon, however, it transpires that ᶜĀshūr himself is not immune to temptation and weakness of the flesh. He falls for Fulla, a barmaid-cum-whore at Darwīsh's place. To the shock of his family and the whole *ḥāra* he takes her as second wife. ᶜĀshūr's full humanity is thus emphasized in spite of the obvious saintly dimension to his character. Emphasized too is the entwined nature of good and evil. Fulla, however, is reformed by marriage and she bears him another son, Shams al-Dīn. For a while ᶜĀshūr is a happy and contented man.

Then the plague[35] strikes the *ḥāra* and death goes on the rampage sparing neither rich nor poor. ᶜĀshūr is frightened and he sees it as 'the wrath of God' (p. 51). He sees a vision in a dream of his adoptive father Shaykh ᶜAfra leading him out of the *ḥāra* into the mountain and the surrounding *khalā'*.[36] He decides to act on the vision. He invites his first wife and his sons by her to accompany him but they refuse and so do the people of the *ḥāra* who accuse him of madness. Thus only ᶜĀshūr, Fulla and their baby son Shams al-Dīn move with their donkey, cart and provisions to the desert, out of reach of death's ravages. They stay there for six months in total seclusion. In the *khalā'* there is ample time for ᶜĀshūr to worship and to meditate. He sees his *ḥāra* 'as a jewel sunk in mud', and discovers that 'he loves it even with its shortcomings'. But he also comes to believe that 'mankind deserves what it suffers'. However, he does not lose his optimism and feels that 'he is being born anew' (pp. 61–2). Eventually they return to a *ḥāra* that is now as deserted as the emptiness they have returned from: the plague has washed it clean of life. Only the *takiyya* remains intact and the singing still wafts over its impregnable walls. Mahfouz has expropriated the story of Noah and the Ark with admirable sleight of hand, augmenting the symbolic value of ᶜĀshūr (who encompasses both Adam and Noah) and greatly enhancing the sense of timelessness necessary for his myth-creating task.

ᶜĀshūr and his family resettle then in what is virtually a ghost *ḥāra*. One day ᶜĀshūr succumbs to the temptation of walking into what used to be the mansion of the wealthiest family in the *ḥāra*. The riches he sees stun him. They decide to abandon their wretched hole of a basement room and live in the deserted palace. ᶜĀshūr silences his pangs of conscience by arguing to himself that the house is without an owner and that wealth is legitimate as long as it is legitimately spent (p. 71). Gradually life starts to come back to the *ḥāra*, with only the houses of the rich remaining vacant. When the *ḥarāfīsh* start to reinhabit the *ḥāra*, ᶜĀshūr is already established in his new palace. He begins to spend lavishly on the poor from his newly acquired wealth until there is no one left without a job or a small business. He also has the *ḥāra* cleaned up, builds a small mosque, a drinking fountain and a donkey trough. Thus ᶜĀshūr becomes the undisputed master of the *ḥāra*. The *ḥarāfīsh*, having never known a rich man who behaved in that manner, 'call him a saint and argue that it was for that reason that God saved him alone from the plague' (p. 72). Thus wealth is redistributed fairly in the post-epidemic *ḥāra* (or post-diluvian world) and human society appears for a while to be at peace with itself.

Before long, however, the government recovers from the aftermath of the epidemic and begins to take stock of the properties and estates of the dead. When ᶜĀshūr is unable to produce proof of ownership, the estate is seized and he goes to prison, the uncrowned hero, nevertheless, of the *ḥāra*'s poor. During his absence, Darwīsh takes control of the *ḥāra* as *futuwwa* and a reign of terror begins for the benefit of the well-to-do and at the expense of the *ḥarāfish*. No wonder then when ᶜĀshūr is released from jail, they give him a hero's welcome, while Darwīsh's gang disappears into thin air. Thus ᶜĀshūr finds himself the unrivalled *futuwwa* of the *ḥāra*. The following extract is the closing paragraph of the story of ᶜĀshūr al-Nājī, the first tale of *Harafish*. I quote it at length because it sums up clearly the essence of what Mahfouz believes good government should be founded upon:

> As the *ḥarāfīsh* expected, ᶜĀshūr established his *fatwana* [strong man's rule] on principles hitherto unknown. He went back to his original job [as cart-driver] and basement flat. He also obliged his men to earn their living by the sweat of their brow, thereby stamping out *baltaga* [living off other people's earnings] once and for all. He levied *itāwa* [protection money] only on the notables and well-to-do in order to spend it on the poor and disabled. He conquered the *futuwwas* of neighbouring *ḥāras*, thereby bringing to our *ḥāra* a respect it had never enjoyed before,

> and so it came to be highly regarded beyond its area as much as it enjoyed internally justice, dignity and security.
> (p. 85)

If we translate mythical language into political language rendering government for *fatwana*, exploitative capitalism for *baltaga*, taxation for *itāwa*, nation for *ḥāra* and neighbouring nations for the other *ḥāras*, then we will have a pretty good, if somewhat simplistic, view of Mahfouz's conditions for the achievement of social harmony as well as harmony among nations.

At 60 but unruffled by his years, still loved and feared and in total control of a happy *ḥāra*, ᶜĀshūr disappears unaccountably. One day he simply does not return from his habitual nocturnal vigil outside the *takiyya*. Already adored by the *ḥarāfīsh* as a hero and a saint, his mysterious disappearance propels him on to an even higher plane of sanctity. After the initial shock, the frantic search and desperate wait, hope of ᶜĀshūr's return is given up and a physical contest for the *fatwana* over the *ḥāra* is won by his youthful son, Shams al-Dīn, whose reign, despite the temptations he is subjected to, continues along the just lines founded by his father. On Shams al-Dīn's death his son Sulaymān takes over unchallenged. For a few years he follows in the footsteps of his father and grandfather, leading a poor and righteous life and putting *fatwana* in the service of the people. Then his eye is caught by the beauty of a wealthy man's daughter. The notables of the *ḥāra* see it as their chance. The girl is offered to him in marriage. Although Sulaymān offers no concessions at the beginning, a *de facto* alliance is effected between the soldiery and the plutocracy of the *ḥāra*. It is only a matter of time before Sulaymān gives up his humble job as cart-driver and gives in to a luxurious lifestyle made possible by his wife's rich family. Gradually the interests of the *ḥarāfīsh* are neglected and Sulaymān becomes the *futuwwa* of the wealthy. His link with the noble heritage of his forebears is severed and his children by his new wife grow up to be successful middle-class merchants. As he indulges in a life of leisure and pleasure, Sulaymān gradually loses his health and fitness (essential assets for a *futuwwa*). He ends up a bedridden paralytic, the wreck of a one-time mighty man. One of his henchmen soon declares himself *futuwwa*. Thus the Nājīs lose the *fatwana* for the first time in three generations and the *ḥāra* enters into an age of darkness not unlike its 'pre-diluvian' days. The divine flame once lit by ᶜĀshūr and maintained by Shams al-Dīn is extinguished.

The above events occupy three of the ten tales of the novel. The rest of the tales are variations on the same theme tracing the history of al-Nājī family from one generation to another and the history of *fatwana* in the *ḥāra*. *Fatwana* is no longer a monopoly of the Nājīs, but it makes no difference any more to the *ḥarāfīsh* who is *futuwwa*, for now the descendants of the great ᶜĀshūr can be as corrupt and tyrannical as any other *futuwwa*. Although the pattern of the book depends on repetition, there is enough variation to preclude tedium and a sense of suspense is maintained, unlike the case in *Children of Gebelawi* where suspense is pre-empted by the external framework of reference.

As we move from tale to tale and from generation to generation, Mahfouz succeeds in conveying a sense of the passage of time through sustained reference in highly poetic language, within and across tales, to the movement of time, the sequence of seasons, time's chariot, the ageing process, the rising and setting of the sun, the changes of climate, the changes of heart, the changes of fortune and the mutability of all things. All this exercises a cumulative but imperceptible effect on us, so that by the time we come to the end of the book we are left with the vague feeling that we have been reading the full story of time and man. The tragedy of humanity through the ages is emphasized by a sense of the immutability of place in the novel. Thus, although the novel spans some sixteen generations on the realistic level (or man's time from Adam till now if we consider the symbolic level), the *ḥāra* evinces little or no physical change throughout, nor do the power structure and the relationship between rich and poor and strong and weak. If anything this is an indictment of the human experience for its ethical failure despite all the material progress it may boast (this is probably why all signs of such progress are absent from the description of life in the *ḥāra* in spite of the huge time span).

Time indeed is of the essence in *Harafish*; it is not there only as the background against which the flux of human misery unfolds. Time itself, with its ultimate manifestation as death, is at the very core of the human tragedy. This of course is a theme that Mahfouz has explored before and after *Harafish*. Nevertheless, one of his most haunting treatments of the subject remains that in the seventh tale of *Harafish*, entitled 'His Majesty Jalāl'. Jalāl is a late descendant of ᶜĀshūr al-Nājī and one of the most powerful and evil *futuwwas* to have controlled the *ḥāra*. His tragedy begins in his boyhood when he witnesses his beautiful and adored mother's head smashed to pieces by a jealous ex-husband of hers. He never forgets the scene or learns to live with its consequences. He grows up with the agonizing questions, 'Why do days not go back as they go forward? Why do we lose what we love and suffer what we hate? Why do things submit to irrevocable ordainments?' (p. 383). One day he puts the question to his teacher at the *kuttāb* or Qur'ān School, 'Why do we die?' he asks. 'It is God's wisdom', replies the Shaykh. 'But *why*?' insists Jalāl. And this time he gets a flogging for an answer (p. 387).

As he advances in his teens he falls in love with Qamar, the daughter of a rich branch of the family. The girl reciprocates his love but the family stands in the way. In the end, however, they succumb to the will of the lovers. The girl becomes the centre of Jalāl's existence and for once he seems on the point of reaching reconciliation with life. Then in the midst of their preparations for the wedding, Qamar is taken ill. Within days 'things submit again to the irrevocable ordainments': death snatches Jalāl's bride. With her Jalāl's soul dies its final death, though he continues to live for many years. In his forlorn state he comes to define death as 'the only truth' and also as the only enemy. He condemns people because 'they sanctified death and worshipped it, thereby encouraging it until it turned into an immortal truth' (p. 404). Sitting in front of the *takiyya* one night he wonders what Qamar looked like in her grave:

> A swollen waterskin giving off foul smell floating in toxic liquids where worms dance. Do not mourn her who was quick to acknowledge defeat! She who did not keep her promise. She who showed no respect for love. She who did not cling to life and opened her chest unto death. We live or die according to our will. How ugly victims are! Advocates of defeat! Those who cheer that death is the end of everything living. That it is the truth. They make death with their weakness and their illusions. We are immortal and only die through treachery and weakness.
>
> (p. 405)

Armed with this vision and his Herculean build, Jalāl does not find it difficult to conquer the existing *futuwwa* and restore *fatwana* to the Nājī family. Soon his power extends unchallenged over his own *ḥāra* and all the neighbouring ones. For a while the hopes of the *ḥarāfīsh* stir, as do the fears of the well-to-do. But nothing is further from Jalāl's mind than the suffering of the *ḥāra*. His thoughts are focused on the ancestral grave awaiting him, notwithstanding the glory and the wealth and the indomitable strength. Overwhelmed with his existential despair, he allows the social cause to recede into insignificance. When told that people are wondering when he will set about restoring justice to the *ḥāra*, he dismisses the matter scornfully: 'Why don't they give in to hunger as they give in to death?' he asks (p. 420). Despite his naturally ascetic temperament, he indulges in the accumulation of wealth and all things worldly 'as if he were barricading himself against death' (p. 412). And all the time he is haunted by the images of his mother's smashed head and his bride's lifeless face. In his obsessive search for a means of fighting death, he obtains an expensive recipe from the herbalist of the *ḥāra* which, in conjunction with moderation in food, drink and sex, should help him prolong his youth and strength. But this is not good enough for him: immortality is his quest. That, he is told, is an aspiration that no believer should entertain as it incurs eternal damnation and is only possible through 'twinning with the devil' (pp. 422–3).

For Jalāl nothing is more damnable than death. Like Faustus in German legend, he accepts the price of mutiny against the human lot. The price of the medium who would effect the twinning process includes Jalāl's largest apartment block, the construction in the *ḥāra* of a grotesque ten-storey-high minaret without a mosque and, as an additional condition, total seclusion for a year, on the last day of which the twinning was to take effect, heralding life without end. Jalāl accepts and endures heroically his solitary confinement for a whole year. On the last day, as the appointed moment approaches, he

> stands naked in front of an open window and welcomes the sunshine washed in the wetness of winter. . . . He feels drunk with a new spirit filling his breast. . . . He has conquered time, having confronted it face to face for so long and without a companion. He shall not fear it any

> more. Let it threaten others with its ill-fated passage! He shall know no wrinkles, no greying of the hair and no weakening of the bones. His soul shall not betray him. Nor shall he be borne in a coffin or laid in a grave. This solid body shall not decompose. It shall not turn into dust. And he shall not taste of the sorrow of departing.
>
> (p. 431)

Jalāl rejoins the world and establishes himself anew as the supreme master of the *ḥāra* and an invincible force beyond its borders. One night he pays a secret visit to the monstrous, red minaret, standing in the midst of a wasteland and towering above everything in the *ḥāra*:

> He climbed its staircase step by step until he reached the top balcony. He defied the biting cold of winter to which the whole universe had surrendered. He raised his head to the plethora of stars keeping vigil above him. Thousands of eyes twinkled high above, while everything below was sunk in the darkness. It might be that he did not climb but that he grew in stature as he should. He must always rise and rise. Purity was only possible through rising. At the pinnacle he would hearken to the language of the planets, the whispers of space and the cravings of power and eternity, away from plaintive moans and foul odours. At this minute the *takiyya* sang its songs of everlasting life; Truth unveiled scores of its hidden faces; and the Unknown laid bare its store of fates. From this balcony he would review the passing trail of generations and prepare a role for each one. Here he could join once and for all the family of heavenly bodies.
>
> (pp. 435–6)

In his description of Jalāl's thoughts in this and the preceding passage, and indeed throughout this amazing tale, Mahfouz dramatizes mankind's most haunting dreams over the centuries, of power, continued life and the solution of the mysteries of existence. In his contempt for the weak and indifference to their suffering, he smacks of Nietzsche's superman who rises above good and evil. He also echoes the great dictators of history in their contempt for human life and pain (a comparative study with Albert Camus' *Caligula* should prove most rewarding).[37]

His ambition is lofty and admirable but his means are selfish and cruel. Mahfouz therefore preserves a horrid end for him to show that he is far from being his ideal of the evolutionary goal of mankind. Nevertheless, he is portrayed as a full tragic hero who commands our sympathy and respect for his stand against time and death and his readiness to pay the price for defying such fearful enemies.

Armoured with his illusion of eternal life, Jalāl drops all his previous moderation and inhibitions. He begins to eat and drink and smoke and fornicate excessively. His lust for life stops at no boundary. Zīnāt, his erstwhile one and only mistress, who loved him madly and had dreamt of bringing him round to marrying her, watches his transformation and the ebbing away of his fondness for her with growing jealousy and uncomprehending despair. Eventually she poisons him. He dies a painful death, incredulous until the end that his powerful foe had triumphed over him notwithstanding. Maddened by the fire in his stomach, he staggers out of the house into the dark sleeping *ḥāra*. He stumbles into the donkey-trough and tries to extinguish the internal blaze by drinking from it. Later under torchlight the gigantic body of what was once the mighty and proud Jalāl was found in a heap at the trough, covered in hay and dung. There was eternity for the beholder! As always, death laughed last.

Since the now myth-enshrouded days of ᶜĀshūr al-Nājī and his son Shams al-Dīn, the down-trodden *ḥarāfīsh* have seen no justice and known no happiness. Was there no way then out of this terrible saga that the *ḥāra* had endured generation out, generation in? The answer to this question occurs in 'Mulberries and Bludgeons', the tenth and final tale of *Harafish*. The *ḥāra* is living through one of its usual dark ages, and in a poor, one-parent family descended from the great ᶜĀshūr al-Nājī, the youngest of three sons is called ᶜĀshūr too (not in vain as we shall see). From an early age he works as shepherd. He grows up to be a strong man, though 'his pleasant manner tended to hide his strength from the eyes of observers' (p. 519). From an early age he is also attracted to the *takiyya* with its mysterious and inspiring songs and to the stories of the exploits of his great ancestor and namesake. ᶜĀshūr's eldest brother drifts away into a world of crime and unlawful wealth and when he is found out, he commits suicide. The ruling *futuwwa* banishes the whole family from the *ḥāra* as a punishment for crimes they did not commit. Soon the second brother drifts away too. Thus only ᶜĀshūr and his mother remain together. Exiled and homeless, ᶜĀshūr decides to live with his mother in the cemetery until the conditions are right to go back.

In his exile he has ample time to contemplate his predicament and that of the *ḥāra*. He comes to the conclusion that 'the worst weaknesses of mankind are their love of money and their love of power' (p. 550). He also thinks hard about why the golden age created by his great ancestor suffered a setback after his death and has never been restored. Through his long meditations in the *khalā'*, his nocturnal vigils by the *takiyya* and a visit in his sleep from his spiritual mentor, he formulates a vision of the answer and the way. Spurred by 'the ever-burning ember in his chest', he sets about putting it into action (p. 551). ᶜĀshūr al-Nājī, his grandfather, was a strong man with a vision and a great heart, he said to himself. He put his strength in the service of the *ḥarāfīsh* and achieved justice in the *ḥāra*, but such justice was a free gift to the people and only depended on the good will of the giver. That was why it did not survive its founder. ᶜĀshūr II (as we might call him) was therefore to approach matters differently. The *ḥarāfīsh* must earn justice for themselves. He could help by providing initiative and strong leadership, but he would not fight their battle for them while they sat back and watched. Thus he begins to proselytize among them and prepare them for the day of confrontation. He teaches them that they should trust nobody, not even him, but only themselves. And he tells them of a strange dream in which he 'saw them carrying bludgeons' (the traditional weapon of *futuwwas* and their men) (pp. 554–5). At the right moment, ᶜĀshūr II ends his exile and leads the *ḥarāfīsh* into battle. Their numerical superiority under the inspiring leadership of ᶜĀshūr II soon brings them victory over their once fearful oppressors. Established as unrivalled *futuwwa* of the *ḥāra*, ᶜĀshūr II does not, however, lose sight of his prime objective: that of making the *ḥarāfīsh* masters of their destiny, and protecting them against setbacks. Thus he ordains that they should train their children in the arts of *fatwana*, 'so that no rascal or adventurer should one day find it possible to dominate them' (p. 564).

Popular revolution then is the answer to oppression offered by Mahfouz. This is perfectly understandable, seen in the context of his apotheosis of Egypt's only popular revolution in its contemporary history (the 1919 revolution) and, conversely, his bitter disillusionment with its later militarily-led, superimposed coup/revolution of 1952. Uncharacteristically in the work of Mahfouz, *Harafish* has a happy, positive ending, as we have seen. It embodies what was hinted at, at the end of *Children of Gebelawi*. There we were left with the vague impression that some day Ḥanash would return with the magical science book and the runaway youths of the *ḥāra* to restore Gebelawi's estate to its legitimate owners. In *Harafish* this is exactly what ᶜĀshūr II does. There is no mention of science in *Harafish*, true. But then is not the organization of society on sound, just and workable principles, as ᶜĀshūr II has organized it, the manifestation of a scientific spirit? Both *Children of Gebelawi* and *Harafish* would seem thus to uphold the ideal of popular revolution.[38]

Points of comparison and contrast with *Children of Gebelawi* constantly emerge from a discussion of *Harafish*. Nor should we end this section without reference to another such point. This concerns the character of ᶜĀshūr II whom the discerning reader will recognize to be inspired by the historical figure of the prophet Muḥammad. Like him, he starts his working life as a shepherd. Muḥammad was an orphan; ᶜĀshūr loses his father at the age of 6 (p. 514). Muḥammad was brought up by a wet-nurse called Ḥalīma al-Saᶜdiyya; ᶜĀshūr's mother is given the name Ḥalīma al-Baraka. ᶜĀshūr is described as enamoured of the *takiyya*, the *khalā*' and the beauty of women (p. 531), and as combining a strong build and a good temperament (p. 519), all of which are attributes that would fit the Prophet too. In addition, ᶜĀshūr's exile period in the cemetery followed by his victorious return to the *ḥāra* and his demolition of the obscene red minaret, built by Jalāl, would easily parallel Muḥammad's forced *hijra* to Madīna and later triumphant return to Makka and his destruction of the idols at the Kaᶜba. All this is on the level of factual detail; the thematic similarities between the objectives and achievements of the two characters are too obvious to need comment. ᶜĀshūr II, then, is Mahfouz's second attempt at portraying the Prophet of Islam in fiction. (His first of course was the character of Qāsim in *Children of Gebelawi*). Artistically, the basic difference between the two portrayals is that ᶜĀshūr's has a life of its own and fits snugly in the larger structure of the book, whereas Qāsim's character draws what artificial life it possesses from its historical model. It is a mark of the extent of Mahfouz's artistic achievement in the second portrayal that the religious conservatives and fundamentalists who had protested so strongly at the representation of Muḥammad and other sacred figures in *Children of Gebelawi* did not so much as mention *Harafish* in this connection: so subtle and independent of its historical model is the portrayal that it completely escaped the notice of those non-literary eyes!

No discussion of *Harafish* would be complete without special attention to the *takiyya* – a prominent motif in the novel and a great Mahfuzian symbol in this as in other works. The *takiyya*, as we have seen, made its first, major appearance in the novelist's work in *Fountain and Tomb*, a work which pre-dated *Harafish* by only two years. Mahfouz had obviously not quite escaped the incantatory power of this haunting symbol. It retains, however, basically, the same symbolic value it had been given in *Fountain and Tomb*. It is an embodiment of man's age-old yearning for Heaven, the hereafter, the supernatural, the metaphysical, the timeless, the infinite, the spiritual, the ideal, the absolute – or God, for the lack of a better and all-encompassing word. A focal point for the spiritual aspirations of the *ḥāra*-dwellers, as well as the source of inspiration for ᶜĀshūr al-Nājī and ᶜĀshūr II, it must be remembered that it was also there, at the *takiyya*, that Jalāl received the revelatory impulse that led him on his destructive quest for power and eternity. This would appear to mean that the *takiyya* is what man makes of it. It is only the embodiment of a mystical yearning – it has no existence outside the soul of man. This interpretation is strengthened by the fact that nobody ever succeeds in establishing any form of communication with the *takiyya* and its dervish inhabitants. The gates are always closed and no one is ever let in or out. Even most catastrophic events, like plagues and famines, seem to pass unnoticed by the *takiyya* in its eternal indifference to the *ḥāra* (pp. 53, 66–7, 499). In the words of Shams al-Dīn, frustrated at the impervious silence of the *takiyya*: 'it is a witness who gives no testimony' (p. 87). Another alienating factor about the *takiyya* is the songs sung by the dervishes and overheard by outsiders. They are captivating and comforting but they are sung in a foreign language, incomprehensible to the *ḥāra*, adding yet more to the general sense of mystery and inaccessibility besetting the *takiyya*. Mahfouz has done extremely well for his purpose to quote those Persian *ṣūfī* verses and scatter them all over the narrative, leaving them in their original tongue, as baffling to the Arab reader as they are to the people of the *ḥāra* in the book.

If the *takiyya* is a symbol of man's highest ideals, then the *qabw* or vault is another symbol for his lowest instincts. Like the *takiyya*, it is a recurrent motif in the novel, always described as dark and filthy, a place for crime and illicit sex, and the abode of jinn and devils.[39] Another motif of evil which joins the *qabw*, two-thirds through the book, is the red mosqueless minaret, built by Jalāl in his mad search for eternity. It survives his ignominious death for a long time: a token, in its crude phallic pride, of man's vanity and ultimate folly.

On the day of the demolition of this evil monstrosity at the behest of ᶜĀshūr II, the *ḥāra* celebrates boisterously well into the night. After midnight, ᶜĀshūr II makes his way to the open space in front of the *takiyya* 'to confer with himself under the starlit sky and within earshot of the songs' (pp. 566–7). Then the impossible comes to pass:

> He squatted on the ground, giving in to a sense of contentment and a gentle breeze. It was one of those rare moments when life shed its veil to reveal the purity of its radiance. Nothing to complain of in body or soul, time or space. It was as if the mysterious songs were giving away their secrets in a thousand tongues – as if he now understood why for so long they had sung in an exotic tongue and kept their doors closed. Through the darkness wafted a creaking sound. Stunned, he gazed at the enormous gate. He saw it open smoothly and steadily. Out of it approached the shadowy figure of a dervish – an embodiment of night's breath. He leaned towards him. 'Get ready with your pipes and drums!' he said. 'Tomorrow the Grand Shaykh will leave his cloister and march through the *ḥāra* in a halo of light. A bludgeon and a mulberry will he give unto each man. Get ready with your pipes and drums!'
>
> (p. 567)

This of course is only an inner vision (Mahfouz uses the word *ru'ya* (vision) to refer to the experience in the last paragraph of the novel). This is as it should be, since all communications between the *takiyya* and those attracted to it have been by means of inner vision or revelation. Nevertheless, it is a unique vision, not hitherto experienced by any of the most faithful devotees of the *takiyya*, not even the great ᶜĀshūr al-Nājī himself. For the first time in its 'history', the *takiyya* opened its haughty, silent doors to a mortal of the *ḥāra* and deigned to speak to him. What was more, a 'walkabout' by the Grand Shaykh himself was promised. This is nothing short of a meeting of the eternal and the temporal. This is the way to eternity. This is the path which Jalāl in his selfishness had been blinded to. Only a humanity that has achieved a total and lasting justice can aspire to eternity, can merge into a timeless union with the *takiyya*. Only then would the Grand Shaykh of the *takiyya* (or Gebelawi of the Great House) come out and give each man a mulberry (his share of the estate) and a bludgeon to defend it with for ever. Only then would God descend to Earth, or Man climb to Heaven, for these are but paradoxically antonymous words with identical denotations. In *Harafish* Mahfouz has created a myth which extends far back into humanity's unrecollected history and far forward into its unforeseeable (but dreamt-of) future. This distant future, in which man's achievement of immortality (once he has achieved justice on earth) is not ruled out, is spelt out by Mahfouz elsewhere. He has argued with reference to *Children of Gebelawi* that 'solving social evils by means of socialism will free mankind to address its prime tragedy, which is mortality'.[40] It appears that ᶜĀshūr II's final vision of a direct communion with the *takiyya* is an intimation of the fulfilment of the dream of immortality. ᶜĀshūr II rather than Jalāl represents Mahfouz's ideal of the superman.

NIGHTS OF THE THOUSAND NIGHTS[41]

Nights (1982) will probably be remembered as Mahfouz's last major novel. Together with *Harafish*, it represents the peak of his episodic period. Rather than create his own myth to portray his vision of the human condition as he did in *Harafish*, here he chooses to adapt for the same purpose one of the most imaginative products of the human mind, namely *The Arabian Nights*. The author chooses some thirteen unconnected tales from *The Arabian Nights* (itself a work of episodic form as readers will recognize) and renders them afresh through the techniques of modernism (symbolism, recurrent motifs, stream of consciousness, and even a kind of magical realism).[42] Tales originally independent of each other are so manipulated that they join up in a narrative continuum. Characters continue to operate across tales and meet up with other characters, unlike in the original, while completely new characters and events are invented and incorporated in the book to serve the novelist's goals. All these technical, unity-forging factors are further strengthened by the work's thematic cohesion, as another Mahfuzian probing of the problems of social evil, time, and the human relationship with the absolute. *Harafish*, as we have seen, was placed in Mahfouz's own timeless mythical setting of the *ḥāra*. *Nights* too is set in the ahistorical mythical setting of *The Arabian Nights*. The effect here, as there, is a widening of the scope of the author's vision beyond historical and geographic borders. Myth, in addition, probably works better on the reader's subconscious than a realistic representation of reality.

The question asked in *Harafish* of why evil existed and how it could be eradicated is posed again here with the stress this time laid on the issue of the extent of the individual's responsibility for evil in his personal conduct as well as in the social environment. In other words: Is Evil a supernatural force able to manipulate man's will? (Does Satan exist? to put it bluntly.) Or is it a purely human phenomenon engendered by man's lust for power and wealth? In the original *Arabian Nights*, teeming as it is with manifestations of the supernatural, evil would seem to have a very positive existence outside man, a fact which would tend to reduce the latter's responsibility for evil-doing. Not so, however, in Mahfouz's *Nights*, even though the jinn play a central role there. (There are two good jinn and two bad ones, respectively influencing his characters to do good or evil.) As we read on, it soon transpires, however, that Mahfouz's jinn are only used to externalize human impulses of good and evil. Evil, then, according to the author is not supernatural, and man is responsible for his deeds and for putting right the evil he sees around him until justice is established on earth.

This philosophy is substantiated in the story of 'Ṣanᶜān al-Jammālī'. Ṣanᶜān is visited by the good afreet, Qumqām, who orders him to murder the corrupt governor of the district.

Ṣanᶜān, a successful merchant, is torn between the instinct of self-preservation and the impulse to succumb to the pressure of the afreet, which could involve the sacrifice of his life. When he finally makes up his mind and kills the governor, Qumqām, contrary to his expectations, leaves him in the lurch. Qumqām congratulates Ṣanᶜān on saving his people from tyranny. But Ṣanᶜān, feeling cheated, flares up at him: 'Who said I was responsible for the people?' To which the wise afreet replies: 'It is a public responsibility that no man should renounce' (p. 34). This sums up Mahfouz's view of the individual's social responsibility.[43] The afreet's role here is to dramatize Ṣanᶜān's internal conflict. One technique that the novelist uses to imply that the jinn are only inner visions is the fact that they are only seen and heard by the person concerned, even when they appear to him while in the company of others.[44] (Ṣanᶜān's story calls to the mind the history of Joan of Arc: she too saw visions and heard voices which motivated her to act heroically, only to deliver her to final loneliness and death at the stake.)

This lesson is reiterated in the novel, tale after tale. Thus in the story of 'Jamaṣa al-Bulṭī', his good jinni refuses again to help him make a choice. He only repeats to him untiringly, 'You have mind, will and soul' (p. 50).[45] Finally, when Jamaṣa, the chief of police himself, makes up his mind and murders the despotic governor (as Ṣanᶜān did in the previous tale), he is tried, sentenced and executed. Nevertheless, he is helped back to life by his jinni with a new face and a new name. From now on Jamaṣa, who survives in all the tales and is given the last lines of the book, becomes an indomitable and almost ubiquitous power of good always able to interfere at the critical moment and save those worthy of saving: an embodiment, as it were, of what we call 'providence'. It is as if Mahfouz wanted to say that the spirit of right and heroism was an omnipresent human spirit that never dies. This or that individual manifestation of it might die, but it lives on in the species, renewing itself from generation to generation. This of course is nothing but Mahfouz's familiar argument about individual time and collective evolutionary time.[46]

In addition to the above the jinn are assigned another symbolic role in *Nights*. In the course of this book we have seen how important the part played by fate or coincidence in the work of Mahfouz is. Some critics tend to see this as a structural deficiency and interference with logical sequence. While this may be true of his very early works, especially the historical novels, it is a mistake to fail to see that as the novelist developed, fate or coincidence came to represent an essential part of his philosophy of life. Although Mahfouz believes, as we have seen, in human volition and responsibility for action, his work shows that he recognizes that the interaction of time and space may equally obstruct and frustrate the human will. The result of the space–time interaction is what we term fate or coincidence. The author's philosophy is best summed up in these wise words from his *Respected Sir*:

> A man in his perplexity may stumble on situations rich with the prospect of happiness in unpropitious circumstances. The place, for instance, may be right but the time wrong: or vice versa. All this confirmed that happiness exists, but that tracks leading to it may not always be smooth. And from the interplay of time and place came either good fortune or absurdity.[47]

This is exactly the second role assigned to the jinn in the novel. They are the embodiment of fate, that mysterious phenomenon which can wreak havoc on men's designs, or alternatively bring them untold happiness (in which case we prefer to call it 'providence') quite independently of their actions. This part is played by the jinn throughout the novel but in a specially prominent way in the tale of 'Nūr al-Dīn and Dunyāzād'. Nūr al-Dīn is an honest and handsome but poor young man, while the beautiful Dunyāzād is placed at the other end of the social scale; she is King Shahrayār's sister-in-law and the daughter of his vizier. In the normal course of things the lives of two such persons are very unlikely to converge. However, the frivolity of two afreets brings them together one night in a dream-like fashion as bride and groom. In the morning they wake up, each in his own bed (and separate world) recollecting at first what they thought was a happy dream only to discover moments later through physical evidence that it had in fact been a reality. They each fall into an abyss of agonized bewilderment and longing for the unknown lover. The two wicked afreets who played the trick on them comment amusedly that 'though they [the two lovers] live in the same city, a gap separates them as wide as that separating earth from heaven' (p. 92). Nūr al-Dīn roams the streets of the city peering hard at women's veiled faces, desperately searching for that of his unknown beloved:

> Could his beloved be one of them?[48] She existed at any rate. No doubt about that. She existed in some *place* and at this very *time*. . . .[49] A dream like that could not just vanish as if it had never been. A yearning so powerful could not flame inside him without cause or purpose.[50]
>
> (p. 99)

The interaction of space and time is not, however, in Mahfouz's world necessarily wholly negative or hostile to mankind. This is demonstrated here when the two lovers are finally united through the good offices of another symbolic supernatural force, viz. that of Jamaṣa al-Bulṭī.

Central to *Nights* and the treatment of the theme of evil in it is the character of the *ṣūfī* or mystic, Shaykh ᶜAbdullāh al-Balkhī. The *ṣūfī* as a character type with a symbolic role was introduced for the first time in Mahfouz's *The Thief and the Dogs*.[51] In works like *Fountain and Tomb* and *Harafish*, the role of the *ṣūfī* was given to the *takiyya*, as has been shown. In *Nights*, however, the *ṣūfī* of *The Thief and the Dogs* is reincarnated in the form of Shaykh Balkhī. In the author's work generally, the *ṣūfī* character type is used to probe in symbolic terms the role of the absolute in the life of both individual and society.

Shaykh Balkhī, as portrayed by Mahfouz, is a paragon of wisdom and purity of spirit. He is above human wishes and beyond joy and sorrow as his words show: 'he who rejoices in what is transient will be sorry when it passes away. All is vain save the worship [of God]' (p. 197). The social context in which this *ṣūfī* lives is that of a city whose tyrannical king rapes and beheads a new girl every day, while his deputies and the rich of the city plunder and repress its impoverished people. But Shaykh Balkhī is untouched by all this. He creates for himself a paradise of the mind and shelters there from the evil reality. As he puts it to one of his disciples:

> Blessed is he who has turned his heart from objects to the God of all objects. The world does not cross my mind. How can the world cross the mind of one who has known the Maker of the world?
>
> (p. 198)

Unlike Ṣanᶜān al-Jammālī and Jamaṣa al-Bulṭī, Shaykh Balkhī chooses to escape from, rather than confront, evil. And while he appears to achieve salvation, it remains a personal, haughty salvation with little significance or value for anyone else. His is an escapist route, a heightened form of the solipsist example, consistently condemned by Mahfouz.[52] Nor is he shown to have accomplished total immunity from the impact of reality, as his daughter is widowed by the wrongful execution of her husband for a crime he had not committed. The position of the *ṣūfī* or religious escapist in relation to society is aptly described by Fāḍil Ṣanᶜān (the revolutionary type of the book): 'Worshippers save themselves, whereas fighters save the people' (p. 196).[53]

This Fāḍil Ṣanᶜān, who figures secondarily in most of the book's tales until he assumes protagonist status in the tale of 'The Invisible Hat' is Mahfouz's character type for the revolutionary hero gone astray. Fāḍil Ṣanᶜān is the son of Ṣanᶜān al-Jammālī, whose story was discussed above. Reduced with his family to a life of poverty, after the execution of his father and seizure of his estate, Ṣanᶜān grows up to hate the regime that has so wronged him.[54] He joins an underground opposition group in the belief that only 'the sword' can put right corruption. Fāḍil leads the usual life of an active revolutionary, suffering endlessly the cycle of arrest, torture and release. One day, however, he is visited by a jinni who makes him a present of the 'invisible hat' which hides its wearer from view. The hat of course is a means of absolute power – of the ability to act with impunity. The whole situation becomes a metaphor for the revolutionary's attainment of government with sole and boundless authority. The jinni stipulates that Fāḍil should use the hat in any way he wishes except for actions 'dictated by conscience' (p. 213). Rather than reject the hat under such a condition (quite the opposite of what he has been struggling for), Fāḍil accepts it. In other words the revolutionary surrenders to the temptation of power. Soon enough he is involved in an escalating series of crimes, first with harmless intentions, then intentions cease to matter. As his crimes acquire a momentum of their own, Fāḍil ends as a captive rather than master of his power – doomed if he stops, doomed if he goes on. Thus Fāḍil's story becomes not only a metaphor for the revolutionary corrupted by power,[55] but also one for the total isolation of the absolute ruler. Mahfouz sums up beautifully the siege mentality at the pinnacle of power:

> Fāḍil Ṣanᶜān realized that he was a dead man. He could not live any longer except beneath the hat – an accursed soul drifting in the dark, capable only of frivolous and wicked actions, and forbidden to repent or do good. He had become a devil. And like the devil he was foredoomed. (p. 222)

In this state of utter loss, all that is left him is, as his jinni tells him, to amuse himself every day 'with an event to shock the people' (p. 223).

The next tale in the novel is that of 'Maᶜrūf the Shoemaker'. We do not have to read far before we begin to realize that it is there as a foil to Ṣanᶜān's story. One evening Maᶜrūf, while sitting in the café, claims (falsely) that he has found King Solomon's ring. His friends call his bluff and ask him to prove it by performing a miracle. Maᶜrūf persists in his joke and orders the jinni-servant of the ring (which he did not have) to raise him up to the sky. To everybody's horror, not least Maᶜrūf's own, he begins to levitate until he disappears into the upper darkness. After a while he descends safely back to the spot where he had been sitting in the café. Though stunned by the experience, he manages to control his surprise and keep up the pretence that he had the ring. Later, try as he may, he is not able to summon up that mysterious force again. What has happened is quite enough, however, to establish him as the most powerful man in the city. Everyone is in awe of him from King Shahrayār downwards. He exploits the situation by taking money from the wealthy to better the condition of the poor, and by watching over the authorities to make sure that the values of honesty and fairness are observed. Having established justice and security in this way, Maᶜrūf naturally becomes the idol of the poor. Things do not, however, go on in this ideal way. One day Maᶜrūf is visited in his palace by an impressive-looking man who turns out to be the very jinni who performed the café miracle on his behalf. The evil jinni instructs him to murder Shaykh Balkhī and ᶜAbdullāh al-Majnūn (i.e. Jamaṣa al-Bulṭī in his latest incarnation) – the two most powerful forces of good in the city. The price of refusal, Maᶜrūf is told, is his betrayal to the authorities. A good man by nature, Maᶜrūf declines. But another surprise is in attendance when he is arrested. The people he has served and brought dignity and welfare to, rise up *en masse* to save him.[56] Thus, rather than face the executioner's sword, Ma^{c}rūf is appointed governor of the district. Unlike Fāḍil Ṣan^{c}ān in the previous tale, whose authority was founded on the use of force, Ma^{c}rūf here draws democratic legitimacy from the love of the masses, who actually place him in office. One must wonder whether Mahfouz has meant Fāḍil's story as a model of Nasser's authoritarian regime (which came to power by a coup, and of which the author has always been critical), while presenting Ma^{c}rūf's story, on the other hand, as a model of the 1919 popular revolution, which democratically brought to power Sa^{c}d Zaghlūl, the author's most revered national hero of modern Egypt.

I have referred at the beginning of this discussion to some of the techniques used by Mahfouz to forge these disparate tales into a united whole that bears clearly the unmistakable Mahfuzian stamp. The most unifying technique he uses, however, is one that he did not have to invent. He simply uses the technique employed in his ancient source. By this I mean the technique of the frame-story of Shahrazād and Shahrayār which holds the whole of *The Arabian Nights* together. We must note, however, that while in the original work the relationship between the frame-story and the rest of the tales remains a mechanical one, in Mahfouz's *Nights* it becomes organic, so that all the stories are both fused together and fused with the frame-story. It is this fact which makes the book a novel, unlike its original source.

The novel begins where *The Arabian Nights* stopped. In other words, it is an attempt at portraying the conditions of Shahrayār, Shahrazād and their subjects after the end of the original frame-story, i.e. after Shahrazād had finished telling her last story, fathered the king's children and earned his pardon.[57] The massacre of the virgins has now been over for some time and Shahrayār's lust for blood has abated and given place to a pensive mood. He is still, however, an unhappy man and his kingdom is a haven for injustice and corruption. Shahrazād is equally unhappy. Her marriage to him had been an act of self-sacrifice to stop the flow of blood. She does not love him: 'I smell blood whenever he gets near me', she tells her father (p. 8). Mahfouz indeed draws Shahrayār's character with great care, showing in a gradual and convincing fashion his development from a bloodthirsty tyrant to a just ruler and finally a bewildered man who renounces power and sets out on a journey in search of the meaning of existence – a development which appears to reflect that of mankind down the ages from early primitivism to the complexity of twentieth-century consciousness.[58] The moment of truth in Shahrayār's life arrives as he listens to Sindbād's account of his amazing voyages. In his retelling of the adventures, the novelist stresses the lessons learnt rather than the strange happenings. Thus Shahrayār learns from Sindbād that man often 'takes illusion for reality'; 'that traditions represent the past and that some of the things of the past should be forgotten for ever'; and 'that man's spirit cannot live without freedom; for Heaven itself will avail man nothing if he loses his liberty' (pp. 247, 251). Shahrayār listens, all the time his humility increasing in proportion to his sense of wonder. By the time Sindbād comes to the end of his story, Shahrayār's vicarious suffering has reached a climax and the barrier between lived experience and conveyed experience is lifted. At this moment the truth is laid bare before his eyes and the full horror of his past life is recognized: the art of storytelling has exercised its cathartic effect.

After anagnorisis comes peripeteia. Shahrayār considers himself unfit to govern. He abdicates and 'wanders about in the land in search of salvation' (p. 256), ironically leaving behind a Shahrazād who now loves him and does not want him to go. Mahfouz sets aside the last tale of the book, 'The Weepers', for an account of Shahrayār's search. From the beginning Shahrayār realizes that he has to choose one of two paths: 'either to travel like Sindbād or to take the path leading to Shaykh Balkhī's house' (p. 260). Sindbād's path, as we have seen, is that of experience and knowledge, whereas Shaykh Balkhī's path is the one of renunciation and escape into the religious unknown. Shahrayār, needless to say, chooses Sindbād's path. His wanderings lead him to the Weeper's Rock by the river. The rock opens to him. He enters and the door shuts behind him. He is overwhelmed by the beauty of the place, which 'was bright without a light, cool without a window and redolent with the scent of roses without a garden' (p. 261). The description goes on deeper and deeper into the realm of fantasy until it becomes clear that Shahrayār has stepped into Heaven itself where there is only joy and timelessness. But alas! Shahrayār stumbles into a little golden door with a warning on it saying, 'Entry forbidden' – the one and only prohibition in that blissful eternity. One day Shahrayār's resolve weakens. He opens the door only to find himself back on earth. Thus the cycle of sin (motivated by the desire to know) and punishment is completed.[59] But we must note here a meaningful omission from the Biblical account: there is no snake, no evil and no woman. Shahrayār's fall is of his own making: responsibility for man's choices rests with no other force than himself, Mahfouz would have us believe. Shahrayār returns to earth, but his soul remains attached to Heaven – to the ideal world that he has seen with his mind's eye.

THE TRAVELS OF IBN FAṬṬŪMA

Published in 1983, *Travels* constitutes Mahfouz's last panoramic review of human history. Although a short novel of some 160 pages, the broadness of its scope puts it on a footing with works like *Children of Gebelawi* and *Harafish*. Like them, it is episodic in form, and like them too, its episodes represent progress in time. Time here, however, is not only that of the novel's action, but rather mankind's time from the dawn of organized society to the present day. For the 'travels' of the novel, as we shall see, are, on the allegorical level, made through time rather than space. In essence, the book is nothing but a conducted tour in social history.

Travels evokes the atmosphere and format of medieval Arabic *riḥla* or travel literature, particularly the journeys of Ibn Baṭṭūṭa, the illustrious fourteenth-century Arab traveller, as recorded in his famous book *Riḥlat Ibn Baṭṭūṭa*. Now Ibn Baṭṭūṭa's name is one that every Arab school-leaver would be familiar with, while Faṭṭūma is a pet name for Fāṭima, fairly common in Egypt and not without a humorous connotation. It would thus appear that by giving his novel the title *Riḥlat Ibn Faṭṭūma*, as it is called in Arabic, Mahfouz aimed at making the immediate association in the mind of the reader between his novel and the historic book, since Ibn Faṭṭūma and Ibn Baṭṭūṭa are of the same consonant-vowel pattern. It would also appear that the modern title is somewhat deliberately irreverent towards the classical work it invokes. From the title-page, then, we are in a frame of mind to conceive of *Riḥlat Ibn Faṭṭūma* as a parody of *Riḥlat Ibn Baṭṭūṭa*. The novel is given a further pretence to historical verisimilitude by a prefatory note saying that the text is 'reproduced from the manuscript written by the hand of Qindīl Muḥammad al-ᶜAnnābī, known as Ibn Faṭṭūma'.

It is divided into seven chapters covering six journeys, the first chapter being devoted to *al-Waṭan* or the homeland from which the journey begins. We know that *al-Waṭan* is part of *Dār al-Islām* (the Abode of Islam) but we do not know which part. Similarly, all the other six countries are given fictitious names, though we can tell from the context what they stand for. There is no specific reference to time either, though the context and the means of travel, etc., suggest that it is medieval times. Thus it appears that time and place are intentionally defaced. This, as we have seen, is an artistic technique previously used by the author to underline the universality of his themes – that of this book being the search for the ideal human society and the political/economic system capable of achieving it. *Travels* is thus a journey in the mind despite its spatio-temporal apparel; it is a bewildered itinerary among different socio-political systems rather than countries and peoples.

Ibn Baṭṭūṭa's original motive when he left Tangier in 1326 at the age of 21 was to perform the religious duty of the *ḥajj* (the pilgrimage to Makka).[60] In the event he went round most of the known world of his day and returned some twenty five years later. His fictitious descendant, however, knew his own mind better and had his journey planned out in the minutest detail before he set out. Nothing, though, was further from his mind than *ḥajj*. He is a man of an inquisitive mind, a perturbed soul and a socio-political awareness. Though himself well-to-do by inheritance, he is dissatisfied with *Dār al-Islām* because it is full of 'injustice, poverty and ignorance' (p. 11), and because there 'every action whether beautiful or ugly is initiated in the name of God the Compassionate, the Merciful' (p. 5). He thus curses *Dār al-Islām* as an 'abode of falsity' (p. 18), and is determined to travel in order 'to learn and bring back to my sick country the healing remedy' (p. 19). Having a more ambitious goal for his *riḥla* than his historic progenitor, Ibn Faṭṭūma meets with less success. He never returns to his homeland and the novel ends with the quest as yet unfinished. Within the allegorical framework of the book, with its very contemporary message, this ending is perhaps the only conceivable one. Apart from this political motive, Mahfouz also gives his traveller a personal motive to get away from his homeland (betrayal by his beloved and disappointment with his widowed mother who consented to marry again (p. 18)), but this is not significant because it is obviously there only for cosmetic reasons and is barely picked up again beyond the first chapter.

Ibn Faṭṭūma's first journey is to *Dār al-Mashriq* (the Abode of Sunrise). He adopts a pattern here to which he will adhere in all subsequent journeys. On arrival he rents a room in the city's inn for ten days, gathers some elementary information about the place from the innkeeper, then wanders on his own in the city and finally seeks a meeting with the city's *ḥakīm* or sage. This is obviously meant to parallel Ibn Baṭṭūṭa's famous eagerness to meet mystics and holy men in all the places he visited. But whereas Ibn Baṭṭūṭa revered his holy men and believed their wisdom and alleged miracles without question,[61] Ibn Faṭṭūma's attitude to his sages is, by contrast, inquisitive and critical.

Dār al-Mashriq is a pagan land where the moon is worshipped. Its people are simple, poor and naked. They are a matriarchal society without sexual inhibitions. Their religion is simple, natural, pleasure-seeking and devoid of both a moral code and belief in afterlife. As for the political and economic system of this land, it is summarized thus to Ibn Faṭṭūma by the Innkeeper: '*Dār al-Mashriq* consists of a capital and four cities. Each city has a "lord" who owns it with its pastures, animals and herdsmen . . . and the palace you have seen is that of the Lord of the Capital. He is the strongest and richest of the lords, but has no power over any of them' (pp. 32–3). From this it becomes apparent that *Dār al-Mashriq* stands for a very early stage of the development of human society; a pre-agricultural, tribal, material society with a natural religion. All the time Ibn Faṭṭūma has *Dār al-Islām* at the back of his mind and it pains him to see that his country is morally not superior to this pagan land (pp. 29, 33, 47).

Deflected from his lofty goal by sexual attraction, Ibn Faṭṭūma spends five years in *Dār al-Mashriq*, during which he marries and fathers children, until he is separated from his family and expelled from the country on the charge of trying to bring up his children as Moslems. Thus he finds himself embarking on his second journey, which takes him to *Dār al-Ḥayra* (the Abode of Bewilderment). There, he finds that the people worship a god-king who owns all the land and apportions it to regional lords who run it in his name and share the revenue with him (pp. 61, 68). By now it must be clear that Ibn Faṭṭūma's journey is more of a journey in time than in space. For here we are obviously a few steps further in the history of human society, where feudal lords reign over their serfs and owe allegiance to a central king who has a divine right to rule. As before, our traveller's thoughts are with his homeland, *Dār al-Islām*. He reflects wistfully that there is no evil that he encounters in his journey which fails to remind him of his sad country, and when he sees the impaled heads of so-called rebels, he is certain that their owners died for justice and freedom as happens in his country (pp. 64–5).

In *Dār al-Ḥayra* he spends twenty years in prison on a false charge. When he is released he embarks on his third journey, to *Dār al-Ḥalba* (the Abode of the Arena). From the first moment it captures his imagination and he seems nearer his dream of finding the ideal state than ever before. *Dār al-Ḥalba* is the land of freedom, wealth and sophisticated civilization. There he feels that for the first time he has met people 'who took pride in themselves' (p. 91). He comes across a protest demonstration and is surprised to see it protected (rather than coerced) by the police, and is even more surprised when he learns that the demonstration was about demanding the legalization of homosexual relations. He is also surprised to learn that the State has no official religion and that equal rights are accorded to worshippers of different faiths, that the head of government is elected for a certain period of time, after which he has to leave office, and that the economy is free and mostly in the hands of individuals. Finally, when he meets their sage, he learns from him that their religion consists in belief in reason 'which should preclude the need for all else' (p. 104). We are obviously here in the heartland of the modern democratic capitalist West. But the Western capitalist model, after initial fascination, proves far from perfect too. For Ibn Faṭṭūma observes that *Dār al-Ḥalba* houses poverty and crime too and when he faces their sage with this fact, the latter replies: 'Freedom is a responsibility that only the capable can shoulder. There is no place among us for the weak.' He also refuses to accept 'compassion' as a human value comparable to freedom (pp. 106–7). Ibn Faṭṭūma ends by rejecting the Halbite (i.e. capitalist) system as lacking a 'moral basis', but he admits that *Dār al-Islām*, with its despotic rulers, sycophantic men of religion and hunger-subdued people is equally without a moral basis (p. 118).

Having despaired of finding his first wife, Ibn Faṭṭūma settles in *Dār al-Ḥalba*, marries again and starts a successful business.

Eventually the old dream of finding the ideal state and taking the cure back home lures him again and he sets out on his fourth journey, this time to *Dār al-Amān* (the Abode of Security). On his arrival at the gates of *Dār al-Amān*, city officials welcome the caravan to 'the land of total justice' (p. 124). Ibn Faṭṭūma is appointed a compulsory escort to show him around the city and to watch over his every movement, not excluding visits to the bathroom at the hotel. By now we have got enough clues to suspect that our traveller must have arrived in the pre-Gorbachovian Soviet Union. What follows confirms the reader's suspicion. In the morning, Ibn Faṭṭūma wakes up to an elegant, but deserted city. This is because every person, man or woman, is working; nobody is unemployed. The escort explains to his captive traveller: 'Every individual is brought up to do a certain job, and every individual is suitably rewarded. We are the only country which knows neither rich nor poor. Here is justice which no other nation could achieve, not even in part' (pp. 128–9). Ibn Faṭṭūma is temporarily impressed, but at the end of the day when the people come out of their workplaces onto the streets, he notices that their faces are grim, tired, lifeless and without a trace of merriment. He is concerned and perplexed (pp. 132–3). At the end of a political rally, he sees severed human heads impaled on spears and is told that their crime was to criticize the regime. He is very dejected to realize that 'individual freedom was punishable by death' (pp. 140–1). His final judgement on *Dār al-Amān* is a mixed one: 'It is an amazing country. It aroused both my admiration and disgust in the extreme' (p. 137). This was the only country where Ibn Faṭṭūma did not exceed the ten-day standard period of stay: he was too bored to want to, nor were visitors welcome to overstay the prescribed period.

With the communist ideal rejected as well, Ibn Faṭṭūma's *riḥla* through the history of the development of human society and its systems of government seems to have taken him as far as the present day and yet to have left him with his ideal unattained: no perfect society and no tried cure for the social and political evil to take back home to *Dār al-Islām*. Have Ibn Faṭṭūma and his author reached a dead-end? Not quite; there is yet *Dār al-Jabal* (the Abode on the Mountain). *Dār al-Jabal* is a place steeped in mystery, or perhaps it is no place at all, but only an ideal in the mind. Ibn Faṭṭūma first hears of it from his tutor in *Dār al-Islām* (himself once a traveller) before he sets out on his journeys. What the tutor (who had himself failed to reach *Dār al-Jabal* in his past travels) tells him about it fires his imagination and gives him the determination to make it the ultimate goal of his travels. 'It is the miracle of nations; unsurpassable perfection,' his tutor tells him and laments that he has never come upon anyone who had visited it, nor seen a book or manuscript about it (p. 10). This mystifying account is maintained throughout the book. In every city where Ibn Faṭṭūma arrives he enquires about *Dār al-Jabal*, but nothing is ever added to his scant knowledge about it. He even meets those who doubt its very existence, not to mention those who believe that their own cities are the very *Dār al-Jabal* (i.e. the Ideal State). He himself, however, never wavers in his faith in *Dār al-Jabal* or his determination to reach it.

Thus when Ibn Faṭṭūma leaves *Dār al-Amān*, he heads in the direction of *Dār al-Jabal*, but first he must visit *Dār al-Ghurūb* (the Abode of Sunset).[62] This is now the fifth leg of his marathon journey. *Dār al-Ghurūb* is described as a land of peace, beauty and plenty. There he meets a guru of tremendous spiritual power who tells him that all the people he sees there are emigrants from all over the world, come to prepare themselves for the journey to *Dār al-Jabal* (p. 150). The guru trains them through singing, but he tells Ibn Faṭṭūma, 'they must bring out of themselves their latent power' (p. 151). Ibn Faṭṭūma decides to stay on in *Dār al-Ghurūb* and receive the spiritual training necessary for the final journey to *Dār al-Jabal*. The guru's first lesson to his disciples is: 'Love work irrespective of result or recompense!' (p. 154), a moral integral to Mahfouz's vision of social salvation.[63] He also tells them: 'There, in *Dār al-Jabal*, through [use of] the mind and [other] hidden powers, they [who live there] discover facts, cultivate lands, build factories and achieve justice, freedom and total purity' (p. 155). The guru's words, looked at closely, are nothing but Mahfouz's own, long-familiar social creed. 'Use of the mind' means the renunciation of the grip of the supernatural over the political, economic and social organization of society, while 'the hidden powers' simply means 'science', another integral part of Mahfouz's vision of social progress.[64] It is also worth noting that his vision of *Dār al-Jabal* (i.e. the Ideal State) seems to combine the two main achievements of both *Dār al-Ḥalba* and *Dār al-Amān* (i.e.

capitalism and communism), namely individual freedom and social justice. As for 'total purity', it is perhaps a pinch of spiritual spice which Mahfouz adds to his utopian recipe, and which is automatically attainable on the accomplishment of perfect social harmony.[65] Another typical Mahfuzian moral was also soon to be learnt, namely that however reclusive or ascetic the individual becomes, however much he seeks to extricate himself from the cobweb of the real world, the real world will finally reimpose itself on him and force him to face up to reality. This is a lesson which was central to the earlier novel, *The Beggar* (see chapter 5), and is repeated here when the spiritual bliss of the inhabitants of *Dār al-Ghurūb* is ravished by the country being invaded by the neighbouring *Dār al-Amān*. They are thus forced to proceed to *Dār al-Jabal* in a state of unreadiness, as their training is still uncompleted.

The final chapter of the novel deals with the progress to *Dār al-Jabal* and is significantly entitled '*al-Bidāya*' (The Beginning). The journey proves long and arduous. They have to cross a desert, climb a mountain and descend on the other side, cross another vast desert and then climb yet another mountain at whose top stands the promised jewel of human endeavour. The novel ends with the travellers standing at the foot of the second mountain and looking up to the top, soaring in the clouds. Will they reach the top? Will they gain entry to the Heaven on earth? We shall never know because here the manuscript on which we have been told the novel was based stops. This in fact is a very natural ending to the novel, for since the book is a journey through historical time from the dawn of human society to the communist state, it is only fitting that it should stop at the present and leave a question mark over the future.

The Travels has both its strength and weakness in its attempt at fusing the entire social experience of humanity in so short a space. Over-simplification is the almost inevitable result of such ambition. That said, the novel is still interesting, if only for the new experiment in form that it demonstrates and its successful parody of *Riḥlat Ibn Baṭṭūṭa*, a parody which consists in two elements, as I hope I have shown: first, that the novel is a *riḥla* in historical time rather than geographical space, and second, that *Dār al-Islām*, which is idealized in *Riḥlat Ibn Baṭṭūṭa*, contrary to historical evidence,[66] is harshly criticized and shown to be in need of radical reform in *Riḥlat Ibn Faṭṭūma*.

7

MATTERS OF FORM: A CASE STUDY OF *RESPECTED SIR*

Reduced to its basics, the study of any creative writer must consist of an examination of the elements of his attitude to the human condition and the methods he employs to translate this attitude into artistic form. This is what I have tried to do here by looking at Mahfouz's *oeuvre* through the stages of its evolution over a fifty-year period. In a study that is essentially an attempt at an overview of the total significance of the author's voluminous output, dwelling continually on matters of structure and technique was neither possible nor desirable. However, no appreciation of an artist's achievement would be complete without close attention to his workshop mannerisms: in the case of a novelist, how he structures plot, portrays character, uses language, etc. I have therefore sought to offer an insight into Mahfouz's craft as a novelist by singling out for close inspection one of his mainstream later short novels, namely *Respected Sir*, published in 1975.[1]

THE PLOT

The story of *Respected Sir* is a simple one, centred on one character, through whose eyes everything is seen and round whom everything revolves; all other characters in the novel are important only inasmuch as they serve to throw light on him, whether by comparison and contrast, or by just being a catalyst in his life. The novel begins with the protagonist in his late teens. This is not stated in the text, but as we are told he is appointed archives clerk immediately after his attainment of the diploma of secondary education (p. 4); it will not therefore be wrong to assume that he was then around the age of 17 or 18. The book ends with the protagonist on his death-bed, near retirement age. Thus the novel almost covers the whole lifetime of the main character, or perhaps one should say 'career', since ᶜUthmān's career has been the very focus of his life. Indeed, it is not without significance that the story opens with ᶜUthmān, submissively standing in 'the blue room', among others, in front of the Director-General, on the day he begins his civil servant's career at the lowest point in the service, as archives clerk; and that it closes with him awaiting death in a hospital room, his thoughts focused on that other room which he knew he was never going to occupy, despite his appointment as director-general. Thus the contrast between the two rooms emphasizes the basic irony in the protagonist's end. In the following pages I will attempt to review the elements of the story in *Respected Sir* and examine their relation to theme and character.

The theme of ambition or, in other terms, the protagonist's obsession with the advancement of his career decides for the novelist the angle from which he tells the story as well as the nature and amount of detail that he weaves into its texture. Thus the story begins with the first day in ᶜUthmān's employment; more particularly, it begins with the moment he is received by the Director-General in 'the blue room' – that moment which gives him the vision that is to determine the course of his life until the very end. What happened before that is largely irrelevant, and therefore the novelist reveals of it, only what is contributory to the understanding of the protagonist and his motives, but later and in the form of intermittent flashbacks.

The epiphanic scene of 'the blue room' in the first chapter is immediately followed by a down-to-earth one in the second, where ᶜUthmān descends to the Ministry's basement to begin his work as an archives clerk. Chapter 3 takes us to the protagonist's humble flat in a poor back street of old Cairo. There, through the use of narrative description and flashbacks, the novelist quickly acquaints us with ᶜUthmān's humble origins and his utter loneliness; all members of his family have died. But even at home, the focal point of his existence is still work; he writes down his eight-point 'Guide for work and life' (pp. 13–14) to study every morning before going out to work. Though he calls it a 'Guide for work and life', all eight points are concerned only with various methods to advance his career.

Chapter 4 introduces us to Sayyida, his first love, who is soon to become his first sacrifice at the altar of ambition. Significantly, the new appointment dominates the conversation and we see ᶜUthmān ruling out the question of marriage, which Sayyida gently broaches, on the pretext that he wants to complete his higher education (p. 18). By the end of this chapter, we have been introduced to all the basic facts in ᶜUthmān's past and present. The choice and presentation of detail all serve to show the protagonist's growing obsession with the advancement of his career, an obsession which is, from the first moment, crystallized in a specific and well-defined target: to become director-general. He even counts the number of years of service required for 'the miracle' to take place (p. 9). All subsequent developments in the story can be seen as an expansion, a deepening of this basic situation. His life will be shown to consist of periods of waiting for the next promotion; each promotion is a station on the road to his ultimate desire, and the sacrifice of Sayyida is only the first in a long series of moral degradations that will bring misery to himself and others.

Thus one can argue that the plot in *Respected Sir* achieves its effect through a cumulative build-up of dramatic tension. The episodes from which the narrative is constructed are similar in nature though different in detail. This episodic similarity creates a repetitive pattern which pervades the novel and serves to underscore the obsessional nature of the protagonist's goal in life. Furthermore, this repetitive pattern of the plot enhances, and is itself enhanced by, the protagonist's lack of character development; for the ᶜUthmān of the last chapter is much the same as the ᶜUthmān of the first chapter, with little or no change in his character. The state of utter ruin that he is brought to at the end of some forty years does not seem to shake his belief in the correctness of his fundamental ideal (p. 186). The repetitive pattern of the plot is broken only twice; and in each case the breach is of paramount importance in its development. The first breach occurs when ᶜUthmān marries Qadriyya, the prostitute, and the second when he discovers the deceit of his second wife.

Now one can talk about two main lines in the plot, which for convenience's sake I will refer to as the professional line and the marital one. The first is concerned with the protagonist's preoccupation with the advancement of his career, and the second with his attempts at marrying above his station in life in order to give his career a push: a fact which shows that the two parallel lines are indeed strongly linked. Thus when ᶜUthmān, who betrayed the only two women he ever loved (and ruined a third in the process) because he thought none of them would help further his career, finally takes a whore for wife, his desperate action comes as an anticlimax and a great irony. At this point the two lines of the plot cut across each other; in fact, this dramatic development in the marital line is a direct result of a negative occurrence in the professional line: the protagonist's failure to obtain a promotion that he had long waited for. ᶜUthmān's marrige to Qadriyya signals the first crack in his resistance and heralds his final defeat. On the other hand, this anti-climactic development in the marital line anticipates the ultimate irony in the professional line, when ᶜUthmān receives the news of his appointment as Director-General only too late, as he lies in his bed waiting for death.

The second breach in the repetitive pattern of the plot constitutes its moment of anagnorisis, to use the Aristotelean term. It occurs when ᶜUthmān discovers that his second wife, who is also his secretary at work, has married him, not out of love, but only to further her own career (pp. 181–2). The discovery is immediately followed by the peripeteia which leaves the protagonist, who had then nearly recovered from a heart attack, in the grip of another, virtually on the brink of death and unable to assume the position for which he had sacrificed everything. Thus again, we see a further complication in the marital line of the plot, this time reaching the major climax, bringing about a corresponding crisis in the professional line. The two lines have ultimately converged in one point of high tension, allowing the plot to reach its denouement.

The structure of the plot is thus seen to have been carefully designed to bring into focus the moral irony of the novel. The protagonist who has always wanted a wife who was a means to an end, but never found one, is used in the same manner by an equally Machiavellian woman. On the other hand, and as a consequence of this, the official position, at whose altar many a noble value had been made an offering, is never practically attained: poetic justice is done. Naguib Mahfouz, always a strict moralist, could not have allowed otherwise.

THE VIEWPOINT

The story of *Respected Sir* is told from an external and restricted viewpoint, i.e. the third person. It is the viewpoint that the author began to use from the time of *The Thief and the Dogs* in preference to that of the omniscient author employed in all his previous novels (except *Mirage*). Everything in the novel is seen through the eyes of the protagonist, who is the centre of gravity, holding together the entire work. This restriction of the viewpoint to that of the main character combines the advantages of both the internal and external methods; for while it maintains the relative freedom of the external, it brings in the intimacy of the internal, or first-person, method.[2] However, one must record that Mahfouz further confines an already restricted viewpoint. He uses the authorial licence accorded him by the narrative method of his choice very sparingly. In point of fact, he only uses it to introduce the external bits of the narrative which cannot be given through ʿUthmān's consciousness, but he never uses it to give us a glimpse into another character's mind. This is so much the case that one might argue that, to all intents and purposes, the viewpoint in the novel is internal, rather than external. This confinement of the viewpoint to the mind of the protagonist adds to the aesthetic force of the novel, giving it, on the one hand, a very concentrated form, and on the other placing the task of judging the character, as it should, in the hands of the reader.

Occasionally, Mahfouz shifts the viewpoint from external to internal in a subtle, almost furtive manner. Examples of this are at the opening of chapters 2 and 31. The first begins with the passionate statement 'I am on fire, O God', and the latter with the furious repetition of the sentence substitute: 'No . . . No . . . No . . .' In both instances the shift is dictated by the strength of the emotion experienced by the character. The use of the first, rather than the third, person here conveys the force and immediacy of the feeling experienced to the reader and brings him closer to the mind of the character. A subtler use of the shifting viewpoint can be seen at the opening of chapters 6 and 33, where the exclamation: 'How wonderful is the turning year!' and the jussive 'Let the days go by!' – seemingly bits of authorial narration – are in fact the thoughts of the character, and respectively introduce the train of thoughts that follows.

Another example, yet, of the use of the shifting viewpoint, this time an overt one, is the letter to the Director-General which opens chapter 11. The importance of the occasion on which the letter is written, namely when ᶜUthmān obtains his university degree, on the one hand, and his establishment of some form of communication with the Director-General for the first time since his appointment, on the other, is in this manner underlined and endowed with more life than it would have if it were reported in the third person.

However, the author's principal method in the internalization of the viewpoint is the use of the stream of consciousness or, as it is sometimes called, the internal monologue which he employs extensively, alongside action, for character revelation. Having said that, one must observe that what Mahfouz uses is a very modified form of this novelistic technique, popular among modern writers in the West since the beginnings of this century. It is nothing like the stream of consciousness as used by, to mention but two, James Joyce or Virginia Woolf,[3] writers whose names are almost synonymous with this technique. Unlike them, Mahfouz does not let us loose in the character's mind and leave us there to fend for ourselves in that vast and dark labyrinth, nor is he interested in the incoherence of the human mind, or its ability to travel, unhampered, across the boundaries of space and time, nor yet, in stressing sensory impressions, all of which are modes of experience that this technique has mostly been used to explore.[4] What Mahfouz does is to guide our steps carefully into the protagonist's mind, beaming his torchlight only on those parts of it that are immediately relevant to theme and situation. His grip on his character's mind is firm, and his search into it meticulously logical and coherent; his prime concern is the internal analysis of motives for behaviour.

In fact, a more suitable term to describe Mahfouz's method of probing into the character's mind may be that coined in 1912 by the linguist Charles Bally, viz. *style indirecte libre*, or free indirect speech.[5] The term is used to indicate the practice, common among novelists long before the heyday of the stream of consciousness, of incorporating features of direct speech into ostensibly narrative discourse.[6] This is exactly the term to describe Mahfouz's account of his character's mind, not only in *Respected Sir*, but indeed in many of his post-realistic novels.

Thus, all the time, the ostensible speaker is the novelist, but what we have in reality is not the author's account of what goes on in the character's mind: it is the actual thoughts of the character. Examples of this can be found on almost every page of the novel. The following one is chosen at random:

> He chided himself for failing to study meticulously His Excellency the Director-General's room and print on his mind's eye a full picture of the man's face and his person, for not trying to unravel the secret of the magic with which he dominated everyone and had them at his beck and call. This was the power to be worshipped. It was the ultimate beauty too. It was one of the secrets of the universe. On earth there existed divine secrets without number for those who had eyes to see and minds to think. The time between hello and goodbye was short. But it was infinite as well. Woe betide anyone who ignored this truth.
>
> (pp. 8–9)

This mode of the internal monologue must have proved more appropriate to Mahfouz's purposes, as types of experiences traditionally associated with the stream-of-consciousness technique were largely no concern of his. The novelist himself has something to tell us on this point:

> The internal monologue . . . is a method, a vision and a way of life; and even though I use it, you cannot say that I belong to its school as such. All that happens is that I sometimes encounter a Joycean moment in my hero's life; so I render it in Joyce's manner with some modification.[7]

Mahfouz frequently uses the shift from narrative discourse to free indirect speech in order subtly to redirect the mind of the reader from the realistic to the higher level of meaning, to find the sublime in the banal, poetry in the prosaic, or significance in what is seemingly trivial. The use of this device is sustained, with varying effect, throughout the novel. I quote one example here:

> One Friday morning he bumped into her [Sayyida] in al-Khaymiyya in her mother's company. Their eyes met for an instant before she turned them away indifferently. She did not look behind her. He had a revelation of one

> meaning of death. Like the voluntary exodus of his ancestor from Eden. Like his own lofty struggle with agony.
>
> (p. 38)

In the extract above, the narrative section describes, in plain terms, an accidental meeting between Sayyida and ᶜUthmān after their separation. The free indirect speech that follows gives us ᶜUthmān's inner reaction to the indifferent look in her eyes: it is a kind of death. His desertion of her is like Adam's desertion of Heaven, while the pain resulting from that act of betrayal is shown in the heightened terms of the suffering of a proud soul. The effect of the quick shift from one narrative mode to another serves to emphasize the contrast between the character's actions as they seem from outside and the justification he finds for them in his heart.

THEMES AND PRESENTATION

I have already suggested that the main theme in *Respected Sir* is ambition. In addition to that, one can talk about two subordinate themes in the novel: one is time, and the other I will call, for convenience's sake, the theme of isolation, meaning by that, isolation from the social scene. The three themes are closely related, and while, for the purpose of analysis, we can discuss them separately, it must be noted that, in the novel, they are indivisible. I will begin with the central theme.

One of the first things that draws the reader's attention in the novel is the language in which the protagonist's thoughts about his professional aspirations are rendered. It is an extremely heightened language, a language that, if used in real life to describe such thoughts, would be tantamount to madness. Indeed, when at one point in the novel, ᶜUthmān speaks, in a conversation with the Director of Administration, in that language, the man doubts his sanity (p. 89). This peculiar use of language pervades the whole book; it sets the tone of the novel, and examples of it can be found on almost every page. Indeed, the mood of the entire work is established in the opening paragraph of the first chapter: the Director-General's office is an 'infinitely spacious room' whose entrants 'were swallowed up, melted down'; the Director-General himself is 'the god sitting behind the magnificent desk'; and as ᶜUthmān enters the room, an electric shock goes through him, 'setting off in his innermost heart an insane love for the gloriousness of life on the pinnacles of power' and he feels that 'he stood in the Divine presence' (pp. 3–4).

The vocabulary used here is religious; it is deliberately used by the author to transfer what is essentially a mundane experience (the first meeting of a small, new appointee with the top official in his department) to a much higher plane: that of religious experience.[8] In other words, Mahfouz employs the vocabulary of one linguistic register to render an experience not usually associated with or expressed in terms of that register. To what effect, then, does Mahfouz mix registers? The answer is: irony.[9] Mahfouz creates an intricate pattern of verbal irony which he weaves into the very texture of the novel and maintains throughout. Thus, all the time, the protagonist's professional ambition is presented in vocabulary and imagery which evoke an exalted and arduous religious quest, as though the attainment of the position of director-general were a sacred mission ordained by divine will, and for whose sake no sacrifice was too dear. The following is a random selection of clusters of such evocative words and phrases strewn over almost every page of the book:

> The sacred aspirations. The holy flame. The sacred fire. The sacred ambition. The sacred apparatus of the state. Infinity. The gates of infinity. The Divine and infinite path. The voice of Destiny. The Divine mysteries. The Divine joy. The threshold of Divinity. God's will on high. The arduous path attended by the blessing of God and His lofty glory. The power to be worshipped. The dreams of eternity. The eternal wisdom. The miracles. Man's glory on earth. The path of glory. The pinnacle of glory. The pomp and circumstance of royalty. Sacrificial offering. Worship. The sky. The clouds. The stars in their courses.

This pattern of verbal irony engenders in the reader an awareness of the incongruity between the object and mode of expression, i.e. the realistic situation and the hyperbolic terms in which it is rendered. This awareness creates and sustains, all the way through, a sense of dramatic irony where the reader is, as it were, cognizant of a basic fact of which the protagonist is ignorant, namely, that his obsession has led him astray; that there is nothing holy about his ambition; and that, in his quest for salvation, he has only fallen into a hell of his own making. Finally, the sense of incongruity, inherent in the presentation, prepares us, all the time, for the great moral irony of the book discussed earlier.[10]

I will now turn to what I have called the theme of isolation. To Mahfouz individual morality is inseparable from social morality, as I have argued elsewhere in this book.[11] In other words, according to the author's moral code, those who only seek their own individual salvation are damned,[12] while those who show concern for others and demonstrate a kind of awareness that their particular predicament is part of a more general one are saved.[13]

To which character type, then, does ᶜUthmān Bayyūmī, our protagonist, belong? Within the framework of Mahfouz's morality, he pertains, unequivocally, to the ranks of the doomed. He is an individualistic self-seeker, whose motives and goals are egoistic; who tramples on human values that stand in the course of his ambition; who never for a moment perceives the glaring fact that a considerable part of his suffering is a direct result of the common social injustice; and that his own self-centred struggle to improve his lot in life would have been more meaningful, and possibly capable of redeeming him, if he had put it in its social and human perspective.

This takes us back to the starting-point of the present argument: the theme of isolation. Mahfouz presents this theme in the form of a recurrent motif which periodically interrupts the main theme. The motif casts the image of the protagonist as a careerist, the epitome of the self-made individualist, with boundless belief in himself and his ability, and deep scorn for all those around him who do not possess his determination and single-mindedness. He stands aloof from both his immediate circle and society at large; what does not touch him personally is no business of his, and as long as his materialistic success is secure, God is in His Heaven and all is well with the world. This attitude of ᶜUthmān's is clearly set out in the novel at an early stage:

> He knew about history from the most ancient times up to the eve of the Great War. He knew about revolutions, but he had never lived them nor reacted to them. . . and he was

> always bewildered by the way groups of eminent statesmen and their supporters fought each other. . . . Today, he was conscious of one goal only, a goal at once profane and sacred, which had nothing to do, as far as he could see, with the strange events that took place in the name of politics. He told himself that man's true life was his inner life, which governed his every heartbeat and which called for toil, dedication and enterprise. It was something holy, something religious, and through it he could achieve self-fulfilment in the service of the sacred apparatus known as the Government or the State.
>
> (p. 21)

Again, he tells a newly appointed employee, by way of advice, that to rely on *oneself* is better than blaming society, that 'God addresses His commandments to us as *individuals* and brings us to account also as *individuals*'.[14] When the girl asserts her belief in the importance of socio-political thought, he tells her 'this means you don't believe in *yourself*' (p. 86). Ironically, ᶜUthmān never sees the relevance of political thought and struggle to his own predicament. He never realizes that his own arduous struggle and many sacrifices could have been avoided had he lived in an equitable society. He accepts the status quo and works within it and according to its axioms, to promote his own existence, without for a moment questioning its validity.

In addition to ᶜUthmān's explicit thoughts on the subject of society, which leave us in no doubt as to his isolationism, Mahfouz makes subtle use of realistic detail in order to enhance our awareness of the protagonist's isolation. By this I mean his use of what one might call the 'room motif'. ᶜUthmān's life is confined to a number of rooms: the room he lives in in al-Ḥusaynī Alley, the room in which he makes love to Qadriyya and, above all, the room he dreams of occupying one day: 'the blue room' of the director-general. Finally, he ends in a hospital room, waiting for death, with his thoughts focused on another kind of room: his 'new tomb' (p. 186). Thus the phases of his life take him from one room to another, but never to the one he had prized above everything. In this way ᶜUthmān's social isolation is emphasized by his physical confinement.[15] Furthermore, the moral irony is emphasized by the irony in the room motif.

In his treatment of the theme of isolation in *Respected Sir*,

Mahfouz was treading on familiar ground. In a way, ᶜUthmān Bayyūmī is a reincarnation of *The Thief and the Dogs'* Saᶜīd Mahrān, for both Saᶜīd and ᶜUthmān opt for the individual way out. The first has a personal vendetta against an unjust regime, while the second chooses to ignore the inherent injustice of the regime and tries to draw from it the utmost personal benefit possible through his devoted cooperation with it. Mahfouz's moral stance in relation to both options, i.e. individual violence on the one hand and complete isolation on the other, is patently illustrated in the failure of the two characters to achieve their ends and in their final defeat.

The next point of discussion is the theme of time. Mahfouz's concept of time as a metaphysical force of oppression in the life of individuals has been expounded in chapters 4 and 6 of this study. In *Respected Sir*, however, time has a more concrete presence than in any of the novels discussed above, where its presence is mostly felt as one of a *force majeure*, acting invisibly behind the scenes, wreaking havoc everywhere and steadily leading characters to their perdition. The difference in *Respected Sir* is that time appears here as almost a physical force, of which the protagonist, and not only the reader, is aware, and with which he is all the time contending. Here time is seen as the major external force with which the hero has to battle. All other forces in the novel, such as poverty, social discrimination, love and the temptation of a quiet happy life are eclipsed by the overpowering magnitude of ruthless time. In fact, with his tremendous willpower, ᶜUthmān does defeat all these secondary forces; what really 'gets' him in the end is time. Now, this does seem to weaken the socio-political content of the book, which the novelist has been at pains to put across, as has been shown earlier. For the social system, supposed to be unjust, does grant ᶜUthmān his hard-earned position of director-general; what really prevents him from assuming it is the fact that it has come too late, after time has struck its final, deadly blow. Thus, though he is punished, the moral core of ᶜUthmān's punishment seems to be lost, or at least rather diluted, as the punitive instrument is, in fact, a *deus ex machina*. One can very well imagine a social utopia, where a man can still be prevented from achieving a legitimate desire through sudden disability or death. More appropriate for Mahfouz's intent here would have been for ᶜUthmān's ultimate defeat to have been inflicted at the hands of what he himself called 'the sacred apparatus of the State', and to which he virtually sold his soul. As it stands, the ending of the book seems an ill-conceived gimmick which leaves us with an existential, rather than a social vision, namely that human effort is futile, and that nothing in life is worth the trouble, since in the end time will come and grab it all. This is not the message we have been prepared for; it might have been acceptable had social isolation not been one of the themes of the novel.

I will now attempt to substantiate the above argument from the novel by examining the manner in which Mahfouz presents his theme to us. The conflict between the protagonist and time, against whose constant background are shown the other conflicts he has to enter in his pursuit of his ambition, is continually evoked through the repeated use of words, phrases and sentences which permeate the whole novel. In their persistence they almost personify time as ᶜUthmān's one and only enemy. Here are a few examples of these evocations picked from various places in the novel:

> Days went by incessantly and stealthily. Days went by as they always would. Life flitted by. Youth flitted by. The river of time flowed on and would not rest. He carried time on his back moment by moment and suffered patience drop by drop. Make sure time does not cheat you! Nothing is more treacherous than the passing years. The chariot of time was going ever faster. Time is like a sword: if you do not kill it, it kills you. Ambition needed time and life was short. It seemed he did not resist death with sufficient fortitude. Here was grey hair advancing on him – how much time was left for him? The fearful race against time, glory and death. His birthdays served to intensify his apprehension of the future. The whip of time continued to lash his back, and he could run no longer.

Paradoxically, time is made to seem both a positive and negative force, simultaneously a builder and a destroyer. For although it is the final vanquisher of ᶜUthmān, it is also the force to whose perpetual flux he owes his relative successes, and without whose movement no aspiration of his can be fulfilled. Thus ᶜUthmān's every promotion is basically a gift from time: 'With the passage of time in its eternal course a post in grade seven became vacant in the Archives Section' (p. 43). Again:

> Out of the stream of days there rose, quite unexpectedly, a high and powerful tide which changed fortunes and created the world anew. For one morning the whole Ministry learnt of a decision to appoint Bahjat Nūr, the Director-General, as Under-Secretary of State. Thus the position of director-general became vacant for the first time in a very long period.
>
> (p. 147)

But, significantly, where time is benevolent in a certain quarter, it is sure to be concurrently playing havoc in another, for several of ʿUthmān's promotions are achieved only thanks to other people's retirement, serious illness, or death. The role of time is best defined by ʿUthmān himself, who perfectly understands the nature of his adversary: 'It is time we must thank for every achievement, and time we must blame for every loss' (p. 153).

CHARACTERIZATION

Like most of Mahfouz's novels since *The Thief and the Dogs* (the episodic works excepted), *Respected Sir* revolves round one character. Other characters have no importance of their own; their only significance is to provide a context in which the protagonist is to act and react, and in which, by means of comparison and contrast, his own character can be understood and his motives and actions morally judged. It follows, therefore, that these characters are completely flat and sketchy in their portrayal. Only those aspects of them which bear relevance to the protagonist are revealed. We do not even know what some of them look like, let alone what they think or believe. All we know, for instance, about Ismāʿīl Fā'iq is that he is 'weak and ignorant' (p. 125) (he undeservedly attains a position of which ʿUthmān is more worthy). All we know again about ʿAbdullāh Wajdī is that he is 40 years old, is corpulent and loves food and drink (p. 150) (40 is a long way to retirement, but the health hazards of corpulence and gluttony are a source of hope for ʿUthmān, eagerly awaiting the removal of this obstacle from his path). Another character of relatively more importance in the novel, Ḥamza al-Suwayfī, is not physically depicted at all. This may be an oversight on the part of Mahfouz. However, it is a mark of his general impatience with detail in his post-realistic novels.

The male character best sketched in the novel is that of Saᶜfān Basyūnī, the Head of Archives. The reason for this is that the author uses him as a foil for the protagonist. He obviously belongs to the same social stratum as ᶜUthmān and comes from similar humble origins (p. 55). What distinguishes him from our protagonist is the fact that he lacks his ambition and willpower. He is a typical example of the man contented with the role and position assigned to him in life by whatever forces are at work. He confides to ᶜUthmān that the headship of archives was more than he could dream of and that 'common people' could not aspire to higher posts than that (p. 54), beliefs which are diametrically opposed to those of ᶜUthmān, who has nothing but contempt for him: 'There were people who never moved, like Saᶜfān Basyūnī. Well-meaning but miserable, paying tribute to a wisdom of which he had learned nothing. But not so those whose hearts had been touched by the sacred fire' (p. 9). But though Basyūnī is obviously without ᶜUthmān's moral flaw, and though he is portrayed as a pleasant, fair and kind-hearted man, he can only command our pity, but not our respect. Nor is he spared a miserable end by his creator, for, in spite of his goodness, he spends the last years of his life in sickness and destitution, and his death is precipitated by the lack of money to buy medicine (pp. 78–9). So, although he is a foil for ᶜUthmān, he clearly is not Mahfouz's pointer to the road to salvation. In fact, his punishment is no less than ᶜUthmān's. What, then, was his crime? Within the framework of Mahfouz's morality, there can only be one answer: social passivity. If you are satisfied with your lot in life without questioning it, if you do not seek to improve it, and co-ordinate your effort with that of other people like you, then you have no chance of being saved. Thus, while ᶜUthmān tried alone, Basyūnī did not try at all. Both types are rejected according to Mahfouz's social ethics.

A point of characterization worthy of notice is the fact that none of the senior officials who directly control the fate of ᶜUthmān is delineated in unpleasant terms. They all seem to enjoy, considering the prevailing social climate, an admirable sense of justice. They all recognize and reward to the best of their ability, and sometimes in the face of external opposition, ᶜUthmān's talent. Even the cabinet minister concerned, who is not really a character in the novel, we learn through his deputy, Bahjat Nūr, firmly stands behind ᶜUthmān's right to accede to the vacant office of director-general. One wonders here: if all symbols of authority, i.e. the top slice of society, directly involved in the action, are shown to be fair people, does this not detract from the force of the book's message as implied in the theme of social isolation discussed earlier?

As for women characters, they are used mainly to uncover certain negative facets of ᶜUthmān's personality. Sayyida and 'Unsiyya are the two women he has truly loved at different times of his life but cruelly sacrificed, because to him love counted for nothing if it was of no practical value to his ambition. What he craved for was a wife to help him up the social ladder. Aṣīla, the woman he ruins without mercy, shows how exploitative of weakness and morally irresponsible he can be. On the other hand, Qadriyya, the prostitute he eventually marries, is herself, like ᶜUthmān, the victim of a corrupt social system but displays a social awareness that he never acquires. When she tells him that once she had gone on a political demonstration, he cannot believe it (p. 51). Nor is he prepared to find excuses for her on the grounds of social injustice: for did he not grow up like her in poverty and deprivation, and did he not discover in good time 'the divine secret in his weak soul' (p. 153)? Finally, we come to the woman who was a match for ᶜUthmān's moral degenerateness: Rāḍiya ᶜAbd al-Khāliq, his secretary and second wife. A Machiavellian like himself, she is the one who in the end holds up the mirror for him to see his true image, thereby giving the novel its great ironic twist.

Having dealt with the minor characters, we can now turn our attention to ᶜUthmān Bayyūmī himself. I have already examined certain aspects of his personality in the course of talking about themes and other characters. I will now examine how he is portrayed.

With a few exceptions in his very early work, Mahfouz's characters are usually morally complex; being neither wholly good nor wholly evil, their portraiture generally reflects the intricacy of human nature. In their depiction, Mahfouz is usually objective, giving the reader a full picture of their inner and outer lives, and leaving him to draw his own conclusions and pass judgement. In other words, he has no direct presence in his novels. He describes his attitude *vis-à-vis* his characters in terms of what he calls a 'technical neutrality', which

> makes it possible for the reader to contemplate things in all their different aspects. I do not point the way to the reader, nor do I pre-empt his judgement of ideas and situations. Rather, I prepare him to judge by himself. But this process of preparation is only seemingly neutral. Within it is, of necessity, my own view.[16]

He goes on to say that in order for him to judge characters, he has to examine their circumstances, and having done that, he can no longer judge them.[17] This statement does not, however, appear to be substantiated by the author's actual treatment of his characters. The merest glance at the endings of Mahfouz's novels shows that poetic justice is always done. No character who fails to fit into his strict moral system can hope to escape his sword. Where his statement appears true is in the examination of circumstances, a task which he performs with a great deal of care, objectivity and comprehensiveness. Such is the case with ᶜUthmān Bayyūmī. He is presented to us as a young man with a certain ambition: to become director-general. This ambition soon turns into an *idée fixe* which consumes his entire existence and goes with him to the grave. His unconditional devotion to the achievement of this goal dominates his decisions and actions, and is responsible for his moral lapses. Is *Respected Sir*, then, a psychological study of the nature of obsession? Only partly so, because ᶜUthmān's obsession is not seen in isolation from his humble social background. In a way, it is a radical rejection of the station in life imposed on him by his social inheritance. The poverty and deprivation he grew up in, and the suffering of his parents and their miserable end are all adequately substantiated in the novel in order to place his ambition within a social framework. Nevertheless, within the author's ethical system, none of this is a valid reason to acquit his protagonist of responsibility for his actions: ᶜUthmān is portrayed as a free agent, perfectly aware of his choices, and prepared to bear the consequences. The moral conflict he goes through before each sacrifice, and the suffering and feelings of guilt he experiences each time after the event are all vividly rendered.

LANGUAGE

I have shown at the beginning of chapter 5 of this study the new turn in form and technique that Mahfouz's work has taken since the early 1960s. The new form necessarily brought along its own new language, one which, in the words of one critic, no longer wanted 'to portray everything in plain words and to report conversations in full', but one 'infinitely more concise and evocative'.[18] While the general features of Mahfouz's new language that started in the 1960s feature in *Respected Sir* as in all the novels published since that period, it is my opinion that the author's language has reached here a peak hitherto unknown in Arabic fiction: it stands as a unique experiment in the novelist's achievement. Nowhere else in his work does Mahfouz attempt to render the central experience of a novel in terms of a linguistic order other than the one it belongs to in the orthodox use of the language. In what amounts to a *tour de force*, the author succeeds in completely subjugating realistic language to psychological language, and sustaining that for the length of the novel.

I have illustrated earlier in this analysis certain salient aspects of Mahfouz's use of language in *Respected Sir*, particularly in the presentation of the theme of ambition, where religious language is used, to ironic effect, to render an experience of a mundane nature. The use of this special linguistic register is also brought to bear in a subtle way on the theme of social isolation. This is achieved by the use of a pattern of imagery drawn from fire and light, and often encountered in *ṣūfī* literature, where the mystic seeks the 'light' of God and is 'burnt' with the 'fire' of the 'sacred yearning' which 'consumes' his soul. I can only quote one example here of what is a consistent pattern of imagery:

> I am *on fire*, O God! *Flames* were devouring his soul from top to bottom as it soared upward into a world of dreams. In a single moment of revelation he perceived the world as *a surge of dazzling light* which he pressed to his bosom and held on to like one demented. He had always dreamed and desired and yearned, but this time he was really *ablaze*, and in *the light of this sacred fire* he glimpsed the meaning of life.
>
> (p. 6) [My italics.]

The expression of the protagonist's ambition through the use of a language imbued with *ṣūfī* connotations enhances the theme of isolation since *ṣūfism* is, in essence, an individual experience, where the mystic abandons the world in his search for the salvation of his own soul.[19]

Mahfouz's prose in *Respected Sir* is terse and pithy, as it generally is in his post-realistic novels. Almost every word has a function and every image or minute detail is, to borrow a term from the world of technology, precision-built to fit into the elaborate structure of the novel. The crispness of the prose with its generally short, staccato sentences matches the often highly tensed mood of the protagonist and his persistent, relentless quest.

Finally, there is the question of dialogue, which Mahfouz has always rendered in standard rather than Egyptian Arabic. This policy has naturally given rise to the criticism that dialogue is thus made to sound unrealistic, i.e. not true to life. The issue, in fact, is not peculiar to Mahfouz: the division between *fuṣḥā* (standard) and *ᶜāmiyya* (colloquial) Arabic is a vexed question that every serious creative author writing in Arabic has had to address since the beginning of the century. Today in the theatre the use of colloquial seems to have gained supremacy. This is easy to understand as the question of realism of speech on the stage is obviously a more vital one than elsewhere. In the novel and short story the problem has not yet been clearly settled, though younger Egyptian authors appear more and more inclined towards the use of *ᶜāmiyya* for dialogue. Mahfouz's opinion on this matter has been tirelessly repeated over the years to critics who put the question to him time and again. He is decidedly in favour of *fuṣḥā*:

> I adopted *fuṣḥā* [when I started writing] because it was the [accepted] language of writing. The question [of *fuṣḥā* and *ᶜāmiyya*] has become problematic only in relatively recent times. Many people consider it a serious problem, and it may well be so in the theatre or cinema. But in the novel and short story, it is much less serious and time alone will settle the question. In point of fact I feel that to disregard a language that unites a group of people [i.e. the Arabic-speaking countries] is to disregard art itself and a sacred human relationship at the same time.[20]

In another statement he recognizes the problem of having 'to describe everyday life in a language that has long been used only to deal with thought, politics, philosophy and religion'. He goes on to describe the continuous struggle he had to go through in order to adapt that language to the requirements of the art of the novel: 'I was,' he says, 'like one burdened with heavy loads but every day I cast off one.'[21]

As in all Mahfouz's novels, dialogue in *Respected Sir* is written in *fuṣḥā*. And, as in his post-realistic novels, it is terse, lively and always to the point. The archaisms and clichés, which cluttered the historical novels and continued to exist in a certain measure in the early realistic novels, have long been disposed of. The effort exerted by the novelist in trying to reach a compromise language between the Arabic of writing and that of speech is evident in his willingness (one which increased over the years) to adapt his use of *fuṣḥā* in dialogue in such a way as to accept occasionally colloquial glossary and structures where *fuṣḥā* would be less effective.[22]

8

IMAGES OF GOD, DEATH AND SOCIETY: THE SHORT STORIES AND THE PLAYS

If Mahfouz had not written any of his novels, he would still have merited a place of high prominence in the history of modern Arabic letters on account of his short stories alone, of which he has written some 200 spread across fourteen collections[1] and a lifetime. As it happens he has also written, as we have seen, thirty-three novels,[2] many of which are masterpieces of craft and vision. The inevitable result of this has been that his short stories have mostly been accorded second place in the study of the author's work and treated all too often as footnotes to the novels. The fact that this brief chapter occurs at the end of this book is unfortunately as 'good' an illustration as any of the situation. One critic has described the relationship of the short stories to the novels in terms of 'the little pieces of clay left over after the manufacture of earthenware . . . the remainder of characters, events and thoughts from his long works'.[3] This statement should not be taken as dismissive of the short stories; it only seeks to point out that both the stories and novels draw from the same intellectual substance. Indeed, while the novels will always remain the critic's main source for composing the jigsaw of the author's world-picture, the short stories will be immensely valuable in highlighting particular aspects of his vision and reassuring the critic on the soundness of his interpretation of the novels. It is in this sense (and only in this sense) that the stories may be seen as subordinate to the novels. But as works of art to be read and enjoyed, and as edifiers of the human soul, their independence and importance in their own right can only be self-evident.

THE BEGINNING

Mahfouz started writing stories while he was still an undergraduate. His first known published story goes back to 1932.[4] Regular publication, however, did not begin until after his graduation in 1934. By 1946 he had published seventy-four stories altogether in the various literary and general magazines of the day in Cairo.[5] At a date that has so far been difficult to determine with precision[6] (but which we know must be at least later than April 1945)[7] he collected twenty-eight[8] of these stories and published them under the title *Whispers of Madness*.[9] The rest remain uncollected to date and reports of scholars who have taken the trouble to look them up in their original sources indicate that they are largely naive juvenilia with little artistic merit,[10] which probably explains why Mahfouz has been happy to leave them be. In common with the late Professor Badr, one can only assume that the stories chosen for inclusion in the collection must represent in the view of their writer the cream of the total of seventy-four stories.[11] Be this as it may, today these stories, very like the early historical novels, are only of 'historical' value, as the primitive stages in the evolution of a prodigious talent. They are written in a prose style as yet unliberated from classical ornateness and cliché and the influence of al-Manfalūṭī's sentimentalism.[12] Structurally, they are weak, tending to rely heavily on coincidence and improbable situations,[13] while the author is ever intrusively present with cumbersome didactic comment. Nevertheless, for all their faults and artistic immaturity, one can see (in their preoccupations at least) that these stories were written by the Mahfouz-to-be. The roots of the author's socialism[14] and nationalism[15] are there, as are those of his life-long obsession with time and the ironies of fate, however simple and less than half-formed.[16] There, too, are the blueprints for some of his typical characters and situations.[17] Finally, there too are the roots of the author's tragic sense of life and his profound sadness for the individual, twice crushed by the injustice of society and the less tractable harshness that is at the centre of existence.[18]

THE SECOND BEGINNING

By the time Mahfouz came to collect and publish the stories of *Whispers of Madness*, he had already published his first six novels[19] and made the shift from historical romance to realism. For the next fifteen years or so it would appear that the short story was but a fleeting passion of early youth or the training ground for the author's real mission. Those years were spent in perfecting the techniques of realism up to *The Trilogy* and the allegorical *Children of Gebelawi*. They also saw the increasing use of the stream-of-consciousness technique and the final shift from traditional, omniscient narration to the restricted viewpoint; from the sprawling novel to the condensed plot and the poetic, taut and symbol-strewn prose style such as *The Thief and the Dogs* had to offer. During that period, too, the author's metaphysical quest for God and the meaning of existence had begun to dominate his work (beginning with his exploration of Kamāl's spiritual crisis in *The Trilogy*) and probably played an important role in determining the new aesthetic form that his work was to take. In 1963, however, much to the surprise of his critics, Mahfouz (now a mature, established novelist) published a second collection of short stories, namely *God's World*,[20] on which all the above accomplishments were brought to bear. Moreover, the following years were soon to prove that this newly rediscovered passion was there to stay and effloresce, mostly in line with his novelistic development, but sometimes taking wild turns of its own and unleashing in the author fresh powers of creativity untapped in the novels (as happened in the post-1967 Absurd explosion). From 1963 to date thirteen collections have been published.

God's World is predominantly an awed and bewildered contemplation of the mysterious phenomenon of death: seven of its fourteen stories deal with the subject through haunting metaphors and situations. I am only able to look briefly at two of them here. In '*Qātil*' (Murderer), the story explores the psyche of a one-time petty criminal, cornered finally by beggary and unemployment after release from a term of imprisonment into accepting a murder contract. On the day assigned for the crime, the protagonist follows his would-be victim through the activities of his day awaiting the right moment for the attack. As we too follow him with the protagonist, we find ourselves in the frightful position of becoming privy to the secret intrigues of fate. The ironies of the situation hit us as we see the victim go to the funeral of a friend, unaware that before the end of the day he will be joining him in death, and as we eavesdrop on him later at a café talking to various companions about his plans for the next day and the longer-term future. The murderer, completely unknown to the victim and lacking a personal motive, becomes a powerful symbol of death as an abstract agent stalking human beings relentlessly, as they go about the business of living, before it strikes out of nowhere.

In 'Ḍidd Majhūl' (By a Person Unknown),[21] a police detective is involved in investigating a mysterious murder case without apparent motive and with not a trace of evidence. Soon more murders are committed in exactly the same style, leaving the diligent detective and his assistants entirely helpless before the riddle of this serial killer who makes no distinction in his choice of victim between rich and poor, old and young, healthy and ill. The unstoppable killer, it dawns on us as we go along, is none other than death itself; death 'with its silence, mysteriousness, unfamiliarity, cruelty, irony and impossibility' (p. 108). Finally, the killer strikes the investigating detective himself (who has felt the increasing strain of the case all the time), as he sits in his own office. Horror sweeps across an already shaken community, with the result that the new investigator announces a news blackout on future developments of the case. 'No talking of death after today,' he tells his team. 'Life must go on as usual. . . . Meanwhile, the investigation shall continue' (p. 119): death is the one certain fact in our lives, yet it is the most taboo subject of conversation and the thought furthest from the mind until it is forced to confront it. As for the 'continuing investigation', this must be seen in the context of Mahfouz's famed belief in the unlimited potential of science:[22] there are symbolic references in the story to forensic examinations, while the police detective stands of course for the 'detective' powers of science. Death, we have seen, is a recurrent subject in the author's novels, but it is in short stories like these that he is able to confront his readers, with admirable intensity and clarity, with a painful realization of mankind's at once most personal and most common experience. Finally, the subject of 'God' is never too far from that of 'death': both are related aspects of the metaphysical. No wonder then that in the proximity of so much death in *God's World*, we encounter 'Zaᶜbalāwī'[23] the author's most celebrated metaphor for a sick humanity's persistent search for an ever-elusive God, a search which is at once its pain and its hope.[24]

In 1965 the collection *A House of Ill Repute* was published to show the author still haunted by visions of death and trying to purge his awe in one metaphor after another: eleven out of the eighteen stories of the collection are treatments of the fearful subject, with death here mostly shown in the context of time, as the final episode in an inevitable process. Interestingly, the stories in the collection generally display in their artistic conception and execution a strong affinity with the author's contemporaneous novels. They too are metaphors well grounded in realistic detail, while pointing at a higher symbolic meaning. 'Qubayl al-Raḥīl' (Shortly before Departure), to take one example, tells the story of a government official being transferred after four years of service from the beautiful city of Alexandria to the desolate and remote Asyūṭ in Upper Egypt. Before his departure he decides to spend a night in the company of an attractive prostitute he has always seen in his habitual café but never got round to inviting her to his flat, just as he never got round to visiting any of the Alexandrian attractions. After they make love, she returns to him her fee already paid in advance. She explains that when she is especially gratified, she makes no charge. For the rest of the night, the man is unable to contain his joy. He takes her for an evening out, and in enthusiastic demonstration of his virility engages in one fight after another with men he believes truly or falsely are making advances to the woman. He takes her back to his flat still feeling on top of the world and in her warm embraces seeks shelter from an awful storm raging outside. The following morning the woman demands her fee back: it was all a trick to make him happy before his departure, she explains. 'What an idiot you are!' he exclaims. 'Don't you see it is a trick you can't play twice?' 'Who said we would meet again?' says she (p. 14).

The woman is significantly named Dunyā (i.e. life, time, the world, etc.), not an uncommon female proper name in Egypt. This free clue, however, was hardly needed. The texture of the story is sufficiently enriched with suggestive signs that hint at the symbolic understratum of meaning. The 'departure' of the story is one from life to death, symbolized by the transfer of the official from north to south, the movement deeper into the country being the descent into the underworld. Similarly, the unvisited sights of Alexandria are the many lost opportunities and unfulfilled wishes of life. The prostitute, on the other hand, stands for the fickleness of time, the changes of fortune. But fickle as life or *dunyā* may be, its lure is all-powerful and we want to cling on to it, as the man does to the woman. And like him we are flattered by our little achievements in life, 'our virilities', as it were, and are happy to enter into endless conflicts to safeguard them from others, only to be confronted in the end with the sobering realization of the ephemerality, the unreality of our 'virility', and the knowledge that 'life', like the prostitute of the story, can only be enjoyed once, and only for a short time 'before the departure'.[25]

THE FLIGHT INTO ABSURDITY

In 1969 Mahfouz published two collections: *The Black Cat Tavern*[26] and *Under the Bus Shelter.* The first of these two collections comprises nineteen stories, which mostly share with the two previous ones their thematic and stylistic features, with God, death, time and above all the ironies of fate dominating the stories. Though published in 1969, it appears, however, that most of the stories in this collection were written prior to the national trauma of 1967, since none of them (with the possible exception of the title-story)[27] demonstrates the tremendous effect that the events of 1967 were to have for a while on Mahfouz's work. This effect is in fact to be found, to start with, in the second collection of the same year, *Under the Bus Shelter.*[28] Indeed, the author goes out of his way to ensure that his readers are aware of the specific historical context against which the stories were written: on the back of the flyleaf he records uncharacteristically that 'these stories were written in the period between October and December 1967'. That is to say, they were his first reaction in art form to the national catastrophe of 5 June 1967. The collection contains six stories and five one-act plays. Two of the stories, namely 'Al-Ḥāwī Khaṭaf al-Ṭabaq' (The Conjurer Made off with Dish)[29] and 'Thalāthat Ayyām fī al-Yaman' (Three Days in Yemen), are very likely to have been written before June 1967 despite their inclusion in this collection. They are completely out of tune with the rest of the book, the first being a subtle metaphor equating the loss of innocence and parental protection attendant on growing up with the insecurity and sense of loss resulting from living in a Godless world, while the second is a fictionalized record of the author's impressions from a short official visit to the Yemen during the involvement of the Egyptian army there. Both stories are written in the author's familiar realistic style.

The rest of the stories (and for that matter the plays too) represent, however, a substantial departure from the author's habitual way of recreating external reality in his work up to that time. What we experience here is an expressionist or even a surrealist reality characterized by a total collapse of rationality and structure. The world these works present us with is one where conclusions bear no relevance to premises and where language is no guarantee of communication. It is also a world without a sense of purpose, a world where anarchy, futility and violence reign supreme. In short, it is a world depicted in the best traditions of the literature of the absurd. The fatal passivity of a society of indifferent onlookers is recreated in 'Taḥt al-Maẓalla' (Under the Bus Shelter), where a group of people waiting for the bus (which never arrives) watch, taking place under their noses, thefts, murders, deadly car crashes, burial of the living, sex orgies, decapitated heads rolling at their feet – all without lifting a finger. When finally they approach a policeman, who has been happily looking on all the time, he charges them with illegal assembly and guns them all down on the spot. National passivity is denounced again[30] in 'Al-Nawm' (Sleep),[31] where a man is shown shamefully dozing off in a café while the woman he loved was being murdered as she called out to him only a few steps away. Again in 'Al-Wajh al-Ākhar' (The Other Face), we see the conflict between the values of 'reason and moderation' on the one hand, and 'instinct' or 'the life force' on the other, personified by two brothers: one a police officer and the other an outlaw. When Ramaḍān (Instinct) refuses to abide by the laws of ᶜUthmān (Reason), he is hunted down and killed. When this happens, the narrator, a friend of both brothers and so far one who conforms to the laws of reason, loses his faith and decides to 'abandon good conduct and rules and rituals'. Instead he turns into a bohemian artist and 'unfolds [his] sails in the face of the storm' (p. 53). This is quite uncharacteristic of Mahfouz – to come down in favour of unruly passion over reason, law and order! A momentary despair perhaps at the famed moderation and submissive conformity of his people, who happily suffered the authoritarian rule which finally led them to defeat.[32]

It is, however, in 'Al-Ẓalām' (The Darkness) that Mahfouz makes his bitterest ridicule of authoritarian rule and popular stupor at once. The force of the metaphor he creates exercises maximal effect through the abstraction, in the manner of the theatre of the absurd, of the situation to its very bare rudiments. The author reduces the conditions of existence under a police state to a gathering in the dark by a group of drug-addicts in a remote and secluded room – a haven provided by a master drug-pusher who has his clients totally under his control. In the total darkness his well-trained eyes can see them, but they cannot see him nor each other. They come from all walks of life but nothing binds them together except the common darkness and the promise of 'security and protection' by the *Muᶜallim* or Chief. He extols to them the advantages of 'darkness' which shields them both from the external world and each other: 'Look at your different religions and convictions, yet you are able to have a good time in perfect harmony thanks to the darkness and the silence' (p. 32). The Orwellian big-brother portrait of the Chief is undoubtedly a satire of Nasser, the darkness a metaphor for the information blackout characteristic of a totalitarian regime, while the drug-induced stupor epitomizes the nature of the relationship between a charismatic autocrat and his mass-hypnotized people. One evening the Chief, who always monopolized speech (the dictator as educator of his nation), falls silent. The men, who are entirely dependent on him for safe conduct out of the place, are terror-stricken. They grope in the dark and establish that his place is vacant, that the door is securely locked and that the room is without windows. Trapped, they summon up their courage to strike matches and dispel the darkness, only to find that their match-boxes have been stolen (people deprived of means of access to information). They also discover the theft of their identity cards (people turned into a featureless mass, their identity melting into the personality cult of the leader). This episode appears to conjure up the helpless, infantile dependency of a people on their dictatorial leader, with the temporary disappearance of the Chief possibly modelled on Nasser's short-lived resignation from the presidency on 9 June 1967, which was popularly rejected in a massive display of emotion.[33] The parallelism, however, is not followed through in the story, because the Chief who reappears (much to the relief of his captive clients) is far from repentant (unlike the Nasser returned by the people on 10 June). He admits to stealing their matches and ID cards, but assures them that he had not left his place for one minute and that in fact they had been unconscious under the influence of a curious narcotic mixture of his invention. When they argue that they 'groped his empty place with their hands . . . , banged on the walls and called out in voices like thunder', he tells them that 'you had only imagined actions which never actually took form outside your brains' (p. 38) (in totalitarian regimes boundaries between reality and illusion cease to exist). The Chief goes on to tell them that before dawn they will have lost their memory under the influence of his narcotic (in a totalitarian system the past is obliterated or falsified in the cause of glorifying the present). Finally, he tells them that it is time 'to try my madness': 'Lie down like corpses on your cushions,' says he, 'for tomorrow the emptiness will welcome your youthful bodies dampened with the dew of the fields' (p. 39). He also promises to take the same narcotic and to follow them. (The relationship between a totalitarian ruler and his nation is in the last analysis a suicide pact.)

Mahfouz's sudden headlong dive into surrealist and absurdist modes of expression left his critics reeling from the impact of the surprise. True, he had earlier given expression to issues of an absurdist, existentialist nature (such as in *The Beggar* and *Chatter on the Nile*), but this was mainly done through a rationalist mode of narrative which showed a certain respect for external reality. This was now no longer the case, with the artistic reality badly distorted to reflect the disintegration of the society it sought to comment on. The author was showered with questions from astounded critics and curious interviewers. Always happy to comment on his work, he provided the answers. In his pronouncements on the subject he appears well aware of what I hope the above analysis of 'The Darkness' has gone some way to show, namely that his version of *absurdity* is one that is highly structured and fraught with *meaning*. He refers, almost apologetically, to the period in which he wrote the stories as one during which he 'had lost his balance' and thus came 'to write works which were *seemingly*[34] absurd'. He goes on to say:

> However, my insistence on [social] commitment spoiled their absurdity. . . . In those works I painted a world that was confused, fragmented and devoid of logic or reason. But it was apparent, despite this, that there was a certain meaning that I was driving at. . . . It appears that I had not completely given in to the absurd.[35]

Mahfouz's affair with the absurd was in fact to prove a passing though intense infatuation but it was not to spill over from his stories and playlets into his novels. By the early 1970s the whole episode was over and for a long time after, the author was at pains to distance himself from it:

> I do not believe in the philosophy of the absurd. . . . Absurdity believes in nothing, whereas I have many things that I believe in. Absurdity finds no meaning in life, whereas to me it is full of meaning. Absurdity, in its grief before death, is oblivious of civilization, whereas before civilization I tend to ignore death.[36]

THE PLAYS

Mahfouz's absurdist phase coincided with another no less astounding development in his creative life. Nearly 60 years of age with some thirty years of writing behind him, during which he had established himself as the unrivalled novelist in Arabic, he started to publish in *Al-Ahrām* a series of one-act plays which he collected later in *Under the Bus Shelter*, as mentioned above. The plays, if anything, are even more steeped in absurdity than the contemporary stories. But, as in the stories again, it is Mahfouz's own brand of 'meaningful absurdity'. All five plays appear to be concerned with examining certain negative and positive values, which by their presence in or absence from Egyptian life, led, in the author's view, to the 1967 debacle. This is achieved from behind a screen of abstraction and distortion. No particularly Egyptian scene is evoked, nor is the 1967 defeat mentioned. The characters are nameless, while the stage settings are mostly frugal and expressionistic in nature.[37] The dialogue, which is written in simple standard Arabic,[38] is often witty and racy, maintaining a quick rhythm through generally short speeches and occasional repartee. 'Yumīt wa Yuḥyī' (Death and Resurrection) examines the trepidations of a young man faced with a menacing danger and torn between his love for life and sense of dignity. In the end the play appears to laud freedom as an absolute value that should be maintained even in the face of death. 'Al-Tirka' (The Legacy) examines the debilitating tensions between the spiritual 'legacy' of the past and the necessity of scientific progress at the expense of this legacy. The ironically titled 'Al-Najāt' (Rescue),[39] on the other hand, dramatizes with great intensity the fear, the despondency, the sense of siege, and finally the gratuitous death of the individual living under a police state. 'Mashrū^{c} lil-Munāqasha' (A Project for Debate) portrays a dogmatic tyrannical playwright, who refuses to consider the views of his actors and director on a play he is writing. In this respect at least, the play is a variation on the theme of 'The Darkness', the story discussed earlier.

'Al-Mahamma' (The Task), the fifth and last play in this collection, is in line with the general purport of the four stories previously discussed. Fantasy and abstraction are again placed in the service of a sharp intellectual message, which consists in the disparagement of passivity, inaction, the shunning of responsibility and resignation to a presumed destiny – a message that the author appeared anxious to 'rub in' to his people in the aftermath of 1967. I will look at the play in some detail. A youth arrives at an empty spot in the desert for a rendezvous with his girl friend. Soon after a middle-aged man appears. The youth is upset to see him as he suspects the man has been following him all day. The youth confronts him with a list of all the places he has followed him to from early morning, but the man attributes it all to coincidence and maintains that he has finally come to this spot to watch the sunset. The girl arrives but the presence of the man dominates the conversation and spoils the assignation. They hear the noise of snoring and in their effort to establish whether the man has indeed fallen asleep, they wake him up. He then forces his attention on them and offers to demonstrate to the youth how to make love properly to the girl. When she slaps him on the face, he retreats and engages in a series of asides, in which he argues that his good intentions are always misunderstood by people, who create their own troubles and then blame him for them. When the girl finally leaves in despair, he goes to apologize to the youth saying that he was only trying to make friends, but that his 'bad luck' always stood between him and people. He now admits that he has been following the youth all day to seek his friendship and dispel his own bad luck. The youth in turn rails at him and blames on him his own 'bad luck' all day:

> *Youth* Now I know the secret of the bad luck that kept me company all day.
> *Man* Don't be like the others!
> *Youth* In Citadel Square I slipped and hurt my knee.
> *Man (smiling)* You were looking at a woman in a window.
> *Youth* At the restaurant I nearly choked to death.
> *Man* You were gulping down food as if in a race.
>
> (p. 240)

The list goes on in the same manner: the youth blames his ill luck over one thing or another on the man, and the man offers a perfectly rational explanation for it. The man thus is gradually shown to be a personification of ill fortune on which people blame their own failures. Meanwhile the youth's injured knee gets worse and he is unable to walk back to town. The man (whose friendship he has rejected) now refuses to help him, and at sunset he goes away, leaving him behind in the desert. The sunset is in fact symbolic of the youth's death. In the next scene he is attended by two fierce men, who clearly stand for Nākir and Nakīr, the two angels who, in popular Moslem belief, interrogate the dead in their graves. The young man's interrogation centres on the 'task' he had been entrusted with but failed to do. He denies any knowledge of a task:

> *Man I* What have you done with your long day? Why did you go to Citadel Square?
> *Youth* I was wandering about aimlessly.
> *Man I* You wander about aimlessly when you have been sent there on a task!
> *Youth* It was my day off.
> *Man II* Did the Citadel not remind you of your task?
> *Youth* I slipped and hurt my knee.
> (*Man II lashes youth with a whip. Youth screams.*)
>
> (p. 251)

The interrogation goes on, interspersed with torture, and all pleas for mercy are rejected. The message is clear: life is a 'task', a mission, and it is a morally unforgivable sin to let it slip away in inaction, blaming one's own shortcomings on fate or unpropitious circumstances.

A word of warning to the reader whose only knowledge of these works so far is what he reads here will perhaps not be out of place. These works, because of the expressionist-cum-surrealist style in which they are executed, tend to suffer more than others when summarized and deciphered. They should not therefore be thought to be as didactic or dry as they may seem when subjected to interpretative analysis. They have indeed a life of their own, which is multilayered and open to various readings. This is so much the case that one critic has argued, not without good cause, that the obscurity of these works makes them impervious except to a selected few.[40]

Mahfouz's flirtation with the theatre, which appeared to be an integral part of his short-lived connection with the absurd, came to an end more or less at the same time as the latter did. He explains his shift to drama in the aftermath of 1967 in an interview given in 1970 in the following terms:

> There is no doubt that today we live in the age of the theatre. The present moment [in our history], fraught with ideas and problems, can only be debated through the theatre. . . . The novel needs calmness, consideration and settled conditions, and because of this it must now step aside and let the theatre take control.[41]

He tries, however, to present his switch to the theatre as part of 'a natural and gradual development' in his work, rather than the sudden unaccountable one it may have seemed to be: 'I found that I had to depend increasingly on dialogue in not a small number of my recent stories and novels.'[42]

In addition to the five one-act plays included in *Under the Bus Shelter* and treated above, the author has included three more in later collections (which brings his total output for the theatre to eight plays). The first of these, 'Al-Muṭārada' (The Chase),[43] portrays in expressionistic terms Death's relentless chase of man through the phases of life. The second, 'Al-Jabal' (The Mountain),[44] appears, unlike all the other plays, to stick to a conventional as opposed to expressionistic representation of reality in situation and dialogue. It is, however, a political parable dealing with one of Mahfouz's favourite themes, i.e. revolutionary idealism gone awry on assumption of absolute power – the author's judgement, no doubt, on the 1952 revolution. The third and last play, 'Al-Shayṭān Yaᶜiẓ' (The Devil Preaches),[45] is a fantasy inspired, as the author acknowledges on the title-page, by the tale of 'The City of Brass' in *The Thousand and One Nights*.[46] Here we are given a warning, among other things, against the dangers of placing the limitless power of science (symbolized here by a jinni) under the control of despotic rulers – a warning already forcefully voiced, as we have seen, in the last section (ᶜArafa) of *Children of Gebelawi*.

THE *ḤUWĀRIYYĀT*

In 1971, Mahfouz published two further collections of short stories: *A Tale without Beginning or End* and *The Honeymoon*. Some of the stories are now written in the author's old familiar style of symbolic or two-layered realism, but the majority are still characterized by a wild imagination scornful of observable reality. The themes all come from the author's customary repertoire with its persistent preoccupation with Egypt's immediate political and cultural crises. The stories are at times limited to portraying social disaffection (e.g. 'ᶜAnbar Lūlū' (Cell Block Lūlū) in the first collection), and at others go on to point to the author's vision of a way out, which consists invariably in commitment to responsibility, facing up to reality and the adoption of a scientific outlook (e.g. 'Al-Rajul alladhī Faqad Dhākiratuh Marratayn' (The Man who Lost his Memory Twice) in the first collection and 'Nāfidha fī al-Ḍawr al-Khāmis wa al-Thalāthīn' (A Window in the Thirty-fifth Floor)[47] in the second). Two allegorical stories in the first collection deserve special mention here. The first is the title-story, which denounces institutionalized religion as a fake, self-interested body, whose grip over society is a serious obstacle to the causes of social justice and scientific progress. The second story, 'Ḥārat al-ᶜUshshāq' (Lovers' Alley), traces (through the highly amusing metaphor of a husband ever suspicious of his wife's fidelity), the intellectual evolution of humankind through the stages of animism, belief in God, faith in the supremacy of reason to, finally, scientific empiricism, which (we are given to believe) is not sufficient for a happy coexistence with the world, but is the only tool we have to deal with it at this stage of our evolution.[48] Finally, one must point out that most of the stories in both collections are extraordinarily dominated by dialogue, with narrative interspersions often needing nothing much more than brackets to turn them into stage directions.[49] Conscious of their peculiar quality, the author coined the word *ḥuwāriyya* (a dialogic story) to describe this particular type of stories:

> A *ḥuwāriyya* is in essence a story which depends on dialogue. If you want to read it as a story, you can. And if you think it is suitable for the stage, no adaptation will be needed.[50]

THE RECOIL FROM ABSURDITY

The barrage of short stories which took the shape of four collections published between 1969 and 1971 was temporarily interrupted to herald the author's return to novel writing with *Mirrors* in 1972 and *Love in the Rain* in 1973. The first novel's episodic form and the second's lack of a central plot or character, however, show the author to have been still in a mood which inclined to, as it were, the piecemeal rather than the wholesale contemplation of reality. In 1973 another collection of stories was published under the title *The Crime*. The collection is largely a continuation of the expressionist-cum-surrealist trend discussed above. Thematically, the stories point at a relaxation in the importunate preoccupation with the immediate political reality which characterized the earlier collections. Most of the stories here are forays into the author's usual metaphysical haunts. In retrospect, *The Crime* was largely to mark the end of the absurdist connection in Mahfouz's career.[51]

After *The Crime* there was to be a lull in the publication of short stories for a period of about five years, during which Mahfouz produced five novels including his highly innovative work *Harafish*. In 1979, however, two further collections were published, namely *The Devil Preaches* and *Love under the Pyramids*. Both collections are dominated by longish stories averaging 40–50 pages. The staccato prose, often poetic, pensive and full of a sense of wonder at the nature of things, reveals a close affinity with the style of the contemporarily published *Harafish*. In their socio-political scope, the stories are a testimony to Mahfouz's untiring, almost stoical, effort to keep up with the woes of his nation. This is a task which he undertook for over half a century and under a variety of regimes and social conditions, yet he always managed to sense with an unfailing instinct what was wrong with his country and be the first to give it expression: it is no wonder that he has often been described as the conscience of his nation. In these collections the pain and confusion of the post-1967 years is no longer there. Meanwhile another Arab–Israeli war has come and gone. The Suez Canal has been crossed and the myth of the invincibility of Israel laid to rest. This, coupled with the measured political and economic liberalization initiated by a buoyant and self-confident Sādāt in the mid-1970s, helped boost the public morale for a while. But the Sādāt promise proved a fiction all too soon with the euphoria of the military achievement of October 1973 giving way again to political stalemate; democratization proving to be only surface-deep; and *infitāḥ* or economic liberalization creating a new class of the super-rich rather than bringing plenty to the many.

Mahfouz, whose nationalist and artistic instincts simply rejected the passing euphoria and showed no trace of it in his work, was quick to capture the new frustration and disaffection in his stories of the late 1970s. Official corruption, abuse of power, political manipulation of the justice system, illegitimate wealth, the displacement of the middle class in the consumerist society created by the *infitāḥ* policy, unemployment, shortage of housing, the sexual frustration of a generation of young people crippled on the one hand with a conservative social attitude to premarital sex, and too economically constrained, on the other, to afford marriage – all these issues and, above all, the crack under their pressure in individual morality and the loss of belief in social ideals, are widely recreated by the author in stories like 'Ayyūb' (Job),[52] 'Al-Rabīᶜ al-Qādim' (Next Spring) and 'Qarār fī Ḍaw' al-Barq' (A Lightning Decision) in *The Devil Preaches*, and 'Ahl al-Qimma' (The People at the Top) and 'Al-Ḥubb Fawq Haḍabat al-Haram' (Love under the Pyramids)[53] in the second collection which bears the title of the latter story.

But alert as he is to the crude and humdrum necessities of human life and never oblivious to their importance in determining individual action and shaping social movement, Mahfouz has remained at all times preoccupied to the point of obsession with the pursuit of a truth higher than anything that the physical world or history can offer us for the comprehension of ourselves – that kind of truth we normally call God. In these collections, as elsewhere in the author's work, physical hunger and spiritual thirst go hand in hand. Thus in proximity with the stories dealing with issues of society we find as many dealing with the holy quest or (as often in Mahfouz) inseparably combining the two pursuits. In 'Al-Rajul al-Thānī' (The Second Man), to take an example from *The Devil Preaches*, the author explores the concept of man's God-appointed mission on earth through the intriguing metaphor of a *futuwwa* (thug) who elects one of his men to carry out a mysterious and impossible task, promising him the position of 'second man' in the gang if successful. As the situation grows more complex and one error leads to another, the *futuwwa* offers his man no guidance whatsoever, enigmatically ordering him at each turn to 'continue' with the task. Finally, the aspiring man dies in the pursuit of a mission whose meaning or goal he never comprehended. But until the end he refuses to contemplate the notion that perhaps his chief was playing a practical joke on him – that there was no mission and no goal; that it was all absurd.

The author's untiring pursuit of God continues in 'Nūr al-Qamar' (a female proper name meaning 'Moonlight'). The story, included in *Love under the Pyramids*, must indeed be counted among his best renderings of this favourite theme of his. It is the story of a middle-aged man's obsessive love for a young and beautiful woman singer at a popular cabaret. The girl remains unattainable throughout, despite the countless sacrifices made and risks taken by the besotted protagonist. The whole experience is told in the suggestive terms of *ṣūfī* love. The girl finally runs away from the cabaret and her selfish, overprotective old guardian (God breaking free from the bondage of institutionalized religion?). After a harsh struggle with the self, the protagonist triumphs over his suicidal despair following the disappearance of the girl. He finds distraction in social and political involvement, but never ceases to hope that one day he may find the elusive object of his love. One can argue here that the protagonist of 'Nūr al-Qamar' represents Mahfouz's *modus vivendi* for the relationship between man and God. Unlike Ṣābir in *The Search*, the protagonist here draws back from the brink of despair at the right moment, acknowledging the validity of positive involvement in life as at least a painkiller, if not a proper cure, for the metaphysical ailment. But like Zaᶜbalāwī in the eponymous story (in *God's World*) he is determined to go on looking for the eternal healer. In Mahfouz involvement in life is in fact the only commendable path to God.

In 1982 Mahfouz published a collection titled *I Saw in a Dream*, followed in 1984 by yet another, viz. *The Secret Organization*. The stories of these collections represent yet further variations on the author's familiar repertoire of themes, his inventive powers apparently never failing to find fresh and memorable metaphors for old concerns. The prose is often lyrical and evocative, while the narrative technique tends to depend on dreams, visions and the interweaving of the realistic and the fantastic in a way that smacks of the methods of magical realism in the work of Gabriel Garcia Marquez.[54]

In 1989 Mahfouz published a collection entitled *The False Dawn*[55] which contains no less than thirty very short stories averaging about five pages each. Most of the stories are of a social or political documentary nature, while a few continue with the metaphysical search. One deserving special mention is a four-page story, 'Niṣf Yawm' (Half a Day), which merges, in one moment of time, the consciousness of the protagonist both as a child passing his first day at school and as an old man unable to cross a busy road. It is a technical *tour de force* achieving verbally what even celluloid may find difficult to achieve. Brief as it is, the story must count as the author's most powerful rendering of the dilemma of the gulf between observable time and mnemonic time.[56] This collection remains Mahfouz's latest published book to date. In his eighties, frail in health and with fading eyesight, the author has recently complained of a state of creative barrenness and argued that in the future he would probably only be able to express himself, if at all, through the short-story medium.[57] He continues, however, to write his weekly current-affairs column in the Cairo daily *Al-Ahrām*.

NOTES

1 THE WRITER AND HIS WORLD

1 See ch. 6, n. 31 for the meaning of the word 'ḥarāfish'. Henceforth I will refer to this novel as simply *Harafish*.
2 Jamāl al-Ghīṭānī, *Naguib Mahfouz Yatadhakkar*, introduction to 3rd edition, Cairo: Mu'assasat Akhbār al-Yawm, 1987(?), p. 22. (First published by Dār al-Masīra, Beirut, 1980. The first edition did not contain the 44-page introduction by al-Ghīṭānī added to the later edition.)
3 ibid., p. 56.
4 ibid., p. 57.
5 ibid., p. 107.
6 ibid., pp. 46–7.
7 ibid., p. 47.
8 ibid., pp. 120–1.
9 See interview in *Al-Muṣawwar*, 21 October 1988, pp. 10–19, 68–73.
10 See J. al-Ghīṭānī, op. cit., p. 125.
11 ibid., p. 124.
12 ibid., p. 126.
13 *Takiyya* from the Turkish *tekke*, a religious foundation of a quasi-monastic type. The history of the *takiyya* in Egypt was a continuation of that of the *khānqāh* (a composite word of Persian origin, also denoting a building usually reserved for Muslim mystics, belonging to a dervish order). The foundation of *khānqāhs* in Egypt began under the Ayyūbids after the fall of the Fāṭimids in the later twelfth century and continued under the Mamluks. From the Ottoman period onwards (the sixteenth century), *khānqāhs* were still founded, but they appeared more and more in the form of the Turkish institution *tekke*. Many of these institutions have survived to the present day. See 'Khānqāh' in *Encyclopaedia of Islām*, Leiden: E. J. Brill, New Edition, 1978.
14 J. al-Ghīṭānī, op. cit., p. 47.
15 At the outset of *The Trilogy*, whose action begins in 1917, Kamāl (whose childhood and youth are modelled on the author's) is aged

10, which means that during the events of 1919 he was 12. It is probably the case that Mahfouz has chosen to make his persona in the novel some five years older than himself to allow himself more flexibility in portraying the child's involvement in the events: a 12-year-old is naturally more mature, more observant and capable of independent movement than a 7-year-old.

16 J. al-Ghīṭānī, op. cit., p. 16.
17 ibid., p. 52.
18 In *The Trilogy* I (pp. 420–1), there is a dramatic description of the child Kamāl's first experience of the sound of bullets, fired on a demonstration.
19 Naguib Mahfouz, *Mirrors*, p. 45; see also the episodes on 'Riḍā Ḥamāda' and 'Nādir Burhān' for further treatment of the events of 1919.
20 See p. 4.
21 See J. al-Ghīṭānī, op. cit., pp. 52, 101, 106; see also Naguib Mahfouz, *Ataḥaddath Ilaykum*, Beirut: Dār al-ᶜAwda, 1977, p. 78.
22 ibid., p. 79.
23 ibid., p. 80.
24 J. al-Ghīṭānī, op. cit., pp. 45–6.
25 ibid., p. 46.
26 ibid.
27 ibid., pp. 49–50, 153.
28 See *Al-Hilāl*, February 1970, pp. 98–9.
29 Muṣṭafā Kāmil (1874–1908) championed the call for ending the British occupation of Egypt. He founded Al-Ḥizb Al-Waṭanī (the National Party) in 1907.
30 Muḥammad Farīd (1867–1919) led the National Party after Muṣṭafā Kāmil's death in 1908.
31 Saᶜd Zaghlūl (1860–1927) led Egypt's national struggle for independence from 1918 until his death. His arrest (together with other leaders) by the British authorities in March 1919 and subsequent exile to Malta triggered the popular revolution of the same year. In 1923 he won the general election with a sweeping majority and became prime minister. He was idolized in his own lifetime and became a living symbol of the national aspirations of the nation. After his death the Wafd (i.e. delegation) Party which he had founded was to remain in the forefront of the national struggle until its abolition together with other political parties after the 1952 army coup.
32 *Ataḥaddath Ilaykum*, pp. 80–1.
33 ibid., pp. 79, 84.
34 ibid., p. 79.
35 J. al-Ghīṭānī, op. cit., pp. 49, 153.
36 ibid., p. 52.
37 ibid., p. 53.
38 Mahfouz admits that his evocations of *khalā'* are owed to ᶜAbbāsiyya (see ibid., pp. 57–8).
39 The Arabic title is 'Niṣf Yawm'. See Naguib Mahfouz, *The False*

Dawn, 1989. A translation of this story is included in Naguib Mahfouz, *The Time and the Place and Other Stories*, trans. Denys Johnson-Davies, New York: Doubleday, 1991. For a brief discussion of the story, see p. 212

40 J. al-Ghīṭānī, op. cit., p. 58.

41 See Naguib Mahfouz, *Whispers of Madness*. The Arabic title of the story is 'Ḥulm Sā^{c}a', first published in *Al-Risāla*, 15 July 1940. See ^{c}Abd al-Muḥsin Ṭāhā Badr, *Naguib Mahfouz: al-Ru'ya wa al-Adāt*, Cairo: Dār al-Thaqāfa, 1978, p. 496.

42 See *Mirrors*, pp. 210–12.

43 ibid., p. 214.

44 J. al-Ghīṭānī, op. cit., p. 49.

45 Naguib Mahfouz, *Fountain and Tomb*, 'Tale 6', pp. 15–16.

46 ibid., see Tales nos. 4–7, 10, 17, 24, 25.

47 ibid., pp. 43–4.

48 J. al-Ghīṭānī, op. cit., pp. 60–1.

49 Fu'ād Dawwāra, *Naguib Mahfouz: min al-Qawmiyya ilā al-^{c}Ālamiyya*, Cairo: al-Hay'a al-Miṣriyya al-^{c}Āmma lil-Kitāb, 1989, pp. 211–12. Dawwāra's interview of Mahfouz was first published in *Al-Kātib*, no. 22, 1963.

50 Interview with al-Bannā in *Al-Ādāb*, July 1960; quoted in Sasson Somekh, *The Changing Rhythm*, Leiden: E. J. Brill, 1973, pp. 37–8.

51 J. al-Ghīṭānī, op. cit., p. 77. 'I did not know him closely' are the words used by Mahfouz. In a more recent statement, however, he argues that 'for ten whole years, 1929–39, Salāma Mūsā was my literary patron and tutor' (Ghālī Shukrī, *Naguib Mahfouz: min al-Jamāliyya ilā Nobel*, Cairo: al-Hay'a al-^{c}Āmma lil-Isti^{c}lāmāt, 1988, p. 98).

52 From an interview in *Al-Majalla*, January 1963; quoted in S. Somekh, op. cit., p. 38.

53 J. al-Ghīṭānī, op. cit., p. 62.

54 ibid.

55 Mahfouz, however, changes the details of the situation in the novel. There the choice is between the highly respected School of Law and the much despised Higher College for Teachers which Kamāl chooses. Kamāl, however, justifies his choice to his shocked father by quoting the study of the history of thought and 'the origins of life and its ultimate end' as the reasons behind his wish; subjects of an obviously philosophical nature.

56 F. Dawwāra, op. cit., p. 212.

57 Ibrāhīm Manṣūr, ed., *Al-Izdiwāj al-Thaqāfī wa Azmat al-Mu^{c}āraḍa al-Miṣriyya*, Beirut: Dār al-Ṭalī^{c}a, 1981, p. 86.

58 F. Dawwāra, op. cit., p. 212.

59 *Ataḥaddath Ilaykum*, pp. 87–8.

60 See A. T. Badr, op. cit., pp. 33–72 for a review of the articles, and pp. 489–93 for a bibliographic list.

61 ibid., pp. 46–8. For another brief review of some of Mahfouz's early philosophic articles and their relation to his later work, see also Ṣabrī Ḥāfiẓ, 'Naguib Mahfouz bayn al-Dīn wa al-Falsafa', *Al-*

Hilāl, February 1970, pp. 116–27.

62 For a fuller quotation of Mahfouz's views on time see pp. 70–1.

63 Discussed later in this book in chs 4 and 8 respectively.

64 See 'Bergson' in *The Encyclopaedia Britannica*.

65 For titles of the articles, see A. T. Badr, op. cit., pp. 489–93.

66 J. al-Ghīṭānī, op. cit., p. 75. Mahfouz's inner conflict is externalized in *The Trilogy* III (*passim*) through the lengthy dialogues between Kamāl and his friend Riyāḍ Qaldas, with Kamāl arguing the case for philosophy and Riyāḍ that for art. See also *The Trilogy* II (p. 222) for an early and brief exposition of the issue in a conversation between Kamāl and his friend, Ḥusayn Shaddād.

67 Mahfouz refers to a 1930 edition. However, I have only been able to look at a 1940 edition revised and extended by H. Pollock and C. Nairne (London: George Newnes). The book is a comprehensive survey in two volumes beginning from the Ancient Egyptian *Book of the Dead* up to the modernist movement in Europe. It is written in a simple style and addressed to the uninitiated reader. It must have suited Mahfouz well – a young convert from philosophy at the time.

68 In the following pages I have drawn heavily on the many interviews contained in Mahfouz's *Ataḥaddath Ilaykum*, in addition to F. Dawwāra (op. cit.) and J. al-Ghīṭānī (op. cit.). Where I feel a more specific reference is needed, I will give one.

69 J. al-Ghīṭānī, op. cit., p. 94; see also F. Dawwāra, op. cit., pp. 217–18.

70 *Ataḥaddath Ilaykum*, pp. 94–5.

71 See F. Dawwāra, op. cit., pp. 213–14.

72 *Ataḥaddath Ilaykum*, pp. 52, 154, 161–2.

73 ibid., pp. 95–6; see also J. al-Ghīṭānī, op. cit., p. 110.

74 J. al-Ghīṭānī, op. cit., pp. 93–4.

75 *Ataḥaddath Ilaykum*, p. 95.

76 J. al-Ghīṭānī, op. cit., p. 80.

77 ibid., pp. 100–1.

78 *Ataḥaddath Ilaykum*, p. 72.

79 J. al-Ghīṭanī, op. cit., p. 80.

80 See F. Dawwāra, op. cit., p. 226; see also *Ataḥaddath Ilaykum*, p. 96.

81 Interview given in I. Manṣūr, op. cit., p. 90.

82 ibid., p. 91.

83 Interview in *Al-Qabas*, 11 June 1987.

84 J. al-Ghīṭānī, op. cit., p. 117.

85 *Ataḥaddath Ilaykum*, p. 32. For some recreations of those violent scenes see *Mirrors*, sketches of 'Badr al-Zayādī' and 'Ṭāhā ᶜAnān'.

86 Badr quotes an article written by Mahfouz as early as 1930 in which he hails 'socialism' as a 'compromise' between 'communism' and 'individualism'. He also quotes another (written in 1943), in which he denounces 'the dictatorship of communism' and lauds the non-violent, reformative methods of 'socialist democracy'. See A. T. Badr, op. cit., pp. 43–4, 57–8.

87 For a discussion of this issue, see my article 'Religion in the Novels of Naguib Mahfouz', *British Society for Middle Eastern Studies Bulletin*, vol. 15, nos. 1 and 2, 1988, pp. 21–7.
88 J. al-Ghīṭānī, op. cit., p. 118.
89 See the sketch of ᶜAbd al-Wahhāb Ismāᶜīl' (the fictitious name Mahfouz gives Quṭb) in *Mirrors*, pp. 261–7; see also *Al-Hilāl*, December 1988, pp. 98–101 for confirmation of this interpretation of the character.
90 See ᶜAlī Shalash, *Naguib Mahfouz: al-Ṭarīq wa al-Ṣadā*, Beirut: Dār al-Ādāb, 1990. The book partly deals with the early critical reception of Mahfouz. The Appendices contain four reviews written for various magazines by Sayyid Quṭb during the years 1944–8. The reviews deal with the following novels: *The Struggle of Thebes*, *Khan al-Khalili*, *New Cairo* and *Midaq Alley*.
91 *Ataḥaddath Ilaykum*, pp. 16–17.
92 Mahfouz names the month of April 1952 as the completion date of *The Trilogy* (see J. al-Ghīṭānī, op. cit., p. 98).
93 Ghālī Shukrī, *Al-Muntamī*, Cairo: Dār al-Maᶜārif, 2nd edition, 1969, p. 239; see also F. Dawwāra, op. cit., p. 227; J. al-Ghīṭānī, op. cit., p. 138 (where Mahfouz seems to cast some doubt on his earlier explanation without really offering a new one); interview with Jūrj Ṭarābīshī in *Anwāl*, 31 March 1989, p. 15; *Ataḥaddath Ilaykum*, p. 91.
94 See G. Shukrī, *Al-Muntamī*, p. 239.
95 The only exception perhaps is *The Search*, which poses a metaphysical question within a symbolic framework and is without a direct political message.
96 Mahfouz, in common with other writers of the period, seems to contribute to this opinion. See interview in *Al-Muṣawwar*, 21 October 1988, pp. 10–19, 68–73.
97 *Ataḥaddath Ilaykum*, pp. 98–9.
98 In my discussion so far of Mahfouz's attitude to the 1952 revolution, I have relied considerably on my article 'The Novelist as Political Eye-witness: a View of Naguib Mahfouz's Evaluation of the Nasser and Ṣadāt Eras', *Journal of Arabic Literature*, vol. 21, 1990, pp. 72–86.
99 This is a reference to *Mīthāq al-ᶜAmal al-Waṭanī* (The Charter for National Action), the political manifesto of the state presented by Nasser to the nation in 1962.
100 See, for instance, the two columns titled 'Thawrat Yūlyū' in Naguib Mahfouz, *Of Religion and Democracy*, pp. 153–4, 189–90.
101 See, for instance, the two columns titled '23 Aghusṭus' and '13 Nūfambir' in Naguib Mahfouz, *Of Youth and Freedom*, pp. 160–1, 172–3.
102 ibid., 'Mā Baᶜd al-Jalā'', pp. 86–7; 'Matā Naᶜrif Qīmat al-Waqt?', pp. 108–9; 'Mādhā Taᶜnī Isrā'īl?', pp. 110–11.
103 For more details on Mahfouz's attitude *vis-à-vis* the peace with Israel see p. 236, n. 61.
104 See, for example, *Ataḥaddath Ilaykum*, p. 204; see also Ibrāhīm

^{c}Āmir, 'Naguib Mahfouz Siyāsiyyan', *Al-Hilāl*, February 1970, pp. 32–4.

105 Interview with Jūrj Ṭarābīshī in *Anwāl*, 31 March 1989, pp. 15, 21; see also interview in *Al-Qabas*, 11 June 1987.

106 For information used in the following pages I have drawn on these sources in order of importance (individual references will be occasionally given when this is felt to be particularly useful): J. al-Ghīṭānī, op. cit.; *Ataḥaddath Ilaykum*; Adham Rajab, 'Ṣafaḥāt Majhūla min Ḥayāt Naguib Mahfouz', and Muḥammad ^{c}Afīfī, 'Naguib Mahfouz Rajul al-Sā^{c}a' – both in *Al-Hilāl*, February 1970, pp. 92–9 and 137–41, respectively; Appendix on the author's life and work in *Of Youth and Freedom*, pp. 224–35; 'Ḥiwār ma^{c}a Naguib Mahfouz', *Al-Muṣawwar*, 21 October 1988, pp. 10–19, 68–73.

107 A notable example is his novel, *Respected Sir*.

108 For lists of both sets of films see appendix on the novelist's life and work in *Of Youth and Freedom*, pp. 231–4.

109 For a study on the adaptation of Mahfouz's work for the cinema, see Hāshim al-Naḥḥās, *Naguib Mahfouz ^{c}alā al-Shāsha*, Cairo: al-Hay'a al-Miṣriyya al-^{c}Āmma lil-Kitāb, 1975.

110 This count does not include such works as the collected interviews (*Ataḥaddath Ilaykum*), or the memoirs (*Naguib Mahfouz Yatadhakkar*), as the first was selected and introduced by Ṣabrī Ḥāfiẓ, while the second was prepared by Jamāl al-Ghīṭānī from conversations with Mahfouz. On the other hand, a work difficult to classify, *Before the Throne*, has been counted, for convenience's sake, as a novel.

111 This produced the short story 'Thalāthat Ayyām fī al-Yaman' (Three Days in Yemen) about Egyptian soldiers at war in Yemen (1962–7). The story is included in the collection *Under the Bus Shelter* (1969).

112 Ironically he was obliged to come to London as an old man in the winter of 1991 for heart surgery.

113 Compare the words of Kamāl in *The Trilogy* II (p. 195): 'It seems to me that I am naturally inclined to staying put. The idea of travelling alarms me – I mean the trouble and hassle, not the sightseeing and discovery. If only it were possible for the world to parade past while I stood where I am!'

114 See J. al-Ghīṭānī, op. cit., pp. 25–6.

115 Interview with Jūrj Ṭarābīshī in *Anwāl*, 31 March 1989, p. 15.

116 ibid.

2 LOOKING BACKWARD TO THE PRESENT: THE HISTORICAL NOVELS

1 Mahfouz gives 1932 in the list of publications usually appended to his books. However, Fāṭima Mūsā quotes 1931 as the date indicated on the index of Dār al-Kutub (the Egyptian National Library).

See her *Fī al-Riwāya al-ᶜArabiyya al-Muᶜāṣira*, Cairo: Maktabat al-Anglū, 1972(?), p. 35. This earlier date is confirmed in ᶜAbd al-Muḥsin Ṭāhā Badr, *Naguib Mahfouz: al-Ru'ya wa al-Adāt*, Cairo: Dār al-Thaqāfa, 1978, p. 502.

2 See Sasson Somekh, *The Changing Rhythm: a Study of Najīb Maḥfūẓ's Novels*, Leiden: E. J. Brill, 1973, p. 42, fn.1.

3 See ᶜAlī Shalash, *Naguib Mahfouz: al-Ṭarīq wa al-Ṣadā*, Beirut: Dār al-Ādāb, 1990, p. 40.

4 F. Mūsā, *Fī al-Riwāya al-ᶜArabiyya al-Muᶜāṣira*, p. 35.

5 See S. Somekh, op. cit., pp. 26–30 for a brief discussion of this and other historical trends in the Egyptian novel before Mahfouz.

6 See F. Mūsā, *Fī al-Riwāya al-ᶜArabiyya al-Muᶜāṣira*, pp. 35–7.

7 See Alan Gardiner, *Egypt of the Pharaohs*, Oxford: Oxford University Press, 1961, p. 434.

8 ibid., p. 436; see also p. 102.

9 On this and the earlier historical novels see Mattityahu Peled, *Religion My Own: the Literary Works of Najīb Maḥfūẓ*, New Brunswick: Transaction Books, 1983. He offers an informative comparison between historical fact and Mahfouz's treatment of it in fiction.

10 There have also been attempts by some critics at reading modern politics into *Rhodopis*, namely in terms of a popular revolt against a corrupt monarch. This, however, remains a hypothesis forced on the work and denied by Mahfouz himself. The issue is discussed by A. T. Badr, op. cit., pp. 189–90.

11 M. Peled was probably the first to draw attention to the Turkish factor in his discussion of this novel (see op. cit.), while most Egyptian critics were happy to define the parallelism as being between the ancient Hyksos and the modern British. In an interview given in 1973 Mahfouz expressed his enthusiasm for this interpretation, referring to Peled discreetly as only a 'non-Arab critic' (Peled is an Israeli and the interview pre-dates the Egyptian–Israeli peace treaty). For Mahfouz's comment, see his *Ataḥaddath Ilaykum*, Beirut: Dār al-ᶜAwda, 1977, pp. 88–9.

12 In fact Mahfouz uses very similar words again in a social novel published not very long after, viz. *New Cairo* (1946): 'the best policy with the peasant is the whip' (p. 194).

13 *Ataḥaddath Ilaykum*, pp. 86–7.

14 Here are two examples from *The Game of Fates*, pp. 6 and 50 respectively: 'On that day hidden in the folds of time, and which the gods decreed should mark the beginning of our story' is an example of the author addressing the reader, while the following is an example of authorial commentary on character speech: 'She meant no harm by what she said. It was only a wish, and often does the soul wish for the impossible and for what it would not dare do out of fear or pity.'

15 The more mature Mahfouz has this interesting comment on his own style in *The Game of Fates*:

Today I laugh at myself with regard to the style of that novel. At the time I was imbued with examples of grand style which we used to learn off by heart. I did not realise the necessity of compatibility between style and subject matter. Thus I used grand classical Arabic for a Pharaonic subject – the incompatibility persisted throughout.

(Interview in *Majallat al-Kātib al-ᶜArabī*, July 1970, p. 36; quoted in A. T. Badr, op. cit., p. 152)

16 *Ataḥaddath Ilaykum*, p. 92.

17 For the discussion of *Before the Throne* I have relied on my article 'The Novelist as Political Eye-witness: a View of Najīb Maḥfūẓ's Evaluation of the Nasser and Ṣādāt Eras', *Journal of Arabic Literature*, vol. 21, 1990, pp. 72–86. For a more detailed discussion of this work, see my book in Arabic *ᶜĀlam Naguib Mahfouz min Khilāl Riwāyātih*, Cairo: Dār al-Hilāl, 1988, pp. 82–95.

18 *Ataḥaddath Ilaykum*, p. 90.

19 In an interview with Ghālī Shukrī, Mahfouz spelled out his view of Akhenaton, in the course of commenting on the novel. He argued that Akhenaton may have been an idealist with a particular calling, but that his approach to reality was erroneous: 'It is not the business of a preacher to utilise material power to spread his belief.' See Ghālī Shukrī, *Naguib Mahfouz: min al-Jamāliyya ilā Nobel*, Cairo: al-Hay'a al-ᶜĀmma lil-Istiᶜlāmāt, 1988, p. 70. A similar view may be gleaned from a short story entitled 'Al-Samā' al-Sābiᶜa' (The Seventh Heaven) in the collection *Love under the Pyramids*. There the protagonist encounters, in the purgatory of the First Heaven, Akhenaton. He learns that he had been kept there for thousands of years. Surprised that such should have been the fate of the first monotheist in history, he is told: 'True! But he imposed his god on people with force rather than guidance and persuasion' (p. 106).

20 For a more detailed treatment of this novel, see my book *ᶜĀlam Naguib Mahfouz min Khilāl Riwāyātih*, pp. 107–15.

3 PAINS OF REBIRTH: THE CONFLICT BETWEEN PAST AND PRESENT

1 There is a controversy surrounding the publication dates of Mahfouz's first two social novels, *Khan al-Khalili* and *New Cairo*. One thing is certain however: the dates given by the author himself in the lists at the end of his book are not reliable. Sasson Somekh was probably the first scholar to draw attention to this fact. He established that *Khan al-Khalili* was Mahfouz's first realistic novel, published in 1945, and followed in 1946 by *New Cairo* (see S. Somekh, *The Changing Rhythm: a Study of Najīb Maḥfūẓ's Novels*, Leiden: E. J. Brill, 1973, pp. 198–9). This is contrary to Mahfouz's account which reverses the order and the dates. See also Aḥmad al-Hawwārī, *Maṣādir Naqd al-Riwāya fī al-Adab al-ᶜArabī*

al-Ḥadīth fī Miṣr, Cairo: Dār al-Maᶜārif, 1979, pp. 191–7. Hawwārī cites the full text of Sayyid Quṭb's review of *New Cairo* (first published in *Al-Risāla*, 30 December 1946). In the course of the review, Quṭb refers to *Khan al-Khalili* as an 'earlier' novel by Mahfouz. Hawwārī's bibliography gives us further evidence by listing a review of *Khan al-Khalili* by the same critic published a year earlier, also in *Al-Risāla* (17 December 1945). A more recent study (ᶜAlī Shalash, *Naguib Mahfouz: al-Ṭarīq wa al-Ṣadā*, Beirut: Dār al-Ādāb, 1990) confirms these findings by citing more reviews of *Khan al-Khalili* published in 1945, and of *New Cairo* published in 1946.

2 This negative characterization (especially the lack of intellectual parity between the two characters) may be Mahfouz's way of giving prominence and credibility to the views he favours, i.e. those of the socialist lawyer. In his next novel (*New Cairo*) he is more subtle, allowing intellectual parity to opponent advocates, while devising other means (as will be shown) to express his authorial sympathies.

3 This is probably why Mahfouz portrays him as physically one-eyed to indicate that intellectually he had unbalanced vision. ᶜAbd al-Muḥsin Ṭāhā Badr explains this disability in similar terms. See his *Naguib Mahfouz: al-Ru'ya wa al-Adāt*, Cairo: Dār al-Thaqāfa, 1978, p. 332.

4 The next such character in the author's work will be Ḥusayn, the middle brother in *The Beginning and the End*.

5 The case may simply be that the author could not adequately transform real-life substance into art. Consider his following statement about the source of his character: 'Aḥmad ᶜĀkif was a real person. . . . He was a small official in the administration of [King Fu'ād] University. He thought he knew everything that went on in Egypt. He only held the Baccalaureat, but he thought himself master of all branches of knowledge' (Jamāl al-Ghīṭānī, *Naguib Mahfouz Yatadhakkar*, Cairo: Akhbār al-Yawm, 1987(?), p. 102). In *Mirrors*, Mahfouz recreates the character of Aḥmad ᶜĀkif in the sketch entitled 'Ṭanṭāwī Ismāᶜīl', which is probably a more true-to-life account of the person he refers to above. S. Somekh (op. cit., p. 78) seems also aware of the confusion in the portrayal of this character and rightly accuses Mahfouz of not knowing his protagonist.

6 One critic, however, sees no point at all in Rushdī's death. He argues that 'the author appears always as if he hated characters that bubbled with life and vitality like Rushdī. Thus he punishes them most cruelly . . . and inflicts . . . death on them because he does not want such characters to live.' This appears to be an excessive judgement more concerned with making illegitimate conclusions about the psychology of the author than about the book under discussion. See A. T. Badr, op. cit., p. 356.

7 See n. 1.

8 Mahfouz mentions that at the time of writing the novel, the type of Maḥjūb ᶜAbd al-Dā'im was very common in real life.

(J. al-Ghīṭānī, op. cit., p. 141). He also refers to a friend from his school days who, like Maḥjūb, was an adventurer without principles, and admits that his character and experiences had been a repeated source of inspiration for him (ibid., pp. 54–5).

9 See A. T. Badr, op. cit., p. 308; Alī Jād, *Form and Technique in the Egyptian Novel*, London: Ithaca Press, 1983, p. 152; S. Somekh, op. cit., p. 76.

10 Mahfouz has this comment to make on his character and the situation he puts him in: 'I am against that society [i.e. the one portrayed in *New Cairo*], but I am also against the solution chosen by Maḥjūb. . . . He escapes from a sinking ship by despicable means, [whereas] his two colleagues, the socialist and the Islamist, transcend their own interests and problems in their thinking . . . and as such they are reformists . . . unlike him' (Naguib Mahfouz, *Ataḥaddath Ilaykum*, Beirut: Dār al-cAwda, 1977, pp. 154–5). What Mahfouz ignores, however, is that neither of those two colleagues has been subjected to the hardships of Maḥjūb.

11 This duo (a major improvement on the pair in *Khan al-Khalili*) are introduced again in *The Trilogy* III under the names of the two brothers Aḥmad and cAbd al-Muncim Shawkat.

12 *Ataḥaddath Ilaykum*, pp. 157–8.

13 One critic has argued in the course of commenting on the character of Aḥmad Rāshid in *Khan al-Khalili* that 'he is, as are all the socialists of Najīb Maḥfūẓ, a sterile, uninteresting character. . .'. This, of course, is a sweeping judgement belied by the portraits of both cAlī Ṭāhā, the socialist of *New Cairo* and Aḥmad Shawkat of *The Trilogy* III. As for Aḥmad Rāshid, the judgement appears to stand true, however, as has been shown. See Mattityahu Peled, *Religion My Own: the Literary Works of Najīb Maḥfūẓ*, New Brunswick: Transaction Books, 1983, pp. 135–6.

14 In my discussion of *New Cairo* I have made use of my article 'Religion in the Novels of Naguib Mahfouz', *British Society for Middle Eastern Studies Bulletin*, vol. 15, nos. 1 and 2, 1988, pp. 21–7. See also chapter 6 in my unpublished Ph.D. thesis '*Ḥaḍrat al-Muḥtaram* by Najīb Maḥfūẓ: a Translation and a Critical Assessment', University of Exeter, 1984.

15 One character speaks of suffering 'the horrors of darkness and air-raids for five years.' See (*Midaq Alley*, p. 6).

16 See Fāṭima Mūsā, *Fī al-Riwāya al-cArabiyya al-Mucāṣira*, Cairo: Maktabat al-Anglū al-Miṣriyya, 1972(?), p. 99.

17 'Tale 10' of Mahfouz's semi-autobiographical work, *Fountain and Tomb*, contains in all probability the real-life origin of Ḥamīda. The narrator recollects from the days of his childhood a young woman of their alley (also the daughter of a matchmaker) who was 'violent, daring and obscene', but of 'dazzling beauty'. Her high aspirations cause her to turn down many a suitor of her class. Finally she accepts a well-to-do, 50-year-old merchant already with a wife and children (cf. Salīm cAlwān in *Midaq Alley*). However, she only lives with him for two years before running away from the

whole alley. Later in life the narrator bumps into her – she had become a belly-dancer in a night club.

18 See ch. 3 of the novel (*passim*) where she is first introduced.

19 See ch. 18 of the novel, *passim*.

20 Of tremendous relevance here is the passage (ch. 23, p. 202), where her first journey from old Cairo to Sharīf Pasha Street in the heart of the modern city is described. Words of light, flight and ecstacy abound to reflect the symbolic journey from the old world of death and darkness to the new one of life and glitter. Significantly, the journey is made in a taxi. It was Ḥamīda's first time ever in a car – appropriately the flight to modernity takes place in a product of modernity (in those days horse-drawn carriages were still more common than taxis).

21 Another critic has written of Ḥamīda as a symbol of Egypt, though in completely different terms. He sees her (without offering textual support) as a victim (rather than the wilful agent she is shown to be) of exploitation by the British soldiers and the Egyptian pimp who leads her into prostitution, and thus to symbolize the condition of Egypt in the grip of imperialism and local political collaborators (see Rajā' al-Naqqāsh, *'Udabā' Muᶜāṣirūn*, Cairo: Dār al-Hilāl, 1971, pp. 92–6). Interestingly, Mahfouz denies any consciousness on his part during the writing of the novel of a symbolic aspect to the character of Ḥamīda. He is happy, however, to endorse in retrospect al-Naqqāsh's interpretation, arguing that the condition of Egypt may have influenced his portrayal of the woman subliminally. See Ghālī Shukrī, *Naguib Mahfouz: min al-Jamāliyya ilā Nobel*, Cairo: al-Hay'a al-ᶜĀmma lil-Istiᶜlāmāt, 1988, p. 117; see also interview in *Al-Muṣawwar*, 21 October 1988, p. 71.

22 See ch. 4 of the novel, *passim*, for the juxtaposition of the characters of ᶜAbbās and Ḥusayn.

23 For a similar interpretation see Marius Deeb, 'Najīb Maḥfūẓ's *Midaq Alley*: a Socio-cultural Analysis', *British Society for Middle Eastern Studies Bulletin*, vol. 10, no. 2, 1983, p. 128.

24 Fāṭima Mūsā makes the interesting remark that ᶜAmm Kāmil probably stands for what ᶜAbbās al-Ḥulw might have become had he not been killed (*Fī al-Riwāya al-ᶜArabiyya al-Muᶜāṣira*, p. 97).

25 *Mirage* was published one year after *Midaq Alley.* Mahfouz, however, has said that it pre-dated the latter in writing and that it was the success of *Midaq Alley* that encouraged him to publish it. *Midaq Alley* being a more accomplished work, this argument would seem to make sense. See F. Mūsā, *Fī al-Riwāya al-ᶜArabiyya al-Muᶜāṣira*, p. 43; A. T. Badr, op. cit., p. 372.

26 The novel does not define clearly the time of its action. However, talk about the economic crisis and the change of the Egyptian Constitution suggests the early 1930s (see *Mirage*, p. 176). For a painstaking and more detailed attempt at calculating the possible time of action, see A. T. Badr, op. cit., pp. 369–71.

27 For the real-life character who was Mahfouz's inspiration for

the protagonist of *Mirage*, see J. al-Ghīṭānī, op. cit., p. 102. For an earlier and much shorter treatment of the theme of the novel, see 'Thaman al-Ḍaᶜf' (The Price of Weakness), a very early short story by Mahfouz, first published in *Al-Majalla al-Jadīda*, 3 August 1934; reprinted in *Naguib Mahfouz: Nobel 1988: Kitāb Tidhkārī*, Cairo: Wizārat al-Thaqāfa, 1988(?).

28 It should be mentioned here that Mahfouz's interest in psychoanalysis had its first manifestation in the character of Aḥmad ᶜĀkif in *Khan al-Khalili*, whose mental ravings reveal him as an undoubted megalomaniac.

29 See, for instance, Nabīl Rāghib, *Qaḍiyyat al-Shakl al-Fannī ᶜind Naguib Mahfouz*, Cairo: Dār al-Kātib al-ᶜArabī, 1967. Mr Rāghib classifies Mahfouz's work up to the mid-1960s in three chronological phases (historical, social and what he calls 'plasto-dramatic'). He discusses *Mirage* independently of all three groupings under the heading 'al-marḥala al-nafsiyya al-mabtūra' (the nipped psychological phase). Nevine Ibrahim Ghourab also reads it as a psychological novel but in addition to Freud she holds that Mahfouz came here under the direct influence of D. H. Lawrence's *Sons and Lovers*. For an enlightening comparison between the two works, see her 'The Influence of Three English Novelists, John Galsworthy, D. H. Lawrence and James Joyce on some of the Novels of Najīb Maḥfūẓ', unpublished Ph.D. thesis, Cairo University, 1987, ch. 2, *passim*.

30 A. T. Badr, for instance, reads the novel as being partly a metaphor of the disintegration of the aristocratic, Turkish class of which the protagonist is a descendant (op. cit., pp. 376–8). M. Peled, on the other hand, sees it as 'a call to face reality', although he does not substantiate his argument (op. cit., p. 154).

31 Compare the later and more subtle reintroduction of this duality through the characters of Karīma and Ilhām in *The Search*, where the protagonist, Ṣābir, is again faced with the stark choice between materialism and spiritualism.

32 A. T. Badr (op. cit., p. 397) writes (in what appears like a loss of critical temper) commenting on the deaths of the two women (mother and wife) and the imprisonment of the doctor: 'It is as if there was a vendetta between the author and mankind – as if any possibility of success, purity or innocence, disturbed and provoked him in the extreme.' The critic, usually a scholar of sober judgement, is obviously horrified at the extent of Mahfouz's pessimistic view of the human condition. His horror probably stems from failure to read the metaphoric significance behind the actual happenings.

33 Internal evidence suggests that the action of the novel begins in 1933 (see p. 52) and ends late in 1936 or early in 1937. There is a reference (p. 275) to Ḥasanayn's premature graduation in the Military Academy as a result of the 1936 Anglo-Egyptian Treaty which stipulated an increase in the numbers of the Egyptian Army. The action ends within months of Ḥasanayn's graduation.

A. T. Badr, (op. cit., p. 444) defines the period of the novel, however, as falling between November 1935 and late 1939, without explaining how he arrived at these dates.

34 It is worth noting that Mahfouz is not interested in evoking a strong sense of place except when his fiction is set in his own birthplace, i.e. Jamāliyya and adjacent parts. A strong evocation of place can thus be found in *Khan al-Khalili*, *Midaq Alley*, and later *The Trilogy*, but not in *New Cairo*, *Mirage* or *The Beginning and the End*.

35 The author has this to say about the real-life origin of his characters in *The Beginning and the End*: 'I knew them in my childhood as they struggled to grow up. They all ended up happily. . . . At the beginning I thought of writing a comic novel about them. . . . But when I got wrapped up in writing, I completely forgot their happy attainments . . . and discovered in their life tragedies that had never crossed my mind as a child' (*Ataḥaddath Ilaykum*, p. 158).

36 In one interview Mahfouz argues that human existence is tragic because it ends in death, but that within this tragic framework there are many 'artificial tragedies of man's own making, such as ignorance, poverty, exploitation, violence, brutality, etc. This justifies our emphasis on the tragedies of society, because these are tragedies that can be remedied' (*Ataḥaddath Ilaykum*, pp. 73–4).

37 A notable exception is A. T. Badr (op. cit., pp. 449–51), who sees the social factor in the novel as 'marginal' and attributes the tragedy of the family to fate (i.e. the death of the father) and human nature as shaped by physical and mental heredity.

38 *Ataḥaddath Ilaykum*, p. 153.

39 See, for instance, pp. 175–6 of the novel.

40 See pp. 51–2, for my discussion of the same issue in *New Cairo*.

41 Ḥasanayn is in fact shown to be obsessed with the notion of obliterating the past. Here are some page citations where he makes various frenzied expressions of his feelings towards the past: pp. 277, 278, 302, 313, 318, 336, 344, 347, 366, 373, 381, 383.

42 This conflict continues to rage in *The Trilogy*, as will be shown in the next chapter of this book.

4 TIME AND THE MAN: FOUR EGYPTIAN SAGAS

1 Naguib Mahfouz, *Ataḥaddath Ilaykum*, Beirut: Dār al-ᶜAwda, 1977, pp. 150–1.

2 ibid., p. 46.

3 ibid., pp. 73–4.

4 According to Mahfouz *The Trilogy* took some seven years to prepare and write, starting from 1945 to April 1952 when it was completed. Originally it was written as one piece with the title 'Bayn al-Qaṣrayn', but Mahfouz's publisher rejected it on account of its excessive length. However, when what later came to be

known as the first part of *The Trilogy* was successfully serialized in the then literary magazine *Al-Risāla al-Jadīda* (between April 1954 and April 1956), the publisher changed his mind and suggested to Mahfouz that he should divide the book into three parts with different titles. That was how the work became a trilogy. See Jamāl al-Ghīṭānī, *Naguib Mahfouz Yatadhakkar*, Cairo: Akhbār al-Yawm, 1987(?), pp. 98–9; see also Ghālī Shukrī, *Naguib Mahfouz: min al-Jamāliyya ilā Nobel*, Cairo: al-Hay'a al-^{c}Āmma lil-Isti^{c}lāmāt, 1988, pp. 105–6, 133.

5 ^{c}*Awdat al-Rūḥ* (The Return of the Spirit) (1933) by Tawfīq al-Ḥakīm is an exception. But it does so on a much smaller scale than *The Trilogy*.

6 For a detailed review of features of Egyptian life recorded in *The Trilogy*, see Fawzī al-^{c}Antablī, 'al-Mujtama^{c} al-Miṣrī Kamā Tuṣawwiruh Riwāyat *Bayn al-Qaṣrayn*', *Al-Majalla*, March 1958, pp. 99–106.

7 This issue (i.e. existential obsession with the issue of death and the serious ethical pitfalls it can lead to) was explored in depth many years later in the tale of 'His Majesty Jalāl' in *Harafish*. The tale will be examined at length in ch. 6 of this book.

8 Although cataclysmic time is usually quite haphazard in its infliction of death on individuals, Mahfouz appears somewhat reluctant to allow totally fortuitous death a place in his fiction. Thus though Fahmī's death occurs accidentally in a political demonstration, the portrayal of Fahmī's character suggests that there is something inevitable about it. He is a sad, introverted character, too idealistic, too absorbed in the public cause, too alienated from his family and too heartbroken by his disappointment in love to survive. There is a sense of doom hanging over him so that, when he is killed, it does not come to us as a complete surprise. It is as if the novelist, aware from the beginning of the fate of Fahmī, could not help but prepare us for it. Now all this seems to be in conflict with the twist of irony implicit in Fahmī's death: he had survived many dangerous confrontations only to be killed in a peaceful, authorized demonstration. Mahfouz wanted to show a random death with a purpose. It does not quite work.

9 See the previous note. An exception to this generalization can perhaps be found in some of Mahfouz's short stories.

10 Cf. Matittyahu Peled, *Religion My Own: the Literary Works of Najīb Maḥfūẓ*, New Brunswick: Transaction Books, 1983, pp. 109–18. Peled offers the most detailed and best-argued interpretation of the ^{c}Ā'isha episode to date. Somehow, though, he seems to arrive at the far-fetched conclusion that by extirpating her branch of the family Mahfouz was pointing out the necessity of uprooting the Turkish element in Egyptian society, an argument that is difficult to uphold as ^{c}Ā'isha was neither Turkish nor foreign!

11 See the opening paragraphs of this chapter.

12 After *The Trilogy* (where heredity plays a major role) naturalism seems to vanish from the work of the author without a trace. But

then after *The Trilogy* much else was to undergo change in the work of Mahfouz as I hope this study will show at a later stage. One of the best naturalistic readings of *The Trilogy* is presented by Luwīs ᶜAwaḍ in two articles: 'Kayfa Taqra' Naguib Mahfouz' and 'Bayn al-Qaṣrayn' included in his book *Maqālāt fī al-Naqd wa al-Adab*, Cairo: Maktabat al-Anglū al-Miṣriyya, n.d., pp. 355–73.

13 See ch. 1, p. 19.

14 The symbolism of the situation is only general because Amīna is not the biological mother of Yāsīn.

15 This vision is particularly obvious in *Children of Gebelawi*, an allegory of man's struggle to survive with dignity from the time of Adam to the present. It will be discussed in ch. 6.

16 See *Ataḥaddath Ilaykum*, pp. 73–4 (quoted in full earlier on in this chapter, see p. 71).

17 ibid., p. 157.

18 A few examples are: 'This was her father's irrevocable will. She could only submit, nay she had to be pleased with it too. For mere acquiescence was an unforgivable sin' (*PW*, p. 183); 'Everything in this house was blindly subject to the boundless domination of a supreme will, more akin to religious hegemony' (*PW*, p. 272); 'my father makes no mistakes; he is infallible' (*PW*, p. 311); 'Her father – her worshipped father, has so ordained; he whose ordainments could not be revoked. God's will be done!' (*PD*, p. 265).

19 See *Palace Walk*, ch. 39, *passim*. This archetypal scene drawing on the Biblical scene where Adam eats from the Tree of Knowledge is evoked twice again in Mahfouz's next novel, *Children of Gebelawi* (discussed in ch. 5). The first is when Adham (i.e. Adam) tries to enter the forbidden room where the deeds of the estate are kept, and the second when ᶜArafa (i.e. Science) attempts the same. In the two latter cases the transgressors on the secrets of divinity are caught and punished, whereas Yāsīn's stolen 'knowledge' remains 'unknown' to the supposedly 'all-knowing' God/Father, thereby affirming the breach of his divinity.

20 Here Kamāl is very much reminiscent of Stephen Dedalus in James Joyce's *Portrait of the Artist as a Young Man* who, in his search for a personal truth, also rejects ties of the family, Ireland and Catholicism. For an engaging comparative study of the development of both characters and the influence of Joyce's work on Mahfouz's, see Nevine Ibrahim Ghourab, 'The Influence of Three English Novelists, John Galsworthy, D. H. Lawrence and James Joyce on some of the Novels of Najīb Maḥfūẓ', unpublished Ph.D. thesis, Cairo University, 1987, ch. 3, *passim*.

21 Compare *Chatter on the Nile*, where another car accident forces reality on the escapist inhabitants of the boathouse and shatters for ever their dream world.

22 *Ataḥaddath Ilaykum*, p. 62.

23 Here are some examples. On first hearing his name uttered by her lips, Kamāl feels like crying out '*Zammilūnī*! *Daththirūnī*!' (Wrap

me up! Cover me with my mantle!) (*PD*, p. 22) – the famous words attributed to the prophet Muḥammad, who felt feverish after first receiving the Revelation from Gabriel (in the Qur'ān the Prophet is referred to as the '*Muzzammil*' and the '*Muddaththir*' (see the opening verses of *Sūras* LXXIII and LXXIV)). He also refers to the house of the Shaddāds where she lives as '*manzil al-waḥy wa mabᶜath al-sanā*'' (the place where revelation descended and light emanated) (*PD*, p. 26) – stock phrases again associated with the history of the Prophet. Elsewhere Kamāl draws an image from the Gospels, referring to an event which pre-dated the beginning of his love for ᶜĀyda as having occurred 'before the Holy Spirit had descended on him' (*PD*, p. 81).

24 Compare the words of the narrator (as child) in the semi-autobiographical *Fountain and Tomb*: 'English patrols became a familiar sight to us. We would stare at the soldiers in astonishment trying to reconcile what we hear about their brutality with what we see of their smartness and the beauty of their faces' ('Tale 15', p. 34).

25 The significance of Kamāl's childish experience is enhanced by his eldest brother Yāsīn's similar experience. Yāsīn is stopped one day by a soldier who asks for a match to light a cigarette. Yāsīn obliges and the soldier thanks him. Here is how his feeling is rendered after the encounter:

> He walked towards the house reeling with joy. What good luck! An Englishman – not an Australian or an Indian – had smiled at him and thanked him! An Englishman – that is to say a man who figured in his imagination as a model of the perfection of the human race. He might hate the English as all Egyptians did, but in his heart of hearts he respected and venerated them as if they were a super-human species. A man from that species had smiled at him and thanked him.
>
> (*PW*, pp. 452–3)

26 We might recall here that the two brothers, with what they respectively stand for, had made their first appearance in the work of Mahfouz in *New Cairo*, ᶜAbd al-Munᶜim as Ma'mūn Raḍwān, and Aḥmad as ᶜAlī Ṭāhā.

27 For an exposition of the techniques used by Mahfouz which betray his sympathy for Aḥmad see my article, 'Religion in the Novels of Naguib Mahfouz', *British Society for Middle Eastern Studies Bulletin*, vol. 15, nos. 1 and 2, 1988, pp. 21–7.

28 See ch. 1, p. 25.

29 Although published after the assassination of Sādāt (1981), the novel must have been written during his lifetime, as it makes no mention of the event.

30 In spite of these similarities, it must be stressed that, while *The Trilogy* is a great novel, *There Only Remains an Hour* is mainly of documentary value and before long will only be of interest to social historians. Unlike in *The Trilogy*, no character or situation in this novel is of interest in itself, but only for what it points at.

31 As in *New Cairo* and *The Trilogy* we have here the two usual characters standing for the religious right (Muḥammad Burhān) and the secularist left (ᶜAzīz Ṣafwat). We also have a representative of the nonconformist, amoral type (ᶜAlī), again a descendant of *New Cairo*'s Maḥjūb ᶜAbd al-Dā'im. An additional type here is the corrupt beneficiary of the 1952 revolution (Sulaymān Bahjat).

32 As such Saniyya harks back to the first such type created by Mahfouz, i.e. Tūtīshīrī, the royal grandmother in *The Struggle of Thebes* (see pp. 40–1).

33 My discussion of this novel is mainly taken from my article 'The Novelist as Political Eye-witness: a View of Najīb Maḥfūẓ's Evaluation of the Nasser and Sādāt Eras', *Journal of Arabic Literature*, vol. 21, 1990, pp. 72–86.

34 See ch. 2.

35 The following analysis is largely taken from my article cited in n. 33 above.

36 The technique was used earlier by Mahfouz in two novels: *Miramar* and *Wedding Song*. The points of view there were four as opposed to the three in this novel. There is an element of innovation here, however, in the constant oscillation of the point of view among the three characters. In the earlier novels each character gave its full account of the event in a single piece.

37 He also has links with the royal grandmother Tūtīshīrī in *The Struggle of Thebes* and ᶜAmm ᶜAbduh, the houseboat caretaker in *Chatter on the Nile*: all are manifestations of a recurrent archetype in the work of Mahfouz representing generic perpetuity against individual transience.

38 Works which are concerned with time in a major way during that period include *Nights of the Arabian Nights* (1982), *There Only Remains an Hour* (1982), *The Day the Leader was Killed* (1985), *Tales of Mornings and Evenings* (1987), *Good Morning to You* (1987) and *Qushtumur* (1988).

39 This is a quality which they share with earlier works of reminiscence such as *Mirrors* and *Fountain and Tomb*. In fact, some characters from those works reappear under a different guise in the more recent ones.

40 My discussion of *Qushtumur* is partly dependent on my article, 'Naguib Mahfouz wa al-Zaman al-Ḍā'iᶜ fī *Qushtumur*', *Al-Hilāl*, December 1989, pp. 8–12.

41 The italics are mine.

42 A *jilbāb* is a loose, ankle-long garment, while a *rabāb* is a primitive, single-stringed instrument.

5 THE ABORTED DREAM: ON EARTH AS IN HEAVEN

1 It was not, however, published until 1956–7, as indicated earlier.

2 See p. 25.

3 Naguib Mahfouz *Ataḥaddath Ilaykum*, Beirut: Dār al-ᶜAwda,

1977, p. 91; see also Jamāl al-Ghīṭānī, *Naguib Mahfouz Yatadhakkar*, Cairo: Akhbār al-Yawm, 1987(?), p. 138.

4 He refers to what he calls 'the saturation of my vision' through writing *The Trilogy* (by which he probably means his artistic exhaustion of the potential of techniques used by him up to that time) as another possible explanation for his writer's block, but he hastens to add 'but I cannot be sure of that' (J. al-Ghīṭānī, op. cit., p. 138).

5 Interview in *Al-Qabas*, 31 December 1975; quoted in Ibrāhīm al-Shaykh, *Mawāqif Ijtimāᶜiyya wa Siyāsiyya fī Adab Naguib Mahfouz*, Cairo, 3rd edition, 1987, p. 164.

6 More than twenty years later, Mahfouz was to return to this subject again; see ch. 6 for the discussion of the tale of 'The Invisible Hat' in *Nights of the Thousand Nights*.

7 The story of Saᶜīd Mahrān was inspired by a real-life criminal by the name of Maḥmūd Amīn Sulaymān, who also believed that his wife had betrayed him and was out to get her. His story, which captured the public imagination in 1960, was extensively covered by the press. He gave the police a hard time until he was chased down with the help of police dogs to a cave near Ḥilwān where he fought back until death. Mahfouz was admittedly greatly moved by the whole incident and within months he had written his novel. See *Ataḥaddath Ilaykum*, pp. 112–13; J. al-Ghīṭānī, op. cit., p. 108; Yaḥyā Ḥaqqī, *ᶜIṭr al-Aḥbāb*, Cairo: Dār al-Kitāb al-Jadīd, n.d., p. 113; Fāṭima Mūsā, *Bayn Adabayn*, Cairo: Maktabat al-Anglū al-Miṣriyya, 1965, pp. 132–5; Fu'ād Dawwāra, *Naguib Mahfouz: min al-Qawmiyya ilā al-ᶜĀlamiyya*, Cairo: al-Hay'a al-ᶜĀmma lil-Kitāb, 1989, pp. 52–4; Ghālī Shukrī, *Naguib Mahfouz: min al-Jamāliyya ilā Nobel*, Cairo: al-Hay'a al-ᶜĀmma lil-Istiᶜlāmāt, 1988, p. 41.

8 See my article 'The Novelist as Political Eye-witness: a View of Najīb Maḥfūẓ's Evaluation of the Nasser and Sādāt Eras', *Journal of Arabic Literature*, vol. 21, 1990, pp. 72–86.

9 For a similar view, see Ghālī Shukrī, *Al-Muntamī: Dirāsa fī Adab Naguib Mahfouz*, Cairo: Dār al-Maᶜārif, 1969, p. 281; see also Maḥmūd Amīn al-ᶜĀlim, *Ta'ammulāt fī ᶜĀlam Naguib Mahfouz*, Cairo: al-Hay'a al-Miṣriyya al-ᶜĀmma lil-Ta'līf wa al-Nashr, 1970, p. 87. This view also appears to be endorsed by Mahfouz himself who blames his character for his lack of 'the comprehensive outlook necessary for the revolutionary', and for his preoccupation with only 'those who betrayed him personally'. He goes on to name this as 'exactly the reason for his failure and death' (*Ataḥaddath Ilaykum*, p. 156).

10 Notably Ghālī Shukrī in *Al-Muntamī, passim*; see also Rajā' al-Naqqāsh, *'Udabā' Muᶜāṣirūn*, Cairo: Dār al-Hilāl, 1971, pp. 153–242.

11 In an interview, Mahfouz proclaims, 'I reject any form of *sūfism* [i.e. mysticism] achieved at the expense of man's concern with the world and the life of people.' He goes on to explain that *ṣūfī* principles 'created by the *ṣūfī* to be applied to himself or to a superhuman group [of people] is no good for the rest of humanity'

(Aḥmad Hāshim al-Sharīf, *Naguib Mahfouz: Muḥāwarāt Qabl Nobel*, Cairo: Rūzalyūsif, 1989, pp. 29–30). Compare another pronouncement by the author against *ṣūfism*, this time through the mouthpiece of a character in one of his short stories:

> *Ṣūfism* is a form of aristocracy, but my way is the people's way. The hierarchy of *ṣūfism* consists in repentance, renunciation, piety, surrender to Divine will etc., but my way consists in freedom, culture, science, industry, agriculture, technology, democracy and faith. *Ṣūfism* sees the Devil as the true enemy of mankind, whereas my enemies include poverty, ignorance, disease, exploitation, despotism, falsity and fear.

See Naguib Mahfouz's short story 'Ayyūb' (Job) in *The Devil Preaches*, p. 237; see also n. 33.

12 Compare Shaykh ᶜAbdullāh al-Balkhī who is an extended version of Shaykh Junaydī reincarnated, as it were, twenty years later in *Nights of the Thousand Nights*. See the discussion of this novel in ch. 6.

13 In this connection, see also the discussion of *The Beginning and the End* in ch. 3 of this book.

14 For a further exploration of the role of fate in Mahfouz's work see my discussion of *Nights of the Thousand Nights*, ch. 6; see also ch. 2 for a discussion of the early manifestations of fate in his work.

15 For two examples of such critical approaches, see n. 18 below.

16 The author's attitude to the 1952 revolution was expounded in ch. 1, and also in the discussion of *Before the Throne* in ch. 2 of this book.

17 See my article in n. 8.

18 In his review of the novel, Fu'ād Dawwāra reads in ᶜĪsā's engagement to the daughter of a legal adviser to the Royal Estate a symbol of the decline of the Wafd and its willingness to cooperate with the corrupt Monarch during the Party's last years. Strikingly, he fails, however, to make any comment on the significance of the rush by ᶜĪsā's cousin, Ḥasan (the representative of the 1952 revolution) to marry the same girl, once she had dropped ᶜĪsā. See F. Dawwāra, op. cit., pp. 90–104 (Dawwāra's article was first published in *Al-Kātib*, no. 27, 1963). Rajā' al-Naqqāsh, to take another example, opts to ignore the political meaning of the novel and reads it in purely existentialist terms (see his article 'Al-Wāqiᶜiyya al-Wujūdiyya fī *Al-Summān wa al-Kharīf*', *Al-Ādāb*, no. 3, 1963, pp. 39–42, later collected in his '*Udabā' Muᶜāṣirūn*).

19 The word *angst* here and elsewhere in this study is used in the sense given it in existentialist philosophy. According to Sartre, it is a kind of moral and metaphysical anguish, resulting from a state of heightened self-awareness. The energy generated by this awareness can help the *angst*-stricken individual drag himself out of despair and exercise his power of choice, thereby giving meaning to life. See 'Existentialism' in J. A. Cuddon, *A Dictionary of Literary Terms*, London: Penguin Books, 1982.

20 Here is an example:

> They [^{c}Īsā and a friend] walked together in a semi-deserted road as the half-moon shone above the skyline: a cosmic smile in a clear sky. It occurred to him that that beauty arranged in such wondrous order was nothing but a mysterious mocking power which forced on man an awareness of his misery and the chaos of his [life].
>
> (*Autumn Quail*, p. 162)

21 Sartre believes that man can emerge from his passive and indeterminate condition and, by an act of will, become *engagé*; whereupon he is committed (through *engagement*) to some action and part in social and political life. Through commitment man provides a reason and a structure for his existence and thus helps to integrate society. See 'Existentialism' in J. A. Cuddon, op. cit. For a view of Mahfouz's version of existentialism and the absurd through a comparison with Kafka, see Richard K. Myers, 'The Problem of Authority: Franz Kafka and Nagīb Maḥfūẓ', *Journal of Arabic Literature*, vol. 17, 1986, pp. 82–96.

22 See particularly the last chapter of the novel where ^{c}Īsā's despondent 'I no longer care for anything' is countered by the young man's declaration of *engagement* (or commitment): 'I care for everything and think about everything' (p. 182). The characters' words and attitudes seem an exact illustration of Sartre's ideas stated in n. 21.

23 These keywords in the novel first occur at the close of the first chapter but are repeated many times throughout. The Arabic says *al-ḥurriyya wa al-Karāma wa al-salām*. In my view the context favours rendering 'al-salām' as 'security' rather than the more common English equivalent of 'peace'.

24 An example of a political interpretation of the novel gone wild is offered by F. Dawwāra, op. cit., pp. 105–30.

25 There is a near-consensus of opinion among critics on this broad metaphysical reading of the novel. One of the earliest and most illuminating such readings was Luwīs ^{c}Awaḍ's article 'al-Muḥākama al-Nāqiṣa' (*Al-Ahrām*, 31 July 1964), later collected in his *Al-Thawra wa al-Adab*, Cairo: Dār al-Kātib al-^{c}Arabī, 1967; also included in Fāḍil al-Aswad, ed., *Al-Rajul wa al-Qimma: Buḥūth wa Dirāsāt*, Cairo: al-Hay'a al-Miṣriyya al-^{c}Āmma lil-Kitāb, 1989. Another revealing such treatment is by Jūrj Ṭarābīshī in his *Allāh fī Riḥlat Naguib Mahfouz al-Ramziyya*, Beirut: Dār al-Ṭalī^{c}a, 1973, pp. 42–52. When *The Search* was published, the use of 'the father' as a symbol of God had already been established in the work of Mahfouz: first in *The Trilogy* and then, more conspicuously, in *Children of Gebelawi*.

26 There is also a consensus of critical opinion on the symbolic meanings of Karīma and Ilhām (i.e. matter and spirit, respectively) with one brave exception, namely Rajā' al-Naqqāsh's, who argues, gallantly but unconvincingly, for a reversal of roles between the two women (op. cit., pp. 203–11).

27 Character and place-names (hardly ever without some significance in Mahfouz's work) must be counted among the important clues here. Sayyid Sayyid al-Raḥīmī, the father's name, translates 'lord, lord, the merciful', while Ṣābir's name means 'the patient one' – to name but two examples. On the other hand while the Arabic title of the novel, *Al-Ṭarīq*, commonly means 'the way', it is also the word for a '*ṣūfī* order' – a fact which bears an obvious relevance to the metaphysical aspect of Ṣābir's search.

28 Note that the Arabic title of the novel, means 'the way' rather than 'the search'; see also n. 27.

29 Consider the contrasting attitudes of Ilhām and Ṣābir. Ilhām argues that 'Work is more important than the father and more enduring' (*The Search*, p. 75), while Ṣābir holds that 'There is no value to any work which did not come through my father' (p. 81).

30 See nn. 19 and 21.

31 In this novel, Mahfouz's prose evinces a measure of poetic density probably not previously attained in his work, with the exception of Kamāl's monologues in *The Trilogy* II.

32 The issue of the role of art (and philosophy) in a world dominated by science is a recurrent theme in the work of Mahfouz. One of its most detailed expositions occurs in *The Trilogy* III, *passim* (especially in the conversations between Kamāl and Riyāḍ Qaldas).

33 It is relevant to recall here Kamāl's statement of his new-found vision at the end of *The Trilogy*: '*Ṣūfism* is escapism and so is a negative belief in science. . . . Action is necessary, but action needs faith, and the question is how to create for ourselves a new faith in life' (*The Trilogy* III, p. 391; see also n. 11 above).

34 Poetry here must of course be apprehended in a broad sense as an epithet to describe man's spiritual longings, which stem from the basic view of existence as a mystery.

35 The following story is related by Ghālī Shukrī on the authority of Mahfouz himself. On the publication of the novel, ᶜAbd al-Ḥakīm ᶜĀmir, the then Commander-in-Chief of the armed forces and Vice-President, said to Nasser, 'He [Mahfouz] has gone over the top and must be taught a lesson.' Nasser then consulted with his minister of culture, Tharwat ᶜUkāsha, who advised as follows: 'Mr President, in all honesty I tell you that if art could not enjoy this [little] margin of freedom, it would cease to be art.' 'Point taken; consider the matter closed!' answered Nasser calmly. See Ghālī Shukrī, *Naguib Mahfouz: min al-Jamāliyya ilā Nobel*, p. 56.

36 This is probably an allusion to the Egyptian military involvement in Yemen (1962–7).

37 This in all probability is a reference to the revolution's *nouveaux riches*, who inherited the privileges of the regime they ousted. Compare the character of Ḥasan in *Autumn Quail* discussed above.

38 Ghālī Shukrī writes of Mahfouz with reference to *Chatter on the Nile*: 'Of all our writers who saw the horror before its occurrence, this man was the first prophet of defeat' (*Al-Muntamī*, p. 425).

39 Quoted pp. 70–1. For a detailed discussion of the author's concept of time, see ch. 4, *passim*.

40 This four-sided viewpoint and the fact that the novel is set in Alexandria inevitably called for countless fleeting comparisons with Lawrence Durrell's *The Alexandria Quartet* (1957–60) by commentators of the day.

41 Fatḥī Ghānim's quartet, *Al-Rajul alladhī Faqad Ẓillah* had already been published in 1962. There is an English translation of this novel: *The Man Who Lost his Shadow*, trans. Desmond Stewart, London: Heinemann, 1966.

42 It was not until 1981 that he used the technique again, in *Wedding Song*. His third and last attempt was in *The Day the Leader was Killed* (1985), this time using a three-sided viewpoint, rather than four.

43 His next three novels all fit under this description, namely *Mirrors* (1972), *Love in the Rain* (1973) and *The Karnak* (1974).

44 The remnants of liberal nationalism are represented by the old Wafdist, ᶜĀmir Wajdī; the remnants of the land-owning aristocracy by Ṭulba Marzūq and Ḥusnī ᶜAllām; the remnants of foreign influence by Māryānā, the Greek owner of the *pension*, and the remnants of socialists by Manṣūr Bāhī. The revolution, on the other hand, is represented by Sarḥān al-Buḥayrī. A notable omission is Moslem fundamentalism, a fact which probably reflects the revolution's success in the complete marginalization of the Moslem Brotherhood since the mid-1950s.

45 The following discussion of *Miramar* is largely taken from my treatment of the novel contained in my article 'The Novelist as Political Eye-witness', *Journal of Arabic Literature*, vol. 21, 1990, pp. 72–86.

46 Sarḥān refers to Ṭulba Marzuq, the feudalist dispossessed by the revolution as 'a member of the class we must inherit one way or another' (p. 217). In another revealing thought, Sarḥān admits, 'I may hate his class as an idea, but oh, how they charm me, when I am lucky enough to meet them as individuals!' (p. 221) – a thought which calls to the mind Ḥasan's symbolic marriage to ᶜĪsā's aristocratic ex-fiancée in *Autumn Quail*.

47 Mahfouz's portraits of the socialist idealist began with the lifeless authorial mouthpiece Aḥmad Rāshid in *Khan al-Khalili* and evolved steadily across novels to reach their most perfected and elevated version in the character of Aḥmad Shawkat in *The Trilogy* III.

48 Mahfouz admits that Zahra was consciously portrayed so as to represent Egypt. See interview in *Al-Muṣawwar*, 21 October 1988, p. 71. Compare the longish short story 'Samāra al-Amīr' in *Love under the Pyramids* (1979), where Mahfouz comes back again to the idea of using a poor country girl to represent Egypt, and a host of men standing for different classes and regimes who all exploit her.

49 See the character sketch of 'Aḥmad Qadrī' in *Mirrors*. It actually deals with the torture of political prisoners in pre-revolutionary times, but its more contemporary relevance cannot be concealed. It

is particularly interesting for an attempt at probing the psychology of a torturer.

50 ibid; see the sketch of 'Bilāl ʿAbduh Basyūnī'.

51 ibid; see the sketch of 'Ṣabrī Jād', where the ideals (or rather anti-ideals!) of the post-1967 generation are revealed. This episode can in fact be read as a preamble to *Love in the Rain*.

52 The following discussion is an enlargement of my previous treatment of the two novels in my article 'The Novelist as Political Eyewitness', pp. 72–86.

53 *Love in the Rain* in fact sees a surprising return by Mahfouz to the omniscient narrator's technique, something he had not done since *The Trilogy*. It is perhaps a mark of Mahfouz's concern to move freely among characters and represent a cross-section of the post-1967 Cairo society, rather than concentrate on the consciousness of a single individual as he had done since *The Thief and the Dogs*.

54 *Ataḥaddath Ilaykum*, p. 111.

55 In the early 1970s and prior to the self-confident mood of the State engendered by the 1973 Arab–Israeli war, *Al-Ahrām*, which normally serialized Mahfouz's novels, refused to publish *Love in the Rain*. Mahfouz then serialized it in a minor, low-circulation magazine called *Al-Shabāb* (Youth), published by the Ministry of Information. The novel, however, was censored, with the sections showing the Cairene apathy towards the war raging on the front withheld. It was not published in its complete form until 1973. See Ghālī Shukrī, *Naguib Mahfouz: min al-Jamāliyya ilā Nobel*, pp. 53–5.

56 The parallelism with the role of the car accident in *Chatter on the Nile* is too striking to ignore. It is this quality which, in retrospect, gives the earlier novel its prophetic ring.

57 For a detailed appreciation of *Love in the Rain*, see Trevor Le Gassic, 'An Analysis of *Al-Ḥubb taḥt al-Maṭar*', in *Studies in Modern Arabic Literature*, ed. R. C. Ostle, Warminster: Aris & Philips, 1975, pp. 140–51.

58 See *The Karnak*, pp. 19, 37, 99, for parts of dialogue or narrative which establish the time of the action.

59 In *The Karnak*, Mahfouz comes close to writing another novel with a multiple viewpoint (in the manner of *Miramar*), with the novel divided into four sections, each carrying the name of a character for a title and concentrating on the account from that character's point of view. Rather than let the characters tell their own stories in the first person, Mahfouz actually gives us the stories at second hand through the narrator, in whom the characters confide. This gives the author legitimate scope for commentary on the meaning of events through the narrator. For a somewhat more detailed consideration of this point see T. Le Gassick, 'Maḥfūẓ's *Al-Karnak*: the Quiet Conscience of Nāṣir's Egypt Revealed' in T. Le Gassik, ed., *Critical Perspectives on Naguib Mahfouz*, Washington D.C.: Three Continents Press, 1991, pp. 151–62.

60 Jamāl al-Ghīṭānī recounts how he 'witnessed the conception of *The*

Karnak' in the Café ᶜUrābī in ᶜAbbāsiyya. He, Mahfouz, and a group of friends were gathered one evening at the café when an old man with an imposing appearance entered. A strange silence engulfed the place for a while as the waiter rushed to serve the man. Upon enquiry it transpired that the stranger was none other than the notorious and much-feared Ḥamza al-Basyūnī, former Commandant of the Military Prison. On knowing this, 'Mahfouz's eyes dilated and he kept watching the man secretly', while his friends started telling the horror stories they had heard about the man and the Military Prison. A few years later *The Karnak* was published. See J. al-Ghīṭānī, op. cit., pp. 25–6.

61 Because of his staunch support for Sādāt's 'peace initiative' in 1977 and the Camp David Accords two years later, Mahfouz was vilified in many Arab intellectual circles and his work was banned from many Arab countries for several years. Mahfouz, however, has repeatedly argued that his views on the subject were entirely his own and that he had not simply been playing Sādāt's tune as his accusers maintained. He actually argues that his public call for peace with Israel pre-dated Sādāt's initiative by at least five years. He refers to a meeting held in 1972 between the editorial staff of *Al-Ahrām* (including himself, Tawfīq al-Ḥakīm and other notable writers) and Colonel Gaddafi of Libya, who was at the time on an official visit to Egypt. The Palestinian question was among the issues debated:

> On this subject I said 'If we do not have the ability to go to war, let us negotiate and make peace. . . .' My words came as a surprise, for nobody had thought, let alone spoken, of this solution. . . . That was five years before Sādāt went to Jerusalem.

Mahfouz also refers to an interview given to the Kuwaiti newspaper *Al-Qabas* in late 1975 or early 1976 (he could not remember the date exactly) in which he reiterated the same call (see Ghālī Shukrī, *Naguib Mahfouz: min al-Jamāliyya ilā Nobel*, pp. 59–60). We should recall here that although *The Karnak* was only published in 1974, the author uncharacteristically gives the date of authorship at the end of the text. The date given is December 1971, though in an interview he gives it again as 1972 (see his *Ataḥaddath Ilaykum*, p. 120). What matters, however, is that whatever the date was, the novel was written before the 1973 war and that Mahfouz's belief in the viability of the idea of an Arab–Israeli peace evidently pre-dates the war and the interim agreements on the disengagement of forces which followed; all of which were factors which helped in the final brewing of the 'peace initiative'.

62 In an interview given to Jūrj Ṭarābīshī, Mahfouz argues in support of the idea of God in this manner:

> If you take science, with the secrets of life and the universe that it makes accessible to us, as your starting-point . . . . it becomes impossible to believe in absurdity. Faced with the infiniteness of at once our knowledge and our ignorance . . . .

we will not then find a power which merits the trust of the bewildered mind more than God does.

(*Anwāl*, 31 March 1989, p. 15)

63 The views of Mahfouz's character here agree perfectly with his own. In a statement made not long after the publication of this novel, he argues, 'My personal contention with Marxism is limited to its philosophical, materialistic side only. On the other hand, I reject any kind of dictatorship even if it promises me heaven on earth.' (see *Rūzalyūsif*, 2 February 1976, p. 87; quoted in I. al-Shaykh, op. cit., p. 26).

64 See p. 83.

65 A millieme is one-thousandth of the Pound Egyptian, no longer in currency today.

66 This situation, embodying the ultimate impossibility of communication between two parties, is borrowed lock, stock and barrel from an earlier short story by the author. See his 'Al-Ṣadā' (The Echo) in *The Black Cat Tavern* (1969).

67 By contrast, in the later novel *There Only Remains an Hour* (discussed in ch. 4) the family house with its neglected garden will be successfully used to stand for a rundown country.

68 Some commentators, however, were tricked by Mahfouz's gimmick into believing that the playwright did not commit suicide and criticized the novelist for an unconvincing ending. See ᶜAbd al-Raḥmān Abū ᶜAwf's review of the novel in *Ibdāᶜ*, vol. 3, February 1985, pp. 12–17. See also Mursi Saad El-Din's introduction to the English translation: Naguib Mahfouz, *Wedding Song*, trans. Olive E. Kenny, Cairo: The American University Press, 1984, pp. ix–xi.

6 FRAGMENTS OF TIME: THE EPISODIC NOVELS

1 The most notable attempt in Egypt was made by Muḥammad Ibrāhīm al-Muwayliḥī (1858–1930) who serialized his *Ḥadīth ᶜĪsā Ibn Hishām* in *Miṣbāh al-Sharq* between 1898 and 1900 before publishing it in book form in 1907. For an informative study on the first fifty years or so (up to the second decade of this century) of the evolution of modern Arabic fiction, see Matti Moosa, *The Origins of Modern Arabic Fiction*, Washington, D.C.: Three Continents Press, 1983.

2 Interview in *Al-Fikr al-Muᶜāṣir*, December 1966, p. 112; quoted in Sasson Somekh, *The Changing Rhythm: a Study of Najīb Maḥfūẓ's Novels*, Leiden: E. J. Brill, 1973, p. 187.

3 See Jamāl al-Ghīṭānī, *Naguib Mahfouz Yatadhakkar*, Cairo: *Akhbār al-Yawm*, 3rd edition, 1987(?), pp. 108–9.

4 Naguib Mahfouz, *Ataḥaddath Ilaykum*, Beirut: Dār al-ᶜAwda, 1977, p. 122. For a detailed discussion of *Mirrors*, see Roger Allen, '*Mirrors* by Nagīb Maḥfūẓ', *The Muslim World*, vol. 62, 1972, pp. 115–25 and vol. 63, 1973, pp. 15–27, also included in T. Le Gassick, ed., *Critical Perspectives on Naguib Mahfouz*,

Washington D.C.: Three Continents Press, 1991, pp. 131–50; see also James Roy King, 'The Deconstruction of the Self in Nagīb Maḥfūẓ's *Mirrors*', *Journal of Arabic Literature*, vol. 19, 1988, pp. 55–67.

5 *Ataḥaddath Ilaykum*, p. 34.

6 ibid., pp. 122–3.

7 ibid., p. 83; see also Ghālī Shukrī, *Naguib Mahfouz: min al-Jamāliyya ilā Nobel*, Cairo: Al-Hay'a al-ᶜĀmma lil-Istiᶜlāmāt, 1988, p. 54.

8 Two prominent examples are his portraits of the eminent critic, Luwīs ᶜAwaḍ and the fundamentalist writer and activist, Sayyid Quṭb, who appear as 'Kāmil Ramzī' and 'ᶜAbd al-Wahhāb Ismāᶜīl' respectively. A third is that of Manṣūr Fahmī (the now forgotten professor of philosophy during Mahfouz's undergraduate years), who figures in the book as 'Ibrāhīm ᶜAql'. For an interesting article paralleling fact with fiction and proving the case for reading Manṣūr Fahmī for Ibrāhīm ᶜAql, see Donald M. Reid, 'The Sleeping Philosopher of Nagīb Maḥfūẓ's *Mirrors*', *The Muslim World*, vol. 74, no. 1, 1984, pp. 1–11.

9 In the novelist's own words, 'a spiritual history of Egypt over more than half a century' (*Ataḥaddath Ilaykum*, p. 34).

10 Compare the short story 'Yawm Ḥāfil' (A Busy Day) in the collection *A House of Ill Repute*, where an important man, full of plans and projects, walking to his café for a drink after a long 'busy day' is surprised by a child playfully spraying his stream of urine on the pavement. The man retreats in a reflex action to avoid being sprayed. His foot slips and he falls. His head hits the edge of the kerb and he dies there and then. Compare also the thoughts of ᶜUthmān Bayyūmī in *Respected Sir* (p. 132): 'One felt relatively secure . . . because one believed that death was logical, that it operated on the basis of premise and conclusion. But death often came upon us without warning, like an earthquake.'

11 In a reference to *Fountain and Tomb* made before its publication, Mahfouz admits that it reflects in a 'not inconsiderable measure' his childhood (*Ataḥaddath Ilaykum*, pp. 78–9).

12 For the meaning of these terms see p. 1; see also p. 213, n. 13. The *ḥāra* as a symbol of the world and the *futuwwa* as a symbol of, alternately, despot and just ruler go back of course to *Children of Gebelawi*, but it is here in *Fountain and Tomb* that they are deepened and established as, so to say, fixed assets in the work of the novelist. On the other hand, the *takiyya* and the *qabw*, which were later to play a major role in *Harafish*, make their first appearance here.

13 The *takiyya* and its garden play here more subtly the symbolic role played earlier in *Children of Gebelawi* by Gebelawi's mansion and its garden.

14 For a detailed analysis of this novel which concentrates on its sociopolitical value, see Ṣabrī Ḥāfiẓ's review of it in the London-based daily, *Al-ᶜArab*. The review was serialized over three issues: 19, 25, 30 May 1988.

15 This is probably the significance of the 'mornings' and 'evenings' of

the title: these are tales of 'beginnings' and 'ends', 'births' and 'deaths'. Note the harping on the image in the titles of the next work discussed, where the first story of the collection is called 'Good Morning to You', while the last one bears the title 'Good Evening to You'. It is as if life in its brevity was reduced to the space between the two greetings.

16 In his review of the book, Ghālī Shukrī also sees a connection among the three pieces and calls the collection a new 'trilogy of generations'. See G. Shukrī, 'Ṣabāḥ al-Ward Yā Naguib Mahfouz', *Al-Hilāl*, November 1988, pp. 104–9.

17 Compare for instance the striking similarity between the episodes of 'Āl al-Kāshif' and 'Āl Ḍirghām' in 'Ṣabāḥ al-Ward' and those of 'Riḍā Ḥamāda' and 'ʿĪd Manṣūr' in *Mirrors*, respectively.

18 The author's agony at the enormity of the gap between actual time/space and recollected time/space or, as it were, present space and past space is recaptured in a brilliant short story called 'Niṣf Yawm' (Half a Day), included in his latest collection, *False Dawn* (1989); discussed in the last chapter of this book (p. 212). For a translation of this story see, Naguib Mahfouz, *The Time and the Place and Other Stories*, selected and trans. Denys Johnson-Davies, New York: Doubleday, 1991.

19 See above, n. 15.

20 Compare 'Tale 48' in *Fountain and Tomb* which appears to be the blueprint for the present story.

21 *Ataḥaddath Ilaykum*, pp. 37–8.

22 Interview with Jūrj Ṭarābīshī in *Anwal*, 31 March 1989, p. 15.

23 The novel was first serialized to its conclusion in *Al-Ahrām* between 21 September and 25 December 1959 despite attempts by the conservative religious establishment to stop the serialization. The pressure however succeeded in preventing its publication in book form in Egypt, though it was later published in Beirut in 1967. After the award of the Nobel prize to the author in 1988, there was a strong public call for its publication in Egypt from a majority of writers and critics. The attempt, however, was nipped in the bud as objections this time came not only from the religious establishment but from religious fundamentalists who threatened the author's life. The issue coincided with the international crisis caused by the publication of Salman Rushdie's *The Satanic Verses*, which of course did not help Mahfouz's case. Fundamentalists labelled him an apostate like Rushdie and ill-informed comparisons were held between the two books by self-proclaimed literary critics. If nothing else, the controversy helped revive interest in the book. See Ghāli Shukrī, *Naguib Mahfouz: min al-Jamāliyya ilā Nobel*, p. 55; see also interview with Mahfouz in *Al-Muṣawwar*, 21 October 1988, pp. 10–19, 68–73.

24 See p. 25.

25 The correct transliteration of the name is 'Jabalāwī'. However, I have stuck here to the spelling adopted in the published English translation to avoid confusion.

26 *Children of Gebelawi* marks the beginning of Mahfouz's use of the *ḥāra* and the *futuwwa* as major symbols in his work. On the other hand, Gebelawi's mysterious house, which functions as a focus for the spiritual aspirations of all the heroes of the *ḥāra*, plays here the symbolic role which later in Mahfouz's work will be assigned to the *takiyya*, as I have shown.

27 The fact is deliberately mystified in the novel whether the encounter with the old maid actually happened or was imagined.

28 Compare ᶜAlī Ṭāhā, the socialist protagonist in *New Cairo* who 'came to believe that atheists, like believers, had their principles and ideals . . . and that good was deeper in the human nature than religion' (Naguib Mahfouz, *New Cairo*, pp. 22–3).

29 Compare the ending of *Harafish* (published some eighteen years later) where this scenario, only a potential in *Children of Gebelawi*, is successfully enacted. See the discussion of *Harafish*, pp. 144–59.

30 In my treatment of *Children of Gebelawi* I have partly relied on my article 'Religion in the Novels of Naguib Mahfouz', *British Society for Middle Eastern Studies Bulletin*, vol. 15, nos. 1 and 2, 1988, pp. 21–7. For a more detailed analysis of the novel, see S. Somekh, 'The Sad Millenarian: An Examination of *Awlād Ḥāratinā*', in T. Le Gassick, ed., *Critical Perspectives on Naguib Mahfouz*, Washington D.C.: Three Continents Press, 1991, pp. 101–14. For a study which favours reading the novel as a parable of autocratic government rather than of religious history, see Jarīr Abū-Ḥaydar, '*Awlād Ḥāratinā* by Najīb Maḥfūẓ: an Event in the Arab World', *Journal of Arabic Literature*, vol. 16, 1985, pp. 119–31.

31 The Arabic title is *Malḥamat al-Ḥarāfīsh*. *Ḥarāfīsh* (sing. *ḥarfūsh*) is no longer a current word in modern Egyptian usage, though Mahfouz may have given it some renewed currency (at least in literary circles) by his use of it in the title of his novel and throughout the book. Sources define a *ḥarfūsh* variously as a member of the lower classes, a person of bad character, a ruffian, a scamp, etc. This may have been the meaning of the term in medieval times and up to the nineteenth century at least. Mahfouz, however, uses the term more loosely to refer to the deprived and oppressed classes of society (who would of course be labelled as bad characters and ruffians by the powerful and privileged whenever they rose up in arms to claim their share of the wealth of society). In using the word *ḥarāfīsh* and making them the protagonists of his novel, which is written in the episodic form, indigenous to popular Arabic literature, Mahfouz was in fact reviving, modernizing and endowing with a new vision a well-established popular, narrative form whose tradition includes parts of *The Arabian Nights* and the famous popular *sīras* (heroic exploits) of *ᶜAntara b. Shaddād*, *Ḥamzat al-ᶜArab* and *al-Ẓāhir Baybars*, to name some of the better-known examples. Historical sources which chronicle the uprisings and practices of *ḥarāfīsh* in Cairo during the Mameluke period include Ibn Īyās' *Badā'iᶜ al-Zuhūr fī Waqā'iᶜ al-Duhūr* and Ibn Taghrī Birdī's *Al-Nujūm al-Zāhira fī Mulūk Miṣr wa al-Qāhira*. It

is almost certain that Mahfouz will have read some of these sources before writing his novel. The nearest word in English to render *ḥarāfīsh* in its original meaning is perhaps 'riff-raff', which the *Shorter Oxford English Dictionary* defines as 'Persons of a disreputable character or belonging to the lowest class of a community'. See '*Ḥarfūsh*' in *The Encyclopaedia of Islam*, New Edition, Leiden: E. J. Brill, 1979; see also '*ḥarfasha*' in R. Dozy, *Supplément aux dictionnaires arabes*, Beirut: Librairie du Liban, 1968. For a detailed study of the phenomenon of *ḥarāfīsh* and similar sections of society, both from the historical and literary points of view, see Muḥammad Rajab al-Najjār, *Ḥikāyāt al-Shuṭṭār wa al-ᶜAyyārīn fī al-Turāth al-ᶜArabī*, Kuwait: ᶜĀlam al-Maᶜrifa, 1981, *passim*.

32 On the historical background to the concept and phenomenon of the *futuwwa* in the popular culture of Egypt, see R. al-Najjār, op. cit., ch. 2, sections 3–6, pp. 138–233.

33 Mahfouz describes what he did in *Children of Gebelawi* as the opposite of what Jonathan Swift did in *Gulliver's Travels*: 'he criticized reality through [the creation of] myth, whereas what I did was to criticize myth through [representation of] reality. I dressed myth in the habit of reality, the better to understand the latter' (*Ataḥaddath Ilaykum*, p. 71).

34 For the origin of the mulberry tree as symbol (and the *takiyya* generally) in the work of Mahfouz, see my discussion of *Fountain and Tomb* earlier in this chapter.

35 From the symptoms given (p. 51) we can tell it is cholera, though the author does not mention the disease by name. Cholera struck Egypt on an epidemic scale in 1947, when more than 32,000 cases were recorded with more than 20,000 deaths (see *Chamber's Encyclopaedia*, Oxford: Pergamon Press, 1966).

36 That would be al-Muqaṭṭam Mountain, east of Cairo, though consistently with Mahfouz's reluctance to pin down realistic locality here, it is not named. For the function of *khalā'* (emptiness, wasteland) in Mahfouz's work, see ch. 1, p. 9.

37 On the factual level the devastation of Jalāl's soul by Qamar's death corresponds to that of Caligula's caused by the death of Drusilla (his sister and incestuous lover), while, on the thematic level, Jalāl's quest for eternity parallels Caligula's for the moon, i.e. the impossible. In their demented obsession, both characters suffer a death of the soul and become callously indifferent to human suffering.

38 *The Thief and the Dogs*, as was shown in ch. 5, upholds the same ideal by demonstrating the inevitability of the failure of individual rebellion. On the other hand, the author's advocacy of the notion of popular revolution, or the active involvement of the masses in resisting oppression, as well as his rejection of the principle of absolute government (however well-meaning) will be shown again in the novel which will be discussed next, *Nights of the Thousand Nights*.

39 For some references to the *qabw*, see *Harafish*, pp. 12, 15, 29, 41, 205, 269, 339, 450.

40 *Ataḥaddath Ilaykum*, p. 74.

41 The title of this novel harks back to the Arabic title of *The Arabian Nights* which is known to Arab readers as 'The Thousand and One Nights', or *Alf Layla wa Layla*. Arabic speakers often refer to the work with the shortened title *Alf Layla*, i.e. The Thousand Nights. It is this shortened form that Mahfouz uses in the title of his novel. During the course of my discussion of the novel, I will simply refer to it as *Nights*.

42 *Nights*, being drawn from a source replete with manifestations of the marvellous and the magical, lends itself easily to 'magical realism'. Admittedly, Mahfouz read *A Hundred Years of Solitude* by Gabriel Garcia Marquez at least two years before the publication of *Nights* (see J. al-Ghīṭānī, op. cit., p. 92). (Note that Ghīṭānī's book where Mahfouz admits to reading Marquez was first published in Beirut by Dār al-Masīra in 1980.) For a consideration of Mahfouz's use of the supernatural in both *Harafish* and *Nights*, see Nedal Al-Mousa, 'The Nature and Uses of the Fantastic in the Fictional World of Naguib Mahfouz', *Journal of Arabic Literature*, vol. 23, 1992, pp. 36–48.

43 Compare the narrator's words in the sketch entitled 'Surūr ᶜAbd al-Bāqī' in *Mirrors*. He argues that no man will be able to 'squeeze out of himself his human potentials until he regards himself not as an independent entity, but as a cell able to live only through existing cooperatively in the living body which is the human race' (p. 158).

44 For an example see the tale of 'Jamaṣa al-Bulṭī', where Jamaṣa's servant fails to see or hear the jinni who appears to his master in the water, *Nights*, p. 41.

45 See ibid., p. 161, where a similar statement is made in a similar situation.

46 See the exposition of this notion in my discussion of *The Trilogy* in ch. 4 of this study; see also the discussion of Bergson's influence on Mahfouz on pp. 14–16.

47 Naguib Mahfouz, *Respected Sir*, pp. 158–60.

48 Compare 'Tale 40' in *Fountain and Tomb*, where a madman confined by his family in a room with a steel-barred window is seen by the child-protagonist staring at nothing and murmuring occasionally: 'Where have you gone, my love?' The story circulating in the neighbourhood is that he once saw a pretty girl in a dream, after which he started roaming the streets looking for her. This one-page snippet (a recollection from the author's boyhood) is, in all probability, the origin of the highly developed story of 'Nūr al-Dīn and Dunyāzād' in this work.

49 The italics are mine.

50 Compare the author's own youthful love story retold in the episode of 'Ṣafā' al-Kātib' in *Mirrors*; see also pp. 9–11 of this book.

51 For the discussion of *The Thief and the Dogs* and the role of the *ṣūfī* in it, see ch. 5.

52 For further elaboration of Mahfouz's attitude towards forms of religious escapism, see my discussions of *The Thief and the Dogs*

and *The Beggar* in ch. 5; see also n. 11 of the same chapter.

53 This is a somewhat free translation of the Arabic which says: '*Ammā ahl al-Fanā' Fayukhalliṣūn anfusahum, wa ammā ahl al-jihād fayukhalliṣūn al-ᶜibād*', *Nights*, p. 196.

54 One suspects that this detail is not without significance. Mahfouz probably wants to cast doubt on the purity of Fāḍil's revolutionary motives. There is an element of personal vendetta here, not dissimilar to Saᶜīd Mahrān's in *The Thief and the Dogs*.

55 Compare Mahfouz's earlier short story 'Al-Khawf' (Fear) in the collection *A House of Ill Repute*, where a young police officer courageously rids the inhabitants of an area of Cairo of the powerful *futuwwas* who persecuted them, only to humiliate them himself in the end. Commenting on the story, Mahfouz refers to his preoccupation with the phenomenon of 'the revolutionary, who as soon as he occupies the seat of power, turns into the very image of despotism he had revolted against' (*Ataḥaddath Ilaykum*, pp. 110–11). In the course of the same commentary, the author admits to having modelled the officer of the story on the other 'officer [i.e. Nasser] who came to play the same part in our life' (ibid.). Nasser was probably again at the back of his mind in his portrayal of Fāḍil Ṣanᶜān in *Nights*. For an English translation of 'Fear', see Naguib Mahfouz, *The Time and the Place and Other Stories*.

56 Compare the rise of the *ḥarāfīsh* in support of Fatḥ al-Bāb and then of ᶜĀshūr II in *Harafish* (Tales 9 and 10).

57 Compare Tawfīq al-Ḥakīm's play, *Shahrazād* (1934) (now a classic of Arabic literature), which has the same starting-point.

58 The use of Shahrayār to embody this vision is central to al-Ḥakīm's *Shahrazād* (see n. 57). There is indeed a strong case for arguing that Mahfouz was influenced by al-Ḥakīm's play (which predates his novel by nearly forty years) in his portrayal of Shahrayār's character.

59 Compare, in *Children of Gebelawi*, Gebelawi's banishment of his son Adham from the Great House following the latter's intrusion into the forbidden room where the deeds of the estate are kept.

60 See *Riḥlat Ibn Baṭṭūṭa*, Beirut: Dār Ṣādir, 1964, p. 4.

61 See Ḥusayn Mu'nis, *Ibn Baṭṭūṭa wa Riḥlatuh*, Cairo: Dār al-Maᶜārif, 1980, p. 26.

62 The allegorical significance of all the place names here must not be lost on the reader. 'The Abode of Sunrise' presumably refers to the dawn of human society, while 'the Abode of Bewilderment' may refer to the 'groping' period in social development up to the foundation of industrial capitalist society which, in turn, is given the name of 'Abode of the Arena', the 'arena' being that of competition or conflict and the principle of survival of the fittest – the basic values of capitalism. 'The Abode of Security', conversely, suggests the social security principle, integral to socialist government. Finally, 'the Abode of Sunset' suggests the exhaustion of the potential of all the above models or phases, and the inevitability of

proceeding to the 'highest' ideal, symbolized by 'the Abode on the Mountain' – the as yet unachieved Heaven on earth.

63 Mahfouz's idea of 'work' and social involvement as a moral duty has been discussed at some length in ch. 5 of this study, particularly in my treatment of *Autumn Quail*, *The Search* and *The Beggar*.

64 For a full discussion of this issue see my article 'Religion in the Novels of Naguib Mahfouz', pp. 21–7.

65 In this connection, consider the ending of *Harafish*, where on the final establishment of justice in the *ḥāra*, the *takiyya* opens its gates to it, bringing about for the first time in human history a symbolic union of heaven and earth – ᶜĀshūr II in *Harafish* appears to have attained *Dār al-Jabal*, which continued to elude Ibn Faṭṭūma in *Travels*.

66 See Ḥusayn Mu'nis, op. cit., pp. 24–5, 30; see also *Ibn Battuta: Travels in Asia and Africa*, trans. and selected with introduction and notes by H. A. R. Gibb, London: George Routledge & Sons, 1929, p. 4.

7 MATTERS OF FORM: A CASE STUDY OF *RESPECTED SIR*

1 The following analysis is abridged and adapted from my Ph.D. thesis '*Ḥaḍrat al-Muḥtaram* by Najīb Maḥfūẓ: a Translation and Critical Assessment', University of Exeter, 1984.

2 See 'Viewpoint' in J. T. Shipley, *Dictionary of World Literary Terms*, London: George Allen & Unwin Ltd., 1970.

3 It is interesting to note here that Mahfouz admits to reading Joyce's *Ulysses*, though he calls it 'a terrible novel', which has created a trend. 'It is', he says, 'like someone pointing to a cave that others had to venture into in their own way' (*Ataḥaddath Ilaykum*, Beirut: Dār al-ᶜAwda, 1977, p. 94).

4 See 'Stream of Consciousness' in J. T. Shipley, op. cit.

5 See Raymond Chapman, *Linguistics and Literature*, London: Edward Arnold, 1973 (rpt 1974), p. 42.

6 ibid.

7 *Ataḥaddath Ilaykum*, pp. 95–6.

8 In his review of *Respected Sir*, Muḥammad ᶜAbdullāh al-Shafaqī refers in passing to Mahfouz's use of 'a quasi-mystical language when talking about employees and their positions', but he does not point out to what effect this use is put. See *Al-Kātib*, March 1977, pp. 113–15.

9 On the ironic effect of mixing linguistic registers in literature, see Raymond Chapman, op. cit., p. 18.

10 See the discussion of the plot, pp. 175–8.

11 See my discussion of *New Cairo* in ch. 3.

12 Examples of this type of character are Maḥjūb ᶜAbd al-Dā'im in *New Cairo* and Ḥasanayn in *The Beginning and the End*, to name but two.

13 Examples of this type are Ma'mūn Raḍwān and ᶜAlī Ṭāhā in *New Cairo*, Ḥusayn in *The Beginning and the End*, Ilhām in *The Search* and ᶜUthmān Khalīl in *The Beggar.* Very often, the moral point is stressed by the contrastive presentation in the same novel of characters of both types: the fallen and the redeemed.

14 All italics are mine.

15 In an interview with Mahfouz, Ṣabrī Ḥāfiẓ remarks that the novelist's characters are always seen in 'closed places', and that they achieve self-fulfilment only in such places. He then asks of Mahfouz why his characters do not achieve self-fulfilment in the outside world – in society at large. Mahfouz answers that those who can do so 'must be rebels or revolutionaries who [are prepared to] overturn the regime in order to impose their point of view. . . . But not all people can afford to do that' (*Ataḥaddath Ilaykum*, pp. 117–18).

16 ibid., pp. 157–8.

17 ibid., p. 158.

18 Sasson Somekh, *The Changing Rhythm: a Study of Najīb Maḥfūẓ's Novels*, Leiden: E. J. Brill, 1973, p. 187. For an interesting account of the nature of the new language used by Mahfouz, in which Ghālī Shukrī argues convincingly that the novelist was opening new vistas of expression for the first time in Arabic, see G. Shukrī, *Al-Muntamī*, Cairo: Dār al-Maᶜārif, 1969, pp. 368–70. For a detailed account of the evolution of Mahfouz's prose from archaism to modernity during the first twenty years of his career (1930–49), see ᶜAbd al-Muḥsin Ṭāhā Badr, *Naguib Mahfouz: al Ru'ya wa al-Adāt*, Cairo: Dār al-Thaqāfa, *passim*; see also M. Enani, 'Novel Rhetoric', in *Egyptian Perspectives on Naguib Mahfouz*, ed. M. M. Enani, Cairo: General Egyptian Book Organization, 1989, pp. 97–144.

19 See my elaboration of Mahfouz's attitude to *Ṣūfism* in ch. 5, particularly the discussions of *The Thief and the Dogs* and *The Beggar.* For a perceptive analysis which reads *Respected Sir* in terms of a religious quest akin to that of *The Search*, see Jūrj Ṭarābīshī, *Ramziyyat al-Mar'a fī al-Riwāya al-ᶜArabiyya*, Beirut: Dār al-Ṭalīᶜa, 1981, pp. 67–99.

20 *Ataḥaddath Ilaykum*, p. 61.

21 ibid., p. 212; see also pp. 25, 48.

22 See for instance the telephone conversation between ᶜUthmān and Aṣīla in ch. 25 of the novel. For a discussion of some aspects of the duality of *fuṣḥā* and *ᶜāmiyya* in Arabic writing, see my article 'Khawāṭir ḥawl Arā' Luwīs ᶜAwaḍ fī Qaḍāyā al-lugha wa fī Adab Naguib Mahfouz', *Al-Ḥayāt*, 15 September 1989.

8 IMAGES OF GOD, DEATH AND SOCIETY: THE SHORT STORIES AND THE PLAYS

1 One of those collections, viz. *Good Morning to You*, has been dealt with in the context of my examination of the author's episodic

works in ch. 6 of this study, where my reasons for doing so are explained.

2 This count includes, for convenience's sake, *Before the Throne*, which some may (justifiably) object to being classified as a novel.

3 Maḥmūd Amīn al-ᶜĀlim, *Ta'mmulāt fī ᶜĀlam Naguib Mahfouz*, Cairo: al-Hay'a al-Miṣriyya al-ᶜĀmma lil-Ta'līf wa al-Nashr, 1970, p. 139.

4 The story was entitled 'Fatra min al-Shabāb' (A Period of Youth) and was published in *Al-Siyāsa*, 22 July 1932; it remains uncollected. See ᶜAbd al-Muḥsin Ṭāhā Badr, *Naguib Mahfouz: al-Ru'ya wa al-Adāt*, Cairo: Dār al-Thaqāfa, 1978, p. 494.

5 For a complete list of these stories, their venues and dates of publication, see ibid., pp. 494–8.

6 The date given by Mahfouz in his list of publications usually appended to his works is 1938, but there is no doubt that this is false. Somekh was probably the first to cast doubt on the authenticity of this date, depending on internal evidence which pointed at a later date. Badr, on the other hand, established that some of the stories collected in *Whispers of Madness* first appeared in magazines up to seven years after 1938. When he confronted Mahfouz with the facts, the author admitted that 1938 was not the true publication date, 'but rather one which determined the stories' artistic quality in the context of my output'. More recently, in a conversation reported by Ghālī Shukrī, he blamed the false date on his publisher and admitted that the collection first appeared after *Midaq Alley* (i.e. after 1947; ten whole years after the publicized date). The author has continued, however, to give in his lists '1938' as the publication date. See Sasson Somekh, *The Changing Rhythm: a Study of Najīb Maḥfūẓ's Novels*, Leiden: E. J. Brill, 1973, pp. 46 (fn. 2), 199; A. T. Badr, op. cit., pp. 91–3, 494–8; Ghālī Shukrī, *Naguib Mahfouz: min al-Jamāliyya ilā Nobel*, Cairo: al-Hay'a al-ᶜĀmma lil-Istiᶜlāmāt, 1988, p. 72.

7 This is because Mahfouz's latest story included in the collection, viz. 'Ṣawt min al-ᶜĀlam al-Ākhar' (A Voice from beyond the Grave) first appeared in *Al-Risāla* over two issues, 16 April and 23 April 1945. See A. T. Badr, op. cit., p. 498.

8 And *not* 30 as Badr cites. See A. T. Badr, op. cit., p. 90.

9 Badr names, however, four stories which appear to have been published for the first time in the collection itself. See A. T. Badr, op. cit., p. 499.

10 Badr pioneered the documentation and study of Mahfouz's uncollected stories and to date his research on the subject remains the main access to that period of the author's work. See A. T. Badr, op. cit., pp. 89–148. For an elaboration on Badr's work, see the more recent study, ᶜAlī Shalash, *Naguib Mahfouz: al-Ṭarīq wa al-Ṣadā*, Beirut: Dār al-Ādāb, 1990, chs. 1 and 2, *passim*.

11 A. T. Badr, op. cit., p. 121.

12 See for instance the opening paragraph of 'Al-Hadhayān' (Hallucinations [of Fever]), which creates as 'tearful' a scene as any

written by al-Manfalūṭī in his famous *Al-Naẓarāt* (1910–21). See Naguib Mahfouz, *Whispers of Madness*, p. 76.

13 One lurid (and by no means rare) example is offered by the story 'Rawḍ al-Faraj', where a young man falls in love with an older cabaret actress, who turns out to be none other than his own mother, from whom he had been separated in his childhood (ibid., pp. 119–35).

14 The scene in the title story, where the (functionally) mad protagonist picks up a chicken placed in front of a rich couple dining at a restaurant and throws it to a group of onlooking street children, betrays a concern for social justice (ibid., pp. 3–10). For a translation of 'Whispers of Madness', see Naguib Mahfouz, *God's World* (an anthology of short stories), trans. with introduction by Akef Abadir and Roger Allen, Minneapolis: Bibliotheca Islamica, 1973.

15 His hostility towards the ruling aristocracy of foreign stock is discernible in 'Yaqẓat al-Mūmyā'' (The Mummy Awakes) (ibid., pp. 85–103). For a translation of this story, see R. Allen, trans. 'The Mummy Awakes', in Alamgir Hashmi, ed., *The Worlds of Muslim Imagination*, Islamabad: Gulmohar, 1986, pp. 15–33.

16 Stories in the collection which deal with the ravages and ironies of time include 'Muftaraq al-Ṭuruq' (The Crossroad), 'Ḥayāt Muharrij' (Life of a Clown), 'Iṣlāḥ al-Qubūr' (Repairing Graves) and 'Ṣawt min al-ᶜĀlam al-Ākhar' (A Voice from Beyond the Grave).

17 For example the prototype for the altruistic self-sacrificing brother, as seen later in the characters of Aḥmad ᶜĀkif and Ḥusayn in *Khan al-Khalili* and *The Beginning and the End* respectively, can be found in the protagonist of 'Ḥayāt lil-Ghayr' (Living for Others) (ibid., pp. 243–54).

18 An inkling of this can be experienced in the story of 'Badhlat al-Asīr' (The Prisoner-of-War's Uniform), which critics are unanimous in setting apart from the rest of the collection for its succinct powerfulness and comparatively high artistic quality (ibid., pp. 166–70). For a translation of this story, see the anthology translated by Akef Abadir and Roger Allen, cited in n.14.

19 See n. 6.

20 It must be noted that the anthology in translation by the same title (cited in n. 14) is not a full translation of Mahfouz's *Dunyā Allāh* (i.e. God's World). In fact it is a representative selection, which spans no less than six collections by the author.

21 The story is translated under this title in Naguib Mahfouz, *The Time and the Place and Other Stories*, selected and trans. Denys Johnson-Davies, New York: Doubleday, 1991.

22 See p. 71. for a quotation where Mahfouz does not rule out the possibility of humanity achieving victory over death through scientific 'progress'.

23 Translated into English by D. Johnson-Davies; see n. 21.

24 Many critics have written on this short story. One notable

treatment is that by Jūrj Ṭarābīshī, who tries to place it in the context of Mahfouz's quest for God in other works. See J. Ṭarābīshī, *Allāh fī Riḥlat Naguib Mahfouz al-Ramziyya*, Beirut: Dār al-Ṭalīᶜa, 3rd edition, 1980, pp. 32–41 (first published 1973); see also Sasson Somekh, ''Zaᶜbalāwī' – Author, Theme and Technique', *Journal of Arabic Literature*, vol. 1, 1970, pp. 24–35.

25 In the later collection *I Saw in a Dream* (1982), Mahfouz uses again the same metaphor in the story of 'Ahl al-Hawā' (The Love-besotted). Here too life is embodied in the image of a powerful and voraciously lustful woman, who consumes men, one after another, before discarding them (to death).

26 There are three English translations of the title-story of this collection: the first by Akef Abadir and Roger Allen (see n.14); the second in Saad El-Gabalawy, trans. with introduction, *Modern Egyptian Short Stories*, Fredericton, N.B.: York Press, 1977; and the third by D. Johnson-Davies (see n.21).

27 See Hamdi Sakkut, 'Najīb Maḥfūẓ's Short Stories' in *Studies in Modern Arabic Literature*, ed. R. C. Ostle, Warminster: Aris & Philips, 1975, p. 122.

28 Two translations are available in English of the title story of this collection, the first by A. Abadir and R. Allen, and the second by D. Johnson-Davies with the slightly different title 'At the Bus Stop'. See nn.14 and 21.

29 For an English translation of this story by D. Johnson-Davies, see n. 21.

30 The theme of the passivity leading to catastrophe had then been already explored at length by Mahfouz in *Chatter on the Nile*. See ch. 5.

31 For an English translation of this story by A. Abadir and R. Allen, see n. 14.

32 Here is Mahfouz's assessment of the Egyptian national character. After extolling the Egyptians' historical qualities of patience, steadfastness and peacefulness, he goes on to add that having long been subjected to persecution, 'they ended up getting used to it . . . falling silent when they should have screamed, using sarcasm when they should have used violence and flattery when they should at least have kept quiet' (Naguib Mahfouz, *Ataḥaddath Ilaykum*, Beirut: Dār al-ᶜAwda, 1977, pp. 53–4; see also p. 165 for a similar statement).

33 The subject of Egypt's collective hypnosis under Nasser was first openly broached after his death by Tawfīq al-Ḥakīm in his famous (and, at the time, controversial) pamphlet *ᶜAwdat al-Waᶜy*, first published in 1974. For an English translation see T. al-Hakim, *The Return of Consciousness*, trans. Bayly Winder, London: Macmillan, 1985.

34 The italics are mine.

35 See Fu'ād Dawwāra, *Naguib Mahfouz: min al-Qawmiyya ilā al-ᶜĀlamiyya*, Cairo: al-Hay'a al-Misriyya al-ᶜĀmma lil-Kitāb, 1989, p. 240.

36 *Ataḥaddath Ilaykum*, pp. 210–11.
37 For a short account of the public and critical reception of three of Mahfouz's plays on their first performance in Cairo in 1969, see Naguib Mahfouz, *One-Act Plays* I, trans. with introduction by Nehad Selaiha, Cairo: General Egyptian Book Organization, 1989, pp. 9–12.
38 With the exception of 'Yumīt wa Yuḥyī' (Death and Resurrection), which occasionally labours under the weight of classical rhetoric.
39 All three plays are included in Nehad Selaiha's translation cited in n. 37.
40 See Jūrj Ṭarābīshī, op. cit., p. 99.
41 See *Ataḥaddath Ilaykum*, p. 179.
42 ibid., p. 178.
43 Included in the short-story collection entitled *The Crime* (1973). For an English translation under a different title, see Judith Rosenhouse, '*Harassment*, a Play by Najīb Maḥfūẓ', *Journal of Arabic Literature*, vol. 9, 1978, pp. 105–37; for an earlier translation see Roger Allen, trans. 'The Chase: a Play by Najīb Maḥfūẓ,' *Mundis Artium*, vol. 10, no. 1, 1977, pp. 134–62.
44 Included in the short-story collection entitled *The Devil Preaches* (1979). For a translation of 'Al-Jabal' by N. Selaiha, see n.37.
45 Included in the same collection as in the previous note. The play obviously lends its title to the collection as a whole.
46 See 'Story of the City of Brass' in *The Thousand and One Nights* (vol. 3), trans. Edward W. Lane, London: East–West Publications, 1981, pp. 109–40. Lane mentions that the story begins in the 566th night and ends in the 578th. The Cairo edition published by Muḥammad ʿAlī Ṣubayḥ & Sons shows, however, that the story begins in the 555th night and ends in the 568th. Comparing Mahfouz's play with the story shows his utilization of it to have been indeed minimal. Basically, all he takes from the story is its starting-point, i.e. the caliph's sending of a number of his men in quest for one of those brass bottles in which King Solomon used to imprison offending jinn. Mahfouz seizes on the symbolic potential of the quest as one for absolute power and develops it along lines entirely his own, maintaining the atmosphere of *The Thousand and One Nights*, but neither the events nor the texture of the story beyond the initial situation.
47 For a translation of this story by A. Abadir and R. Allen, see n.14.
48 For a detailed and penetrative analysis of these two stories, see Jūrj Ṭarābīshī, op. cit., pp. 66–111. For an analysis of 'Ḥikāya bilā Bidāya wa lā Nihāya' in existentialist terms, see Mona M. Mikhail, 'Broken Idols: the Death of Religion as Reflected in Two Short Stories by Idrīs and Maḥfūẓ' in Issa J. Boullata, ed., *Critical Perspectives on Modern Arabic Literature*, Washington, D.C.: Three Continents Press, 1980, pp. 83–93.
49 For a similar observation, see Hamdi Sakkut, op. cit., p. 122.
50 *Ataḥaddath Ilaykum*, p. 182.
51 A possible exception is 'Al-Rajul wa al-Ākhar' (The Man and the

Other Man) in *Love under the Pyramids* (1979). The story has been translated by D. Johnson-Davies; see n.21.

52 As in the Biblical Book of Job rather than 'job' as meaning 'a post of employment'.

53 More literally, the title translates 'Love on the Pyramid Plateau'.

54 As pointed out earlier, Mahfouz has read G. Garcia Marquez's *A Hundred Years of Solitude* (see ch. 6, n. 42).

55 For a detailed review of this collection by the present writer, see 'Naguib Mahfouz Yushakhkhiṣ al-Dā' wa Yaṣif al-Dawā'', *Al-Ahrām Al-Dawlī*, 2 April 1990.

56 For a translation of this story and five others from the same collection, see the selection by D. Johnson-Davies cited in n.21. Another story yet from the same collection, namely 'ᶜAlā Ḍaw' al-Nujūm' (Under a Starlit Sky), has been translated by the present writer; see *The Guardian*, 12 December 1991.

57 See interview with Yūsuf al-Qaᶜīd in *Al-Ḥayāt*, 12 April 1990.

THE WORKS OF NAGUIB MAHFOUZ

In the following list I begin with the Arabic title in italics followed by the English rendering used in the text of this book. To avoid confusion, where there are published translations I have adopted their titles, even in those cases where they do not reflect the Arabic. In such instances I will, however, provide in brackets a more literal translation of the original title. All titles available in English will be indicated with an asterisk. The first date given is that of first publication in Arabic in book form. No account is taken of newspaper or magazine serialization dates (very common with the work of Mahfouz after *The Trilogy*). Publication in book form usually came within a year after serialization, except in the case of *Children of Gebelawi* (serialized in 1959, book in 1967). A few of the first publication dates given (indicated with two asterisks) will contradict the dates authorized by Mahfouz. The reasons for adopting different dates can be found in the appropriate sections of this book where such works are discussed. The second column of dates lists between brackets the dates of editions used in this study – it is to these editions that all my page references are made. Where there is an uncertainty about a date, it will be followed by a question mark. Where the edition used is the first published, the second column will be left blank. Unless otherwise indicated, the place of publication is Cairo and the publisher is Maktabat Miṣr.

THE NOVELS

^c^*Abath al-Aqdār*	The Game of Fates	1939	(1982)
Rādūbīs	Rhodopis	1943	(1947?)
Kifāḥ Ṭība	The Struggle of Thebes	1944	(n.d.)
Khān al-Khalīlī	Khan al-Khalili	1945**	(1960)
Al-Qāhira al-Jadīda	New Cairo	1946**	(1974)
Zuqāq al-Midaqq	Midaq Alley*	1947	(1972)
Al-Sarāb	Mirage	1948	(1982)
Bidāya wa Nihāya	The Beginning and the End*	1949	(1973)
Al-Thulāthiyya:	The (Cairo) Trilogy:		
1 *Bayn al-Qaṣrayn*	Palace Walk*	1956	(1970)
2 *Qaṣr al-Shawq*	Palace of Desire*	1957	(n.d.)
3 *Al-Sukkariyya*	Sugar Street*	1957	(1971?)
Awlād Ḥāratinā	Children of Gebelawi*	(1967)	(1972)
	(Children of Our Quarter) (Beirut: Dār al-Ādāb)		
Al-Liṣṣ wa al-Kilāb	The Thief and the Dogs*	1961	(n.d.)
Al-Summān wa al-Kharīf	Autumn Quail*	1962	(n.d.)
Al-Ṭarīq	The Search*	1964	(1965)
	(The Way)		
Al-Shaḥḥādh	The Beggar*	1965	(1978)
Tharthara fawq al-Nīl	Chatter on the Nile	1966	(1973)
Mirāmār	Miramar*	1967	(1976)
Al-Marāyā	Mirrors*	1972	

Ḥubb taḥt al-Maṭar	Love in the Rain	1973	
Al-Karnak	Karnak*	1974	
Ḥaḍrat al-Muḥtaram	Respected Sir*	1975	(1977)
Ḥikāyāt Ḥāratinā	The Fountain and the Tomb* (Tales from our Quarter)	1975	
Qalb al-Layl	Heart of the Night	1975	
Malḥamat al-Ḥarāfīsh	Epic of the Harafish	1977	
ᶜAṣr al-Ḥubb	The Age of Love	1980	
Afrāḥ al-Qubba	Wedding Song*	1981	
Layālī Alf Layla	Nights of the Thousand Nights	1982	
Al-Bāqī min al-Zaman Sāᶜa	There Only Remains One Hour	1982	
Riḥlat Ibn Faṭṭūma	The Journey of Ibn Fattouma* (referred to in this book as *The Travels of Ibn Fattuma*)	1983	
Amām al-ᶜArsh	Before the Throne	1983	
Yawm Qutil al-Zaᶜīm	The Day the Leader was Killed*	1985	
Al-ᶜĀ'ish fī al-Ḥaqīqa	He who Lives in the Truth	1985	
Ḥadīth al-Ṣabāḥ wa al-Masā'	Tales of Mornings and Evenings	1987	
Qushtumur	Qushtumur	1988	

COLLECTED SHORT STORIES

(Titles of collections including plays will be followed by the number of plays they contain between square brackets.)

Hams al-Junūn	Whispers of Madness	1948?**	(1973)
Dunyā Allāh	God's World	1963	(1973)
*Bayt Sayyi' al-Sum*ᶜ*a*	A House of Ill Repute	1965	(1974?)
Khammārat al-Qiṭṭ al-Aswad	The Black Cat Tavern	1969	(1974)
Taḥt al-Maẓalla [5]	Under the Bus Shelter	1969	(1974)
Ḥikāya bilā Bidāya walā Nihāya	A Tale without Beginning or End	1971	(1973)
*Shahr al-*ᶜ*Asal*	The Honeymoon	1971	(1973)
Al-Jarīma [1]	The Crime	1973	
Al-Ḥubb fawq Haḍabat al-Haram	Love under the Pyramids	1979	
*Al-Shayṭān Ya*ᶜ*iẓ* [2]	The Devil Preaches	1979	
Ra'ayt fīmā Yarā al-Nā'im	I Saw in a Dream	1982	
Al-Tanẓīm al-Sirrī	The Secret Organization	1984	
Ṣabāḥ al-Ward	Good Morning to You	1987	
Al-Fajr al-Kādhib	The False Dawn	1989	

TRANSLATIONS

Miṣr al-Qadīma	Ancient Egypt	1931?**	(1988)

COLLECTED INTERVIEWS

Ataḥaddath Ilaykum (ed. Ṣabrī Ḥāfiẓ)	I Say to You (Beirut: Dār al-ᶜAwda)	1977

MEMOIRS

Naguib Mahfouz Yatadhakkar (ed. Jamāl al-Ghīṭānī)	Naguib Mahfouz Remembers (Cairo: Akhbār al-Yawm)	1987

(First published by Dār al-Masīra, Beirut, 1980. The current edition contains an additional long introduction by the editor.)

JOURNALISM

Ḥawl al-Dīn wa al-Dīmuqrāṭiyya	On Religion and Democracy	1990
Ḥawl al-Thaqāfa wa al-Taᶜlīm	On Culture and Education	1990
Ḥawl al-Shabāb wa al-Ḥuriyya	On Youth and Freedom	1990
(All three titles: ed. Fatḥī al-ᶜAshrī)	(Cairo: al-Dār al-Miṣriyya al-Lubnāniyya)	

NOVELS IN ENGLISH TRANSLATION

Midaq Alley (Trevor Le Gassick), Beirut: Khayat, 1966; London: Heinemann, 1975; American University Press in Cairo, 1984; London: Doubleday, 1992.

Mirrors (Roger Allen), Minneapolis: Bibliotheca Islamica, 1977.

Miramar (Fatma Moussa-Mahmoud), London: Heinemann, 1978; American University Press in Cairo, 1985(?).

'*Al-Karnak*', in Saad El-Gabalawy, trans. with introduction, *Three Contemporary Egyptian Novels*, Fredericton, N.B.: York Press, 1979.

Children of Gebelawi (Philip Stewart), London: Heinemann, 1981.

The Thief and the Dogs (Trevor Le Gassick and M. M. Badawi), American University in Cairo Press, 1984; London: Doubleday, 1990.

Wedding Song (Olive E. Kenny), American University in Cairo Press, 1984; London: Doubleday, 1990.

Autumn Quail (Roger Allen), American University in Cairo Press, 1985; London: Doubleday, 1990.

The Beginning and the End (Ramses Awad), American University in Cairo Press, 1985; London: Doubleday, 1990.

The Beggar (Kristin Walker Henry and Nariman Khales Naili al-Warraki), American University in Cairo Press, 1986; London: Doubleday, 1990.

Respected Sir (Rasheed El-Enany), London: Quartet Books, 1986; American University in Cairo Press, 1987; New York: Doubleday, 1990.

The Search (Mohamed Islam), American University in Cairo Press, 1987; London: Doubleday, 1991.

Fountain and Tomb (Soad Sobhi, Essam Fattouh and James Kenneson), Washington, D.C.: Three Continents Press, 1988.

The Day the Leader was Killed (Malak Hashem), Cairo: General Egyptian Book Organization, 1989.

The Cairo Trilogy:

Palace Walk (William M. Hutchins and Olive E. Kenny), London: Doubleday, 1990.

Palace of Desire (William Maynard Hutchins, Lorne M. Kenny and Olive E. Kenny), London: Doubleday, 1991.

Sugar Street (William Maynard Hutchins and Angele Botros Samaan), London: Doubleday, 1992.

The Journey of Ibn Fattouma (Denys Johnson-Davies), London: Doubleday, 1992.

(At the time of going to press Doubleday had scheduled for publication in 1993 and 1994 three new titles, *Adrift in the Nile* (i.e. *Chatter on the Nile*), *Harafish* and *Nights of the Thousand Nights*.)

COLLECTIONS OF SHORT STORIES AND PLAYS IN ENGLISH TRANSLATION

God's World (Akef Abadir and Roger Allen), Minneapolis: Bibliotheca Islamica, 1973.

The Time and the Place and Other Stories (Denys Johnson-Davies), New York: Doubleday, 1991.

(Both of the above collections are selections made across the spectrum of Mahfouz's output of short stories rather than being complete translations of any one Arabic collection. A number of other stories has been translated in a wide variety of publications, some of which have been referred to in the notes to this book.)

One-Act Plays 1 (Nehad Selaiha), Cairo: General Egyptian Book Organization, 1989 (contains four out of Mahfouz's eight one-act plays).

A GUIDE FOR FURTHER READING

The following list in no way aims at being comprehensive. It does not take account of articles in periodicals and chapters in books, or of unpublished dissertations and theses (of all of which copious material exists in both Arabic and English) – many of these, however, have been referred to in the notes to this book. On the other hand, only a limited number of the numerous monographs on Mahfouz in Arabic were thought to be useful to include here. (Again, the titles of some more will have been given in my notes to chapters.) Finally, not all the contents of this list have necessarily been referred to in the text of the book.

IN ENGLISH

Matti Moosa, *The Origins of Modern Arabic Fiction*, Washington, D.C.: Three Continents Press, 1983. On the earliest stages in the evolution of the genre of the novel in Egypt and Syria during the second half of the nineteenth century and the first two decades of the twentieth. Well-researched and highly informative.

Ali B. Jad, *Form and Technique in the Egyptian Novel (1912–1971)*, London: Ithaca Press, 1983. By far the most comprehensive and perceptively argued treatment of the subject. Discusses briefly Mahfouz's fiction up to the late 1960s but excludes the historical novels.

Of lesser scope and now somewhat dated (though still useful) are:

Hamdi Sakkut, *The Egyptian Novel and its Main Trends (1913–1952)*, Cairo: The American University in Cairo Press, 1971. Deals briefly with Mahfouz's fiction up to *The Trilogy*;

Hilary Kilpatrick, *The Modern Egyptian Novel: a Study in Social Criticism*, London: Ithaca Press, 1974. Deals briefly with Mahfouz's fiction up to the late 1960s but excludes the historical novels.

Readers who want to view the evolution of the genre of the novel in Egypt within the wider context of the development of other literary genres can consult:

J. Brugman, *An Introduction to the History of Modern Arabic Literature in Egypt*, Leiden: E. J. Brill, 1984.

Full-length books on Mahfouz:

Sasson Somekh, *The Changing Rhythm: a Study of Najīb Maḥfūẓ's Novels*, Leiden: E. J. Brill, 1973. Methodical and perceptive. Maintains a balanced approach to aspects of form and content. Contains a useful introductory chapter outlining the state of the Egyptian novel before Mahfouz's arrival on the scene. Deals with Mahfouz's fiction up to the late 1960s.

Mattityahu Peled, *Religion My Own: the Literary Works of Najīb Maḥfūẓ*, New Brunswick: Transaction Books, 1983. Generally more interested in meaning than technique. Accords more importance to the novelist's early historical novels than other critics have done, looking at them in terms of utopian fiction. The author's central endeavour to understand Mahfouz's work in the light of the tenets of medieval Islam should be approached with caution: his analyses and conclusions are intellectually engaging but tend sometimes to coerce Mahfouz's work into a preconceived pattern. Considers Mahfouz's work up to the late 1960s.

Haim Gordon, *Naguib Mahfouz's Egypt: Existential Themes in his Writings*, New York: Greenwood Press, 1990. Hardly a literary study! The author is more interested in giving us his own account of what he considers to be the shortcomings of the Egyptian national character, based on personal observations and impressions made during short visits to Egypt over a number of years – Mahfouz's work and interviews come in handy as tailored illustrations. The author is also not conversant with Arabic and therefore his access to Mahfouz was limited to what works were available to him in translation.

M. M. Enani, ed., *Egyptian Perspectives on Naguib Mahfouz: a Collection of Critical Essays*, Cairo: General Egyptian Book Organization, 1989. Some of the essays were written especially for the collection, but most are translations of earlier reviews and articles in Arabic. They range from general discussions to commentaries on specific works by Mahfouz. Mixed quality. Little to be found on Mahfouz's work since the 1960s.

Trevor Le Gassick, ed., *Critical Perspectives on Naguib Mahfouz,* Washington D.C.: Three Continents Press, 1991. Very similar to the above: a collection of previously published articles, mostly originally written in English but some translated from Arabic by the Editor. The articles deal with a selection of Mahfouz's works up to the early 1970s.

IN ARABIC

Ghālī Shukrī, *Al-Muntamī: Dirāsa fī Adab Naguib Mahfouz*, Cairo: Dār al-Ma^{c}ārif, 2nd edition, 1969. A socio-political reading of Mahfouz through a Marxist-cum-existentialist perspective. Sprawling and undisciplined (450 pages) but can be rewarding sometimes. Deals with Mahfouz's work up to the late 1960s.

Muḥammad Ḥasan ^{c}Abdullāh, *Al-Islāmiyya wa al-Rūḥiyya fī Adab Naguib Mahfouz*, Cairo: Maktabat Miṣr, 2nd edition, 1978. The book (first published in 1972) appears to have been conceived as an answer to G. Shukrī's above. An attempt at rescuing Mahfouz from the leftist critics and claiming him for the envious Islamic right: it does not work. Of little value as a critical study, but useful as an indication of the tensions between left and right, secularist and religious, Moslem and Christian (G. Shukrī is a Copt, a fact which the Moslem M. H. ^{c}Abdullāh insinuates influences his reading of Mahfouz), when they spill over to the literary arena. Discusses Mahfouz's novels up to the 1960s and adds *Mirrors*, *Heart of the Night* and *Harafish* from the 1970s. Of late, however, the Islamic right seem to have given up on Mahfouz as the following monograph demonstrates: Muḥammad Yaḥyā and Muᶜtazz Shukrī, *Al-Ṭarīq ilā Nobel 1988 ᶜAbr Ḥārat Naguib Mahfouz*, Cairo: 'Umma Press, 1989. A bizarre, mixed consideration of *Children of Gebelawi*, first through a comparison with the Qur'ān and incidents from the Prophet's *sīra*, then by putting aside all that and disparaging the novel by literary criteria. Conclusion: condemnation of Mahfouz as an atheist.

Maḥmūd Amīn al-ᶜĀlim, *Ta'ammulāt fī ᶜĀlam Naguib Mahfouz*, Cairo: al-Hay'a al-Miṣriyya al-ᶜĀmma lil-Ta'līf wa al-Nashr, 1970. Unmethodical but highly revealing forays into the work of Mahfouz. Author's approach based on study of structure as a unifying element both within single works and in their totality. Illustrates the possible reward of such an approach but does not go on to carry it out on the extensive scale it would require. Stops at end of the 1960s.

Jūrj Ṭarābīshī, *Allāh fī Riḥlat Naguib Mahfouz al-Ramziyya*, Beirut: Dār al-Ṭalīᶜa, 3rd edition, 1980 (first published in 1973). A penetrating and lucidly argued analysis of Mahfouz's metaphysical quest in a number of novels and short stories from *Children of Gebelawi* to *A Tale without Beginning or End.*

ᶜAbd al-Muḥsin Ṭāhā Badr, *Naguib Mahfouz: al-Ru'ya wa al-Adāt*, Cairo: Dār al-Thaqāfa, 1978. A methodical and elaborate study by a seasoned academic; probably the best-researched on its subject in Arabic. A class-conscious reading of Mahfouz with meticulous and rigorous observation of the development of the novelist's craft and prose style. Invaluable for the analysis and bibliographical account of Mahfouz's early uncollected essays and short stories. Intolerant of Mahfouz's fatalistic view of life and occasionally harsh in tone – quite unusual, since Mahfouz has rarely met with anything but acclaim from his critics. It is very unfortunate that this book (originally intended as volume 1 of a comprehensive study) has not been completed. Its detailed and systematic consideration (485 pages) of Mahfouz's work proceeds no further than *The Beginning and the End*, published in 1949.

ᶜAlī Shalash, *Naguib Mahfouz: al-Ṭarīq wa al-Ṣadā*, Beirut: Dār al-Ādāb, 1990. Informative on the early critical reception of Mahfouz before *The Trilogy* established his fame. Includes in an appendix the full text of fourteen early reviews of Mahfouz's work.

Sīza Aḥmad Qāsim, *Binā' al-Riwāya: Dirāsa Muqārana lī Thulāthiyyat Naguib Mahfouz*, Cairo: al-Hay'a al-Miṣriyya al-ᶜĀmma lil-Kitāb, 1984. A structuralist approach to *The Trilogy*. Often reads like a manual in retrospect for the writing of the novel: there is a painstaking description of the structure of the book but hardly any attempt at putting it in the service of interpretation. Perhaps its strongest point is in the comparisons with masters of European realism such as Balzac and Flaubert which go to prove that by the time of *The Trilogy* Mahfouz had already transcended classical realism and embarked on techniques of modernism.

Al-Rajul wa al-Qimma: Buḥūth wa Dirāsāt, selected and classified by Fāḍil al-Aswad, Cairo: al-Hay'a al-Miṣriyya al-ᶜĀmma lil-Kitāb, 1989. A voluminous compendium of articles on Mahfouz (761 pages). Mixed quality. With only a couple of exceptions, there is no consideration of works written after the 1960s.

Naguib Mahfouz: Ibdāᶜ Niṣf Qarn, selected with introduction by Ghālī Shukrī, Beirut: Dār al-Shurūq, 1989. A smaller and more selective compendium than the above. With the exception of only two reviews, all twenty articles deal with Mahfouz's work up to the 1960s.

INDEX